ESSAYS IN QUAKER HISTORY
in Honor of
Edwin B. Bronner

EDWIN B. BRONNER

Seeking the Light

ESSAYS IN QUAKER HISTORY
in Honor of
Edwin B. Bronner

Edited by J. William Frost and John M. Moore

• 1986 •
Pendle Hill Publications & Friends Historical Association
Wallingford & Haverford
Pennsylvania

SEEKING THE LIGHT
Essays in Quaker History
in honor of Edwin B. Bronner

SEEKING THE LIGHT
Includes Index

1. Society of Friends — History.   2. Bronner, Edwin B., 1920-.
I. Bronner, Edwin B., 1920-.
II. Frost, J. William (Jerry William), 1940-.
III. Moore, John Morrison, 1904-.
BX7632.S44   1986   289.6
ISBN 0.87574-909-7
Library of Congress Card Catalog 86-61066

Designs by Barbara Benton and Dion Lerman
June 1986: 750
Printed in the United States of America
by Wickersham Printing Company, Inc.
Lancaster, Pennsylvania 17603

Contents

Contributors

Margaret Hope Bacon, formerly Associate Secretary for Information and Interpretation of the American Friends Service Committee, is the author of several books on the history of the Society of Friends. Her biography of Henry Cadbury, *Let This Life Speak*, will be published in 1987.

Hugh Barbour is Professor of Religion at Earlham College and the author of *The Quakers in Puritan England*.

Kenneth Carroll, Professor of Religious Studies at Southern Methodist University, is the author of *Quakerism on the Eastern Shore* and *John Perrot, Early Quaker Schismatic*.

Barbara Curtis was for many years the Quaker Bibliographer in the Haverford College Library. She is now President of the Friends Historical Association.

J. William Frost is Jenkins Professor of Quaker History and Director of the Friends Historical Library at Swarthmore College. He is the author of *The Quaker Family in Colonial America*.

Craig Horle spent several years on the staff of the Library of the Society of Friends in Friends House, London. He is now Associate Editor of *The Papers of William Penn* at the Historical Society of Pennsylvania.

Paul Kelly was enrolled in the seminar in Methods of Historical Research when he was an undergraduate at Haverford College. He is now studying law at Stanford University.

Jack Marietta is Professor of History at the University of Arizona and author of *The Reformation of American Quakerism, 1748–1783*.

John M. Moore is Professor emeritus of Philosophy and Religion at Swarthmore College. He is the editor of *Friends in the Delaware Valley*.

Alfred Skerpan, a member of the seminar in Methods of Historical Research at Haverford College, is now a graduate student in history at the University of Wisconsin, Madison.

Roger Wilson, Professor emeritus of Education at University of Bristol, has served London Yearly Meeting as General Secretary of the Friends Relief Service and more recently as clerk. He wrote *Quaker Relief: An Account of the Relief Work of the Society of Friends 1940–1948*.

Arthur Worrall is Professor of History at Colorado State University. He is the author of *Quakers in the Colonial Northeast*.

Introduction

When Frederick B. Tolles in 1949 became editor of the *Bulletin of the Friends Historical Association* (later called *Quaker History*) he assessed the prevailing attitude toward Quaker history. Rejecting the common conception, he announced that Quaker history should be viewed not as "the chronicles of a minor sect," but as "an integral part of. . . . the story of modern Western European culture." A genuine understanding of the internal and external history of Friends would involve something more than digging out new facts. It would require inquiry into ideas, social trends, biographies and economics in order to grasp what formed the Society of Friends and enabled it to survive in a hostile and indifferent world.

Edwin B. Bronner, like Tolles, broadened the focus of Quaker history through his studies of the formative years of Pennsylvania, the interaction of British and American Friends, and the varieties of contemporary meetings in the Americas. The essays in the present volumes are intended as a tribute to Professor Bronner honoring him for his contributions to scholarship, for his work as Curator of the Quaker Collection of Haverford College collecting and preserving invaluable documents and books, for his support of the Friends Historical Association and the Conference of Quaker Historians and Archivists, and for his services to the Friends World Committee and the wider community of Friends.

The articles in this volume demonstrate current research in Quaker history in their extensive coverage of the seventeenth and eighteenth centuries and in their concern for more contemporary issues. The first three deal with the rise of the Quaker movement in seventeenth-century England. The next three treat Friends' attitudes toward and relationships with other religious movements in Colonial America. The last four show the impact of major modern events — the Civil War, the rise of liberalism and the onset of the first and second World Wars on Quakers.

Craig Horle's opening essay provides an illuminating discussion of a very significant development in the organizational structure of early English Quakerism. In its formative period, the decade of the 1650s, the

1

Quaker movement spread rapidly from its beginning in the north of England into virtually all parts of the British Isles, to the Netherlands, and to the British colonies in North America. It did so with a minimum of organization and central authority. Traveling ministers and missionaries were so inflamed by direct inspiration that they believed Christ to be their sole guide and leader. They were loath to recognize any human authority or need for ecclesiastical organization or group discipline. As time went on, however, particularly during the period of severe repression, persecution and schism in the 1660s and '70s the need for organizational structure and discipline became clear. In response the Quaker movement developed an elaborate organization which eventually made the Society of Friends one of the most highly centralized of all Protestant churches. Horle describes a crucial step in this process, the formation of the London Meeting for Sufferings, a group originally established to provide legal and other assistance to persecuted Friends but which came to function as the executive committee of London Yearly Meeting. He demonstrates that this body had its origin in the confusion which existed at the time of George Fox's imprisonment at Worcester in 1673–74. In attempting to procure Fox's release, Friends found themselves working at cross-purposes and cancelling out one another's efforts. Hence it seemed desirable to create a small body of influential Friends who would have the responsibility of dealing with the government in cases of persecution.

Hugh Barbour's essay on "Quaker Prophetesses and Mothers in Israel" provides valuable insights into an important subject — the place of women in the early Quaker movement. He contends that they filled two specific roles, both of which had ample Biblical precedents. On the one hand they were prophetesses who gave voice to messages directly inspired by the Holy Spirit. Quakers argued that Paul nowhere forbids such utterances, since his strictures against women speaking in churches were directed against "vain babbling" and other exercises in human self-expression. Quaker women preachers simply claimed the "liberty of prophesying," a liberty which was hard to deny since to do so would be to attempt interference with the operation of the Divine Spirit. Barbour further points out that Quaker women also served as "Mothers in Israel" in caring for and nurturing the flock of Christ. Margaret Fell, who married George Fox after the death of Judge Fell, was especially active in this service. She organized and administered the 'Kendal Fund' for providing financial support and assistance to Quaker ministers and missionaries in the early period.

The third essay in the first section deals with Thomas Loe, the friend and mentor of William Penn. Thomas Loe's preaching was instrumental in the convincement of Penn, and it was Loe who accompanied Penn on an important visit to the Duke of Buckingham in 1668 when they appealed for assistance in alleviating the persecutions then being inflicted on Quakers. Thomas Loe has always remained a somewhat shadowy figure among early Quaker ministers. Kenneth Carroll has here brought together virtually everything that is known about him.

The second group of essays is concerned with Colonial America. It begins with a paper by Arthur Worrall, who describes how a measure of religious liberty was achieved by the Quaker settlers in Sandwich in Plymouth Colony before 1700. The Puritan settlers and authorities of both Plymouth and Massachusetts Bay had a very limited conception of religious liberty. They demanded it for themselves, but were loath to grant it to others, particularly to Quakers whom they regarded as an obnoxious and pernicious sect, subversive alike to church and state. Yet certain circumstances which developed as early as the time of King Philip's War made it expedient for the authorities to permit the Quakers who had settled in the Town of Sandwich on Cape Cod to own land and to hold their religious meetings with a minimum of interference. Worrall concludes that toleration was achieved in practice long before the colonial officials accepted it in theory.

The next chapter in this section is by Jack Marietta who maintains that the years from 1720 to 1750 showed an unprecedented growth in political self-consciousness among the Quaker inhabitants of Pennsylvania. This changed attitude was largely the result of a formidable challenge by non-Quakers to their control of the province. By 1700 Quakers were no longer in a majority in Pennsylvania, and as the new century wore on, their minority situation became increasingly evident. The determination of Quaker leaders to retain political control proved more and more difficult as non-Quaker immigrants poured into the province in ever-increasing numbers. A faction of royal and proprietary officials sought to reduce the power of the Quaker-controlled Assembly. Particularly after the death of William Penn and the return of his sons to the Church of England, the leaders of the Proprietary Party tended to be Anglicans. Most of the new immigrants were either Scots or Scotch-Irish Presbyterians or Germans, who might be Lutheran, Reformed, or adherents of a variety of sects. Some of them settled in Philadelphia, but the larger number headed for the back country where land was cheap and where it was increasingly difficult for the proprietary agents to collect either purchase money or quitrents. The Scotch-Irish were notoriously prone to make trouble; many of them became squatters and tended to ignore or trample upon the rights of the native inhabitants. As increasing numbers of them became qualified to vote, the ability of the Quakers to control the colonial Assembly became more and more problematic. The Quaker politicians had to devise policies which would command popular support and to forge alliances which would enable them to remain in power. Marietta shows convincingly that the election of 1742 was crucial in this respect. The growth of political self-consciousness and sophistication among Quaker leaders in Pennsylvania was thus a natural and perhaps inevitable result of the liberal immigration policy of the early Quaker settlers of the province.

J. William Frost raises an extremely interesting question in the essay which follows. To what extent did colonial Pennsylvania become a secular society in the eighteenth century? He argues that many features of secularization—one of the generally accepted marks of a modern society—had appeared very early in Pennsylvania, long before the Revolutionary War. There is an obvious paradox here, for was not the Quaker colony begun as "an holy experiment"? Yet from almost the beginning of Penn's holy experiment religious pluralism, separation of church and state, and the absence of tithes drastically changed the European pattern of religion. The liberal immigration policy of the early Friends led to their rapidly becoming a minority in an increasingly pluralistic society. While the early Quaker domination of political life bore some resemblance to a religious establishment, the Friends never sought to maintain these features on a permanent basis, and they resolutely opposed attempts to set up such establishments by other churches. Ironically, the very pluralism of religious allegiances combined with separation of church and state and the voluntary support of churches by their members in place of compulsory tithes, all of which became characteristic features of life in Pennsylvania by the middle of the eighteenth century, virtually insured that religious commitments remained strong. Frost shows by many examples how features of secularization, though present in the early history of the state, did not come to characterize colonial Pennsylvania and why religious interpretations of reality remained pervasive in the Commonwealth.

The final group of three chapters deals with Quakerism in the nineteenth and twentieth centuries. The first is a document from the Civil War in America, edited by Alfred Skerpan, when an undergraduate at Haverford College and enrolled in a seminar on Methods of Historical Research conducted by Edwin B. Bronner and other members of the Department of History at Haverford. The document is a communication or bulletin (in the form of a letter) from the Women's Aid Society of Philadelphia to its members and supporters chiefly in the rural areas comprising the Yearly Meeting of Friends of Philadelphia and Vicinity (i.e. the Orthodox Yearly Meeting). As the Civil War progressed and Union armies penetrated more deeply into the South, the problem of dealing with blacks thereby released from slavery became more and more acute. Quakers responded to the situation by organizing to meet the needs of these "freedmen" for food, clothing, and shelter, and for at least a minimum of education. One of these organizations was the Women's Aid Society. The document shows Quakers' attitudes toward the "freedmen" and describes the activities of Friends toward reconstruction in the South. Alfred Skerpan has done a careful job of editing the document located in the Quaker Collection at Haverford, and has also provided an introduction which describes its historical significance.

The next chapter by Roger Wilson, an English Friend, provides new information on the origins of the famous Manchester Conference of 1895. This conference marked the turning point in modern Quakerism from the prevailing evangelicalism of the middle and later nineteenth century to the more liberal outlook and attitudes of the twentieth century, both in Great Britain and in the United States. Roger Wilson has made use of records which have only recently become available and he has shown that the progressive and liberal tone of this conference was made possible by the skillful and persistent pressures of a group of younger leaders in London Yearly Meeting. Their objective was to utilize its Home Mission Committee and to provide a forum for those dissatisfied with home missions and evangelical doctrine. Wilson calls this group "the emancipators," a designation which may not seem entirely felicitous but which accurately describes their objectives and attitudes. For they were seeking to emancipate the Quaker body from what were increasingly being perceived as the trammels of an outmoded past: too much Biblical literalism and authoritarianism, too much suspicion and hostility toward modern science and evolutionary theories. They wanted the Society to come to terms with modern science and with modern thought generally, and they planned the Manchester Conference to bring about these changes. But in order to do so, they had to gain control of the Home Missions Committee. How they accomplished this coup d'etat using Quaker methods is the subject of Roger Wilson's extremely interesting chapter.

The essay by Margaret Hope Bacon describes a test of Quaker values and of academic freedom at Haverford College at the time of America's participation in the First World War. The incident involved one of its younger Quaker professors, Henry J. Cadbury, who later became a distinguished New Testament scholar at Harvard. This situation need not be described, since Margaret Bacon treats it fully in her essay. She brings out clearly that Haverford College repudiated Henry Cadbury's pacifism and infringed his academic freedom. The issue involved both a basic Quaker "testimony" and a principle which is central and sacred to all liberal academic institutions, the right of faculty members to express their ideas freely and openly in all matters of public concern and scholarly discussion. Academic freedom has long occupied an ambiguous position in the United States. It is widely praised and professed in theory, but has often been denied or infringed upon in practice as the files of the American Association of University Professors will attest. Hence Henry Cadbury's defense of academic freedom, first at Haverford and later at Harvard, is significant not only for Quaker history but for the entire academic community and the liberal tradition in America.

The concluding chapter consists of an interesting and significant letter written by Thomas Kelly to his wife and family in the summer of 1938, together with an introduction prepared by Paul M. Kelly, a grandson of Thomas Kelly, who was an undergraduate at Haverford College and a member of the seminar on Methods of Historical Reseasrch. Thomas Kelly spent the summer of 1938 in Nazi Germany at the invitation of the German Yearly Meeting of Friends during which he gave the Richard Cary lecture at their annual session. He spent most of the summer traveling among Friends and investigating the condition of Jews, dissidents, and other victims of Nazi oppression. He wrote frequent letters to his wife and children but most of them were necessarily short and lacking in specific details, for he soon learned that Nazi spies and informers were everywhere. When he got to Strasbourg on the French side of the Rhine on August 16 he felt that he could unburden himself, and he wrote the long and anguished letter which is printed here.

An abbreviated version of this letter was published in the biography of Thomas Kelly written by his son Richard in 1966. This biography gave principal attention to Thomas Kelly's spiritual struggles and treated the summer in Germany as a crucial turning point in that development. Richard Kelly therefore omitted most of the sections dealing with Thomas Kelly's reactions to the Nazi regime and his visits to Jews and other victims of Nazi persecution. These were judged to be "political" and not immediately relevant to the spiritual crisis through which Thomas Kelly was passing. But these sections are included here, and they provide a more balanced and comprehensive picture of Thomas Kelly's reactions to Nazism and to events in Germany during that fateful summer just preceding the outbreak of World War II. The letter shows that Kelly was a careful and sensitive observer. His realistic appraisal of the developing crisis provides information which will long be useful to historians.

Edwin B. Bronner,
A Biographical Sketch

This volume of essays is offered to Edwin Bronner by his colleagues and friends as a tribute to his accomplishments as a historian and published as a mark of their respect and affection. A living example of Quaker integrity, Ed Bronner is a committed teacher, a provocative scholar for academic and lay audiences and a skillful college administrator. Though he is retiring as the Haverford College librarian, he plans to continue his teaching, research and publication in history and Quakerism.

Edwin Blaine Bronner was born 2 September 1920 in Yorba Linda, California. Both parents were deeply committed members of the Society of Friends and active in pastoral work. In the following years they moved to various places in California and Oregon where his father served as a pastor and worked in mills and in construction in order to support his growing family which by 1925 included a brother Robert and a sister Marjorie. When Edwin had finished high school in California, he went on first to Modesto Junior College and then to Whittier College where he majored in history and received his bachelor's degree in 1941. His extracurricular activities included service as editor of the college paper, and his courses included some preparation for secondary school teaching.

With the onset of World War II Edwin registered as a conscientious objector and on 5 January 1943 was inducted into Civilian Public Service at the camp run by Friends at Elkton, Oregon. After six months of forestry work at Elkton where he also edited the camp newspaper, Edwin was selected to go to Earlham College in Richmond, Indiana, to begin training for overseas relief and reconstruction work under the American Friends Service Committee. This opportunity did not develop because Federal authorities decided not to allow C.O.'s to work overseas during wartime. Subsequent assignments within Civilian Public Service brought Edwin to the headquarters in Philadelphia for work in mental health and public health units. He often served as education or personnel secretary of such programs. Finally, in May 1946, he journeyed to Elkton, Oregon, and was discharged from his service as a conscientious objector.

While living and working in the Philadelphia area Edwin Bronner met

Marian (Anne) Phillips Taylor, a Friend from Cheltenham meeting. Their marriage took place on 9 March 1946 at Abington Friends Meeting in Jenkintown, Pa. The young couple set up housekeeping in Philadelphia. Over the next decade a family of four active daughters made their appearance in the family circle. As career paths for the future were explored, consideration was given to secondary school teaching and to becoming a Friends pastor. Edwin Bronner's irrepressible interest in exploring history and writing about it showed itself in the many articles he prepared for a varied group of historical and Quaker publications. Following a decision to concentrate on a teaching career at the college level in American history, Edwin Bronner enrolled at Harverford College and received his M.A. in 1947. About that time his name first appears in the records of the Friends Historical Association and the Historical Society of Pennsylvania as an active member and an author of articles and reviews.

While pursuing his graduate work he gained experience in college teaching by becoming an instructor and later an assistant professor at Temple University. He began with one course in March 1947 and continued to teach there until 1962. Meanwhile he had matriculated in the doctoral program in history at the University of Pennsylvania. In June 1952 he received the Ph.D. degree with a dissertation on William Penn under the direction of the distinguished American historian, Roy Nichols.

Throughout the forties and early fifties Edwin Bronner established a pattern of activity in which he gave generously of his time and thought to many forms of service beside his teaching, his family and his scholarship. He worked with Mildred Scott Olmsted on publications of the Women's International League for Peace and Freedom, for the Danforth Foundation and for the Friends World Committee for Consultation. When the family took vacations or sabbaticals they made extensive trips across the United States visiting friends and Friends along the way as well as relatives in California.

In 1962 Edwin Bronner was appointed Professor of History and Curator of the Quaker Collection at Haverford College. President Hugh Borton cited this appointment as evidence of the intention of the college, then on the eve of an expansion program, to reinforce its commitment to the encouragement of Quaker influences at the college. By the next year Bronner was offering a course in the History and Philosophy of Quakerism. Such a course, modified and further developed in content, has been given regularly ever since. An innovation in the offerings of the history department in which Edwin Bronner had a role was the introduction in 1970 of the junior seminar for history majors on historical evidence. This course makes use of valuable manuscript materials available in the Quaker Collection and other collections of Haverford College. Undergraduate students are exposed to the critical techniques required in the use and interpretation of primary source materials.

At the beginning of the Haverford years the first of Bronner's books was published. *William Penn's Holy Experiment* came out in 1963 and was acclaimed for its contribution to the understanding of the life and thought of Pennsylvania's Quaker founder. A reprint edition appeared in 1978. During the sixties the Bronner family settled into a house on the college campus and Edwin Bronner expanded the scope of his Quaker interests with service to the Friends World Committee, Section of the Americas, as organizer of the fourth World Conference of Friends held at Guilford College, Greensboro, N.C. More than 1,000 Friends from every continent participated in this gathering. From 1972–1978 Bronner served as chairman of the Friends World Committee and supervised its world-wide program. At the end of that time he dedicated a sabbatical leave to journey with Anne Bronner around the globe, meeting with Friends in Australia, India, Africa and Europe.

In 1968, during his first leave from Haverford, Edwin Bronner spent several months in England in research and editorial work in the Library of Friends House, London. This resulted in the completion of his book *An English View of American Quakerism: The Journal of Walter Robson* . . . which was published first in the Annals of the American Philosophical Society in 1970. Upon his return from overseas he was appointed director of the library of Haverford College in addition to his other college duties. As director of the library Edwin launched an energetic program to reinforce its position as a central part of the scholarly activity of the college. In association with David Fraser and the rest of the library staff he encouraged the development of tri-college cooperation with Bryn Mawr and Swarthmore, implemented the decision to computerize many aspects of the library's technical processes, and worked to preserve and enlarge the outstanding library collections available to students and faculty. In 1974 the faculty chose Edwin Bronner to be clerk of that body. During the next five years he presided over meetings of major importance to the future of the college. It was decided to increase the size and diversity of the student body, to strengthen and extend cooperation with Bryn Mawr, and to recommend the admission of women to Haverford.

His historical research continued throughout this time and resulted in the publication of *The Other Branch: London Yearly Meeting and the Hicksites*, in 1975 under the imprint of Friends Historical Society in London. Just before that book appeared Edwin Bronner had completed a unique year as President of the two Quaker historical associations at the same time.

No account of the life of Edwin Bronner can be complete without mention of his service on the boards of the American Friends Service Committee, the Earlham School of Religion and Pendle Hill, as well as of his role in helping establish the Conference of Quaker Historians and Archivists as an affiliate of the Friends Historical Association. Now in 1986 Edwin continues to write and publish in his chosen fields of history and Quakerism. He is currently serving on the editorial panel of three scholars, consisting of Richard Dunn, Mary M. Dunn and himself, which is publishing the complete works of William Penn, under the auspices of the Historical Society of Pennsylvania. Several volumes of this important series have already appeared including, most recently, Volume 5 by Ed Bronner and David Fraser. It is clear that he is ready and willing to pursue active scholarship and productive writing in the years ahead.

Selected Bibliography of Publications of Edwin B. Bronner

Thomas Early as a Reformer. Philadelphia, 1948.

William Penn's Holy Experiment; the founding of Pennsylvania, 1681–1701. New York, 1962, reprinted, 1978.

American Quakers Today. Edited by E. B. Bronner. Philadelphia, 1966, 1967, 1972.

An English View of American Quakerism. The Journal of Walter Robson (1842–1929) Written During the Fall of 1877, While Traveling among American Friends. Edited by E. B. Bronner. Philadelphia, 1970.

"The Other Branch," London Yearly Meeting and the Hicksites, 1827–1912. London, 1975.

Volume 5 of *The Papers of William Penn, William Penn's Published Writings, 1660–1726: An Interpretive Bibliography.* By Edwin B. Bronner and David Fraser. University of Pennsylvania Press, 1986.

CONTRIBUTING AUTHOR

Barbour, Hugh and Arthur O. Roberts compilers. *Early Quaker Writings, 1650–1700.* Grand Rapids, Michigan, 1973. "Foreward" by E. B. Bronner.

Bicentennial Conference on Religious Liberty, Philadelphia, 1976. *Religious Liberty in the Crossfire of Creeds.* Edited by Franklin H. Littell. Philadelphia,. 1978. "Quaker Discipline and Order, 1680–1720: Philadelphia Yearly Meeting and London Yearly Meeting" by E. B. Bronner.

Carroll, Kenneth L. *The Creative Centre of Quakerism.* Birmingham, England, Philadelphia, 1965. "Summary of the Ninth Meeting," by E. B. Bronner.

Comfort, William Wistar. *William Penn and our Liberties*. Philadelphia, 1976. "Introduction" by E. B. Bronner.

Dunn, Richard S. and Mary Maples. *The World of William Penn*. University of Pennsylvania Press, 1986. "Quaker Discipline and Order, 1680–1720: Philadelphia Yearly Meeting and London Yearly Meeting" by Edwin B. Bronner.

Elliott, Errol T. *Quakers on the American Frontier*. Richmond, Indiana, 1969. "Preface" by E. B. Bronner.

Friends in the Delaware Valley. Edited by John M. Moore. Philadelphia, 1981. "A time of change: Philadelphia Yearly Meeting, 1861–1914" by E. B. Bronner.

Friends Quarterly. Special double number to commemorate the 350th anniversary of George Fox's birth . . . Ashford, Kent, England, 1974. "George Fox and the Friends World Committee" by E. B. Bronner.

Haverford College. *The Spirit and the Intellect, 1833–1983*. Haverford, Pa., 1983. "The Sharpless Years" by E. B. Bronner.

Hirst, Margaret Esther. *The Quakers in Peace and War*. . . . New York, 1972. "With a new introduction for the Garland edition" by E. B. Bronner.

Montgomery County: The Second Hundred Years. Edited by Jean Barth Toll and Michael J. Schwager. Norristown, Pa., 1983. Articles on Haverford College and the Religious Society of Friends by E. B. Bronner.

Philadelphia, A 300-Year History, edited by Russell F. Weigley, New York, 1982. "Village into Town, 1701–1746" by E. B. Bronner.

The West Jersey Concessions and Agreements of 1676/77: a round table of historians. Trenton, 1979. "The English Setting" by E. B. Bronner.

FORTHCOMING PUBLICATION

Revision of pamphlet by William Wistar Comfort, *The Quakers, a brief account of their influence in Pennsylvania*, Harrisburg, Pa., 1986, by Edwin B. Bronner.

PAMPHLETS, PERIODICALS AND SERIAL PUBLICATIONS

"Contemporary American experience of conscience and dissent: the peace testimony (Bibliography)." In *Journal of Economics Studies*, Fall, 1977.

"The disgrace of John Kinsey, Quaker politician, 1739–1750." In *Pennsylvania Magazine of History and Biography*, October, 1951.

"Distributing the printed word: The Tract Association of Friends, 1816–1966." In *Pennsylvania Magazine of History and Biography*, July, 1967.

"An early antislavery statement, 1676." In *Quaker History*, Spring, 1973.

"The failure of the 'holy experiment' in Pennsylvania, 1684–1699." In *Pennsylvania History*, April, 1954.

"First printing of Magna Carta in American, 1687." In *American Journal of Legal History*, July, 1963.

"Indian deed for Petty's Island, 1678." In *Pennsylvania Magazine of History and Biography*, January, 1965.

"Intercolonial relations among Quakers before 1750." In *Quaker History*, Spring, 1967.

"Letter from a yellow fever victim, Philadelphia, 1793." In *Pennsylvania Magazine of History and Biography*, April, 1962.

"The New Deal comes to Pennsylvania: the gubernatorial election of 1934." In *Pennsylvania History*, January, 1960.

"Penn's charter of property of 1701." In *Pennsylvania History*, October, 1957.

"Philadelphia County Court of Quarter Sessions and Common Pleas, 1695." In *Pennsylvania Magazine of History and Biography*, October, 1953.

"A Philadelphia Quaker visits Natchez, 1847." In *The Journal of Southern History*, November, 1961.

"Quaker Landmarks in early Philadelphia." In *Transactions of the American Philosophical Society*, new series, March, 1953.

Quakerism and Christianity. Pendle Hill Pamphlet 152. Wallingford, Pa., 1967.

"The Quakers and non-violence in Pennsylvania." In *Pennsylvania History*, Winter, 1968.

"Quakers labor with Jemima Wilkinson — 1794." In *Quaker History*, Spring, 1969.

"Sharing the Scriptures: the Bible Association of Friends in America, 1829–1979." Philadelphia, 1979.

War Tax Concerns. Friends Committee on War Tax Concerns and Friends World Committee. 1986.

"William Penn and John Woolman." In *Friends Quarterly*, April, 1970.

"William Penn, 17th century founding father. Selections from his political writings." Pendle Hill Pamphlet 204. Wallingford, Pa., 1975.

PART ONE

Seventeenth-
Century
England

Changing Quaker Attitudes toward Legal Defense: The George Fox Case, 1673–75, and the Establishment of Meeting for Sufferings

The establishment of the London-based Meeting for Sufferings in 1676 symbolized a dramatic, albeit gradual, change in Friends' attitude toward the law. Although many of the arguments and tactics which Meeting for Sufferings would employ had their genesis in earlier Quaker behavior, Friends' willingness to utilize legal counsel on a broad scale was a decisive step for a group which had generally condemned the legal profession. In effect, the Quakers had undergone a metamorphosis from a radical sect ostensibly contemptuous of legal procedure into one which employed those procedures to thwart their opponents and to procure their own freedom, although without sacrificing their basic principles. The reasons for this change were probably twofold.

First, since there is little evidence that early Friends had been involved in efforts to reform the law, they were probably poorly informed about the legal system and therefore ill-prepared to confront the bewildering complexity of seventeenth-century legal procedure. Quaker testimonies had not considered such procedures as arranging sureties or bail, paying fees, pleading according to form, or traversing to delay proceedings. Only after extended exposure to such concepts would Friends begin to devise strategies in accord with their principles. Initially, their defense against prosecution relied heavily on their scriptural concept of equity ("Do unto others"), and their beliefs that legitimately held religious testimonies should not be prosecuted, and that the "Law of God" took precedence over that of man.[1] Although interesting points for debate, such arguments were scarcely calculated to sway either judges or juries. These early efforts were generally in reaction to specific circumstances and were not systematically developed. Only gradually did the Quakers realize that their survival as a sect might depend as much on the acquisition and utilization of legal knowledge as on their religious message.

Second, by the 1670s the Quaker leadership had shifted away from the rather isolated North to the area around London, in close proximity to Westminster and Whitehall. Many of these leaders represented a newer generation of Quakers whose interests were more commercial and professional and less agricultural—men such as James Claypoole, Thomas Rudyard, William Penn, Thomas Barker, William Bingley, John Elson, Philip Ford, William Mead, John Field, William Crouch, John Vaughton, Francis Camfield, and George Whitehead.[2] London Friends already dominated the vital executive committees of Quakerism—the Secondday's Morning Meeting, Yearly Meeting, and the Six Weeks Meeting. Less millenarian and "enthusiastic" than earlier Friends, these men were pragmatists who realized that organization, lobbying, and legal tactics were imperatives to any strategy of survival in a hostile political and religious environment.

But despite these changes, periodic outbreaks of persecution, and a highly advanced Quaker organization at both the local and central level by 1673, the creation of a Meeting for Sufferings was slow in coming. Such a committee had been seriously considered as early as a December 1668 meeting of ministers in London, which had announced that a body had been established "only to look after the sufferings of the nation and beyond the seas."[3] That a formalized Meeting for Sufferings did not emerge at that time was due, perhaps, to a combination of factors. These included the strict application of the second Conventicle Act which prevented London Friends from perfecting the Meeting; the issuance of the Declaration of Indulgence in 1672 (rescinded in 1673) which temporarily eliminated the necessity for such a body; and the imprisonment at Worcester of George Fox, the most prominent early Friend, and one whose organizing skill and pragmatism equalled those of the newer generation of Quakers. Ironically, while impeding the development of a Meeting for Sufferings, the imprisonment of Fox and the confused efforts of Friends to obtain his release outlined in bold relief the weakness of an uncoordinated, individualistic approach to legal defense. Furthermore, Fox had long been a bitter enemy of the legal profession, viewing lawyers as frauds and charlatans who allied themselves with ministers of the Established Church to persecute dissenters.[4] Yet during his imprisonment at Worcester he showed a willingness to make use of lawyers and legal tactics to gain his freedom. Consequently, this case would become a catalyst for a centralized and concerted Quaker approach to legal defense.

George Fox was arrested on 17 December 1673 after a meeting at John Halford's barn in Armscote, Worcestershire.[5] Of itself, the arrest was not particularly significant since Fox had been detained many times before, and this initially appeared to be a simple instance of harassment. Henry Parker, justice of the peace and recorder of Evesham, imprisoned Fox and his son-in-law Thomas Lower in Worcester gaol for refusing to give sureties to appear at the next sessions. The charge was vague, and induced Fox and Lower to write to Thomas Hickman, seventh Baron Windsor, the lord lieutenant of Worcestershire, informing him and his colleagues that they had not been in the meeting when taken, but had simply been speaking with others. The mittimus (warrant of committal), Fox asserted, was contradictory, stating that they failed to provide a satisfactory account of their residence, yet including one in the same document, and also mentioning complaints made to Parker of previous meetings which, Fox countered, were irrevelant. While admitting that he refused to provide sureties, he insisted that Lower had not been asked to do so, and yet had also been imprisoned. In effect, they had not been truly charged with any crime.[6] The letter was ignored.

Upon hearing of the arrest, the Quakers and their allies moved quickly, for by 7 January 1674 Lower had received several letters from his brother in London, Dr. Richard Lower, a former Fellow of the Royal Society, about his possible liberty. Dr. Lower also enclosed a letter from Henry Savile, brother of George, Marquis of Halifax and a groom of the king's bedchamber, directed to Savile's brother-in-law, Baron Windsor. However, Savile was only pursuing the release of Lower, who, therefore, did not forward the letter.[7] The most serious initial move by a Friend was that of Thomas Moore, a former Surrey justice, who called on Charles II with a copy of the mittimus and a letter from Margaret Fox, George's wife. Moore explained that the prisoner was the same George Fox that Charles had "sometimes delivered out of prison." After showing him the letter from Margaret Fox, Moore asked Charles to request from the sheriff of Worcestershire all information relating to the cause of imprisonment and to order the release of the prisoners if nothing more appeared. Charles refused this request, but allowed Moore to stay for over an hour, and agreed that while he was "not willing to do any such thing of himself," he wanted Moore to appear before the Privy Council. Moore and Ellis Hookes, a prominent London Friend, both attended as requested, but remained outside while the matter was debated. After the council meeting ended, Charles told Moore that as no law had been broken, he could do nothing, but that the matter should be left to due process. Hookes, however, believed that the real reason lay elsewhere. Charles, he wrote, was "very timorous (it being just at the pinch of the parliament's coming) of doing anything to displease them, his occasions being so great for money, which might something impede the business."[8] In fact, this was a very delicate period for Charles in his relationship with parliament, and particularly with the Commons, who were alarmed at the king's lack of commitment to suppressing Catholicism and Protestant dissent. It would also be questionable tactics for Charles at this juncture to intervene blatantly in local law enforcement.

The primary fear of Friends was that Fox would be tendered the Oath of Allegiance, the refusal of which could lead to a sentence of *praemunire* — loss of estate and imprisonment at the king's pleasure. London Friends were hoping that "the old snare of the oath will be waived at sessions," and to that end Ellis Hookes despatched a letter to Fox and Lower from Margaret Penn, mother of William, to her old acquaintance, Baron Windsor. Hookes and George Whitehead, another prominent London Friend, had been diligent "in turning every stone that might be advantageous for obtaining their liberty, nor yet shall not desist in the matter." But Hookes feared that nothing could be done in London until the next law term, "except they should praemunire them at the sessions, & then we must apply ourselves again to the king."[9] Despite Margaret Penn's affectionate letter to Windsor requesting the discharge of the two Quakers, they remained in gaol. Lower acknowledged the failure thus far of all the efforts and that the matter would be left to the justices at quarter sessions where, "unless they be permitted to tender the Oaths of Allegiance and Supremacy, it's thought we may be discharged." It appeared, he added optimistically, that many of the justices in the area disliked "the severity of Parker's proceedings against us" and had declared "an adverseness to ensnare us with the tender of the oaths."[10]

On 17 January 1674 Fox wrote to Whitehead and others in London about the recent quarter sessions. He and Lower had been called on the last day, prior to which "divers eminent Friends being here did speak to the justices," who had implied that the two would be discharged. Some Friends had also spoken with Baron Windsor, "who also promised fair," and they understood that Dr. Richard Lower had influenced Colonel Samuel Sandy's, M.P. for Ombersley, Worcestershire, and a staunch Royalist, to write from London asking some of the justices to discharge the prisoners. However, the chairman of the sessions was "an old Presbyterian," Leonard Simpson, and while the justices appeared satisfied with Fox's account of the events prior to his arrest, they overrode his protestations of loyalty to the crown, and tendered him the Oaths of Allegiance and Supremacy. He refused to take them and was again imprisoned for failing to provide sureties to appear at the next assizes. Interestingly, the bench was willing to release Lower outright, but he refused to leave his companion, nor would he provide security for Fox's appearance at the assizes.[11]

Fox was anxious for Thomas Moore to meet again with Charles II to tell him that the authorities, instead of allowing the law to take its course, had relied on the usual snare. However, if Charles refused to act, then Friends in London, Fox added, were to seek a way *"as touching my removal . . . as privately & suddenly as may be, before Parker get up to prevent it."* Fox was thinking of a writ of *habeas corpus* to remove him into King's Bench where the king might exercise his influence more effectively.[12]

What was to complicate this case was the lack of effective Quaker organization to coordinate information and to press for Fox's discharge: consequently misinformation, confusion, and disagreement characterized the lengthy period culminating in Fox's release. At first, London Quakers were even unaware that Fox's wife Margaret and her daughter Rachel, who had been with him at the time of his arrest, had gone home to Swarthmoor, prompting Fox to write to her complaining that Rebecca Travers in London thought it was "strange that thee hath not written to her, for she and the rest of London Friends generally thinks that thou art with me in prison and did stay, and not gone into the north." Margaret soon heard from Edward Mann in London that Thomas Rudyard and Ellis Hookes on 22 January 1674 had procured a writ of *habeas corpus* to be sent down to Worcester to bring Fox to London "in order to his release if it can be so ordered or to the K[ings's] Bench, a prison of more liberty . . . which will trouble P[arke]r." At the same time John Rous, a son-in-law of Margaret Fox, had spoken with Dr. Lower about Fox's release, but Lower was annoyed that he had secured a release for his brother Thomas only to have him refuse it. Rous, unlike Edward Mann, feared that removal to London would result in worse treatment for Fox.[13]

Meanwhile, Fox was concerned about his wife's reaction to his arrest, leading him to write to her about what had taken place:

Thou seemed to be much grieved when I was speaking of prisons, & when I was taken thou began to fall upon me with blaming of me, & I told thee that I was to bear it & why could not thee be, & be content with the will of God, & thou said some words & then was pretty quiet. . . . It had been well thou had been more over it to me, for when I was at John Rous's I saw that I was taken prisoner & when I was at Bray Doily's, as I sat at supper, I saw I was taken the night before I was.[14]

In the event, the *habeas corpus* arrived at Worcester and the undersheriff allowed Fox to go to London with Thomas Lower as his guard. Leaving Worcester on 29 January 1674, they appeared in King's Bench on 3 February before Justice William Wylde and after the return of the writ was entered, Fox was ordered to appear again on the following day, which he did. After the sheriff had forcibly removed Fox's hat, Solicitor General William Jones, possibly at the behest of the king, spoke, according to Fox, "notably on my behalf," as did a lawyer who followed, probably hired by London Friends. The three judges, Fox added, "were very moderate."[15] Chief Justice Matthew Hale, after hearing Fox's story of his arrest and committal, assured him that he would now be in the custody of King's Bench and that if they found any irregularities in the justices' proceedings, he would be freed. For the present, he would be allowed to stay with a Friend in town. Henry Parker, however, moved the court to send Fox back to Worcester. Privately, Fox complained that Parker had "spread abroad a very false and malicious story, viz. that there were many substantial men with me, and that we had a design or plot in hand, and that Thomas Lower stayed with me in prison, long after he was set at liberty, to carry on our design." At a second hearing, four lawyers spoke on Parker's behalf, while George Strode pleaded for Fox. The court decided to remand Fox to Worcester assizes, but the judges were willing to grant him bail to appear, contingent on good behavior, which Fox refused. Nonetheless, the judges permitted him to travel to Worcester on his own.[16]

In desperation, Fox wrote to Charles II explaining his case at great length. At the same time, Friends had given *The Case of the People Called Quakers Relating to Oaths or Swearing* to members of parliament, to the king and his council, and to the lord mayor, alderman, and common council of London. This was one aspect of a massive public relations exercise which, in part, might create a climate of opinion favorable to Fox's release. Fox also asked his wife to have monthly and quarterly meetings send for copies to be given to all the major law enforcement officers, as well as to jurors. Unfortunately, he added, "the king can do nothing, it being in the judges' and the sheriffs' hands, so they do suppose that I must go to Worcester assizes or sessions."[17] Nevertheless, many Friends, according to Margaret Rous, daughter of Margaret Fox, "were employed in speaking to judges & sheriff, king & council to procure his stay."[18] Those attempts all failed.

Fox, accompanied by three London Friends, travelled leisurely to Worcester, arriving on 31 March. In the interim, Margaret Fox had complained about the way matters had been handled by Friends. Consequently, on 16 March, William Penn wrote to her. "I could have been glad," he lamented, "things had been more advisedly laid at first, but what is past must be borne." In the event, he added, Fox had been pleased "with the good success the little book had with parliament about oaths. T'was believed they might have done something for us."[19]

On 3 April Fox appeared at assizes before Sir Edward Turner. After allowing Fox to explain his case, including his continued refusal to take the oath, Turner heard from Parker that Fox was a ringleader who must be prosecuted. Turner, as an assize judge, needed to avoid inflaming local passions, and so decided to leave the Quaker to quarter sessions. Fox himself was particularly upset with Ellis Hookes and Richard Cannon (another London Friend), who had been told by Parker when in London that he would set Fox free, but coming into Worcester, Parker bragged that he "was too nimble for the Quakers." Fox added, with some uneasiness, that "here you may see Richard Cannon and Ellis Hookes who had such a confidence in deceitful Parker, were lugging at the tail of Parker and plucked me into the ditch." Turner, however, gave Fox the liberty of the town and permitted him to lodge at a Friend's house until the quarter sessions opened on 29 April.[20]

The chairman of the sessions was Thomas Street, M.P. for Worcester, a judge on the Welsh circuit, and later an Exchequer baron and justice of Common Pleas. When Fox was called, Street mentioned the large meeting the Quaker had attended and his refusal to take the oath. Fox countered that Friends had met in peace and unarmed, and that he had been taken while on the road. The oath was again tendered, and Fox again refused to take it. An indictment was drawn up and read, against which Fox protested, probably over the form. He then turned to the grand jury and explained why he refused to swear. Not surprisingly, a true bill was found. Fox wisely traversed[21] the indictment to gain time. (To traverse was to deny or take issue with an indictment. This delayed trial of an indictment until the succeeding term.) Although refusing to be bound to good behavior or allow any Friend to intervene, Fox was permitted to go free until the next sessions. It was rumored that some of the justices, believing Fox was less dangerous than Parker implied, had extracted a promise from Parker to write Charles II for a *nolle prosequi* ending the prosecution. If so, Parker reneged on this promise, for a letter was never sent. Fox, meanwhile, obtained a copy of his indictment and was intending to travel casually to London, ostensibly to attend Yearly Meeting but, he complained, "some that were earnest to get me out of the hands of those envious justices that sought to praemunire me at Worcester, would needs be tampering again, to bring me before the judges of the King's Bench."[22] This complaint by Fox was unfair since he had previously indicated to Friends his desire for legal remedy. On 4 May 1674 before leaving Worcester, he wrote to his wife acknowledging the receipt of several letters from her and from Thomas Lower (who had left him to assist in efforts to gain his release), and noting that many Friends from as far away as London and Bristol had attended the sessions which "was like a meeting." Some Friends, he added, had in fact, procured another *habeas corpus* and he was again to be brought before King's Bench.[23]

Given the great concourse of Quakers coming to see Fox, it was little wonder that the Worcester justices were apparently at odds over what to do with him. Fox confirmed their dilemma when two weeks later he told Margaret that he had been in London for almost a week, but nothing had yet been done, "but the[y] would be willing to get it of[f] & we shall see this term. The people of the sessions was like Friends & the Lord's power was over all and the[y] are very fair." He added that Gerrard Roberts, a London Friend, had been with some of the Worcestershire justices "since the[y] came to London & do pretend much, some of them that moved formerly for my going to Worcester."[24]

When Fox appeared before the judges of King's Bench he gave them a paper explaining what he could say instead of the Oaths of Allegiance and Supremacy, but reiterating that Quakers could not take an oath, although they would not speak falsely and would be willing to suffer if they did, just as those who broke their oaths.[25] The judges, once again, refused to interfere with Fox's case and remanded him to the sessions at Worcester. However, they permitted him to attend yearly meeting. His relations with his wife remained strained, as he chastized her for running into debt in London (probably on his behalf). Uninformed Friends had asked after her and Lower, believing that they had been with Fox, who finally left London on 9 July.[26]

At Worcester sessions, which began on 16 July, the indictment was read to the jury but, according to Fox, "there being some jumble among the jury, some being scrupulous in their minds concerning it, Judge Street caused the oath to be read and tendered to me again." After Fox was convicted and prior to sentencing, he objected to the indictment, apparently utilizing a lawyer, John Ashley who, Fox noted, "was friendly the last time, and spoke for me now, and spoke and pleaded the errors of the indictment." The presumed errors were many. For example, the indictment omitted the king's name, and that Fox was a subject of the realm. Street admitted that there were errors in the indictment, but correctly cautioned that Fox would have to seek remedies "in their proper place," that is, in the King's Bench by means of a writ of error, having failed to obtain a writ of *certiorari* to remove the indictment before trial. Fox and his attorney continued to complain about the indictment: that it had Fox "of Tredington," while the mittimus had Fox "of London;" and that it dated the first tendering of the oath as 28 April instead of the 29th. Street explained that all days were one where sessions was concerned. Fox also employed the usual Quaker contention that he had not "wilfully and obstinately" refused the oath, but only in obedience to the command of Christ. He then moved on to errors of form in the indictment, such as "General Sessions of the Peace held at Worcester for the county aforesaid," when it should have read "General Quarter Sessions held at Worcester for the Lord the King and body of the County aforesaid." Similarly, it stated that the oath was tendered in "open court," but failed to mention that Fox was present, while in another section it left out that it had been tendered specifically to him.[27]

Fox was employing every argument at his command, for he also demanded that the preamble of the statute be read in court, since it made it quite clear that the oath was "for the discovering of Popish recusants," and therefore was not directed against Quakers. Street complained that the prisoner had "rambled away to London," but Fox protested that he had not run away to King's Bench, but had been removed there by a writ of *habeas corpus* obtained by others.[28] That distinction was probably lost on Street, who in fact was demonstrating the annoyance of justices in general over prisoners who endeavored to bring the superior power of the king and common law judges to bear on local law enforcement matters. Fox also heard from others "that Judge Street said I had removed myself to the King's Bench for justice, but now they had done me justice." Fox also complained inaccurately that Street acted unfairly by tendering the oath when he was appearing on a traverse, rather than binding him over for trial. That was all irrevelant, for Street *praemunired* him, albeit after Fox had been taken away, thus preventing any attempts to obtain a stay of judgement.[29]

London Friends had been actively trying to assist Fox. Ellis Hookes had gone with Gerrard Roberts to Hampton Court on Friday, 10 July to deliver a paper on the case, "but the attorney general coming late there, the business was not heard then." Hookes then attempted to use his influence "to make the [lord] keeper our friend." In the event, the clerk of the Privy Council promised to read the paper the "next council day." Thus on Saturday, 11 July, they procured a letter from Henry Parker, then in London, to the justices at Worcester to stay their proceedings against Fox at the sessions until Hookes learned "what the king will do in it." On 17 July Hookes went again to Hampton Court where "the paper was read the first in the council, but the king said he would not meddle with it & so I came away." Six day later, Hookes informed Margaret Fox of further bad news: her husband had been tried and convicted at Worcester sessions, "nothwithstanding Parker's letter." Only now did Margaret visit her husband. Since the assizes were to take place in August, the case was drawn up and she and Thomas Lower delivered it to Judge William Wylde, who explained that the judges could not help Fox, except by writ of error in King's Bench.[30]

By this time, George Fox was growing increasingly alarmed, and he drew up a lengthy paper to Charles II, which included a defense of the Quaker refusal to swear. Fox was also ill. "I seemed to myself to be amongst the graves and dead corpses, . . . [and] I was so weak that I was almost speechless."[31] Among the Quakers, however, confusion persisted. This is illustrated by a letter of 7 August 1674 from Thomas Moore, who had heard about Fox's illness and *praemunire* from George Whitehead and Ellis Hookes, who had been with him the day before. Moore stressed that when last in London, he had wished to assist Fox, but had heard that William Meade "had undertaken to endeavor thy discharge, which for [the] present took me of[f], but now since I hear by G[eorge] Whitehead he despairs of doing thee service." Moore therefore had "ordered" Ellis Hookes to meet with him on 9 August at Kingston "& to ride with me to Windsor where we have appointed G[eorge] Whitehead to meet us & where I hear the king is." Moore then confessed to Fox that he did not know how to help him. "My way seems to me to be hedged up." He hoped that when Charles II found out about Fox's poor health, he would take action.[32]

However, on 14 August Moore wrote again to Fox. He had gone to Windsor "but very unhappily some friends had got thither before me (out of true love to thee) & when I came thither I found they had obtained by Arlington's[33] means an order from the king to set thee at liberty for some convenient time whilst thou shouldst gain health." Unfortunately, Moore added, this would be "on such terms as I know no true Christian can answer them in." After reading the king's order to Lord Keeper Heneage Finch, Moore warned the Friends that they were "quite out in assenting to the delusion by Arlington who takes sometimes an occasion to hurt us rather then to help us, as he hath done at this time." Troubled, Moore returned to the home of John Rous, and the following day went to the king at Hampton Court "on purpose to destroy what was done by Friends before & to put the business of thy release on a new & more firm bottom." Charles received him "with a great deal of kindness, told me he was glad to see me & when I had opened thy condition to him he answered me with much love & seemed to have a little sense of thy sufferings." Charles promised to speak with Finch about it and asked Moore to come back the next morning. At that time, Moore, accompanied by John Rous and his brother Thomas, returned very early, only to find the king was still in bed. Having sent a paper in to him, they lobbied with James, duke of York, Prince Rupert, the duke of Lauderdale, Lord Keeper Finch and others "who seemed in some sense to affect our cause." At the council, "our business was put a foot . . . none being against it that I know, but all for it." Unfortunately as Charles considered drafting an order for Fox's release, Arlington arrived, "who had agitated the business to the king 3 or 4 days before scurvily." Arlington mentioned to Charles that he had already done something for the prisoner "which caused them all to alter their resolutions & concluded that forasmuch as it was done already there was no need to proceed further, & so gave it over." Despite Moore's protestations to Charles, the king refused to "alter what he had done." Moore therefore left the matter in the hands of Gerrard Roberts, Ellis Hookes, John Rous, and Gilbert Latey "to make what use they can of it to the keeper (to whom thy business is referred) . . . who I think intends to try what may be done." Moore, however, preferred that it fall through, "for I can have no hand it it," but would then be free to begin again to assist him.[34]

Latey and Rous, in fact, were primarily responsible for this predicament. In a letter to Fox on 15 August, Latey explained what had occurred prior to Moore's involvement. Latey, Jane Woodcock, Martha Fisher, and William Beech had gone to Windsor Castle to see Charles, and while there had met a member of the king's guard whom Latey knew, who took them to Prince Rupert. Latey showed him a paper he had written about the case, and Rupert promised to discuss the matter with the king who was hunting. But when Charles returned, probably tired and in no mood to hear more of this tedious case, he was greeted by Martha Fisher, who had stayed behind with a friend. She gave him the paper. Rupert and the duke of Monmouth, who had also promised Latey to speak to Charles, then went to the king, but he "denied them." The following morning the Friends, undaunted, returned to the court, but Charles refused to speak with Martha and avoided the others. Latey, undeterred, pursued him and before Charles could reach his coach, the Quaker caught up to him. In the presence of "many of his nobles," Charles was asked by Latey to release Fox for reasons of health. Charles wearily said he would do what he could. Arlington, also present and seeing the two women, asked to know what was going on. They gave him the paper which he then gave to his page to take to his office "to draw it up according to law, and he

27

would mind the king of it to get it done that evening." However, Charles returned extremely tired from hunting and did not wish to be disturbed. On the following morning, the ever-present Friends called on Arlington who in turn called his secretary and had him draw up the case, promising to obtain the king's signature that evening. Arlington was visited that evening by Latey and John Rous but the beleaguered official put them off until the next morning. In the event, Charles refused to sign the paper which Friends had brought, "but granted the paper of Arlington's" which had been drawn up "in the manner of a petition." Charles ordered Arlington "to write so upon it that if what we had said were so," then Fox should be released "during pleasure as we desired." However, Arlington's clerk "wrote in it also that security should be given" that Fox "should be forth coming if called for." Rous added (as Moore had already explained to Fox) that Ellis Hookes was to try to get the order approved by the lord keeper "who has been some days out of town, and what they have done in it I cannot justly tell. But in a few day[s] thou mayest hear further. I was willing to give thee the account of the whole business, having had true peace with the Lord in my soul ever since."[35] In fact, as Thomas Moore had anticipated, Fox would not agree to Arlington's terms. Even further, however, he would not accept a pardon. Fox wished to be released without any implicit acknowledgment of guilt.

On 27 August Fox heard from Ellis Hookes that Moore (although no doubt still annoyed) had expressed his willingness to assist, "but he thinks the king being lately moved in it & doing something (though to no purpose) it is better to let it rest a while." Hookes suggested that if Margaret Fox could come to London and speak with Charles, "it might have . . . some good effect, he having a respect to her." Moore was ready to help her.[36] In a letter the following day, George Fox asked William Penn to speak with Moore about the errors in the indictment "which thee and I had in discourse." Thomas Lower added in a postscript that he had spoken with the sheriff and undersheriff in an effort to get some liberty for Fox, who was "still weakly & sick . . . & wants air very much to refresh him." Although the sheriff was willing, the undersheriff feared that the justices would blame him for any liberty, since they already thought it barely tolerable that one preacher in prison had caused hundreds more to flock into the area. They would view it as intolerable if Fox was permitted to go abroad, particularly as that might result in further conversions. Both officers recommended a writ of error to overturn the proceedings of the justices, "which if so," added Lower, "would much more torment and plague them than if my father [Fox] were freed from his *praemunire* by the king's grant." Lower asked Penn to consult with

George Strode or any other able counsel before doing anything further. If it appeared that the writ was the proper course of action, then Penn should act accordingly. If not, then he was to assist Thomas Moore, "if you both judge it fit," in pursuing "the king's former promise to him" to free Fox when the latter was *praemunired*. Lower emphasized, however, that before going over the heads of the justices Penn must make absolutely certain that these tactics would be successful. Lower added that they had sent a letter to Sir Francis Russell, a Worcestershire justice of the peace, to see if he and Colonel Sandys would comply with the sheriff's willingness to allow Fox to lodge at a Friend's house in the town.[37]

Unfortunately for Fox, all this lobbying at cross purposes had infuriated Thomas Moore, despite the fact the Fox had written to him agreeing that he was right to be upset. Moore replied to Fox on 3 September 1674 and vented his spleen:

> I have not known any Friends so betrayed in any business with the king since I was convinced & do indeed judge that their understanding was taken away or else sure they would never have admitted of an order that did enjoin the keeper to examine the truth of the matter & take sufficient security for thy liberty for some convenient time, or until thou shouldst be required. This must employ security to the sheriff in whose custody thou art & make thee liable to be remanded again at his pleasure, & likewise the order did employ the security must be bond in the mean time for thy good behavior, which I told G[eorge] Whitehead, whom I judge had no hand in the Petition to the king (for such it was also) would be required by the keeper on sight of the king's order & which I suppose Friends found on application to him to [be?] true.

Moore recapitulated what had happened, emphasizing the kindness of Charles, Prince Rupert, Lord Keeper Finch, and the dukes of York, Monmouth, and Lauderdale, and his own success before the arrival of Arlington. Moore stressed that Arlington had duped the other Friends into believing that the petition to Charles would be his own "& yet made it the petition of the Quakers." Although fearing that Charles might "think me subtle to request him in a business which he had done before," Moore tried to rectify a bad situation. "I was forced to tell him (after Arlington's discovery) that his order did hurt us instead of helping us, & did testify against it what I could as being no part of a Christian to give security, our yea being our bond, nor could we be made liable to the wicked requirings of an evil sheriff or any justice of peace or jailer, which I told him that order would bind us unto, being observed." It had been too late. Disgusted, Moore had then advised "those poor betrayed innocent Friends not to proceed further, telling them the danger which might follow to us as men, & also especially as Christians." As for the king and Privy Council, "I am assured this manner of application & matter also of the order will be thrown on me when I shall come amongst them, whom by dear God hath hitherto preserved . . . from their temptations & subtle insinuations." Despite all that had occurred, however, Moore told Fox he was still ready to help, having written to Ellis Hookes "to enquire if the k[ing] be come to Whitehall & to let me forthwith know." He also agreed to go to London to speak with Penn "as thou [Fox] desirest." But he believed that "the remedy will be worse than the disease if error be found, for they having thee in their custody (if that plea be allowed) may find a way to tender the oath again, such malice & mischief hath been hatched by men of corrupt minds."[38]

Despite Fox's desire for Moore and Penn to cooperate, the future proprietor of Pennsylvania, a man proud of his aristocratic connections, was moving in another direction. Penn wrote to Fox on 5 September that he had secured the services of "a person of some quality" who would undertake the case with the king, but who was asking that the Quakers desist for several days. As for Thomas Moore, Penn perceived that "his interest is but flat, & . . . the k[ing] does not much like that he should come to him but," cautioned Penn, "this is private." As for the matter of errors in the indictment, Penn wished to investigate it further with legal counsel: "I love not to give encouragements without grounds."[39] In fact, the "person of quality" that Penn (and William Meade) had approached was Charles Sackville, earl of Middlesex, M.P. for East Grinstead and gentleman of the bedchamber, who arranged for them to meet with James, duke of York, who in turn cited his opposition to religious persecution and promised to bring the case before Charles.[40]

Meanwhile Ellis Hookes, oblivious to these developments and having heard that Thomas Moore was in poor health, wrote to him offering to send a coach to bring him to London if he was willing to meet with Charles. However, as late as 24 September Moore, responding to a letter from George Fox, explained that he was still bedridden, but was hoping to ride up to London in a day or two to meet with William Penn. He would then attempt to speak with Charles who was leaving London for Newmarket on 2 October, and would tell him about the sufferings Fox had undergone during the Commonwealth and his loyalty to Charles I, "for thus I understand thy letter and am glad thou gavest this hint." Neither Fox nor Moore appear at this time to have been aware of the apparent success of Penn's maneuvers. In fact, Moore again advised that it was better to move Charles "for a total discharge (which is in his power only and according to law) then otherwise, which neither his council nor keep[er] can gainsay."[41]

Friends were still concerned about Fox's health. Edward Pitway, a Friend of Bengeworth and a former Evesham magistrate, managed to convince Henry Parker on 8 October to order the gaoler to allow Fox some liberty to get some air "for his health."[42] Matters were not going smoothly in London. Fox wrote to Penn on 10 October in response to letters from Penn and one from Moore "wherein he signifies that it was thy desire he should be still in moving the king as touching my release, thou being pretty confident of effecting of it by another hand." Yet Fox now called on Penn to meet with the late earl of Salisbury's younger son, William Cecil, whose troop of horse was commanded by John, Lord Frescheville, governor of York Castle when Fox was imprisoned there. Cecil, "who is much familiar with the duke of Monmouth," had visited Fox in prison for two hours, took a copy of the alleged errors in the indictment and was, according to Fox, convinced of the "Truth," having often attended meetings at the Bull and Mouth in London. "He is of a pretty natural disposition & knew thee formerly." For stressed that he wished to be released "without the title of a [par]don . . . (concerning which I have written to thee formerly)."[43]

Sadly, Thomas Moore would again feel "betrayed." Writing to Fox on 21 October 1674 he spoke of meeting with Penn "whom thou didst all along wish me to advise with." Moore found that little had been done. He had searched the study of the absent Gerrard Roberts, the London Friend who was coordinating the paperwork, but found little relating to the case. Nor, he added pointedly, "did I perceive William Penn had received any of thy papers or very few, nor did I find at my coming anything done by counsel's advise or otherwise about thy indictment." Moore thereupon decided to address the king "until I was stopped by William Penn's relation that a person or persons had, as it were, effected thy liberty, or such like words, wishing me to desist . . . now lest the king should have denied me & so I might have been thought to have interposed unreasonably & so have been judged to have hindered that said person if he should have miscarried." Moore agreed to wait and Penn had promised to give him an account shortly thereafter. But he had not heard from Penn and now requested advice from Fox, having already written to Penn "to perform what he gave me great assurance in words would be done."[44]

The matter dragged on. The ever-optimistic Penn wrote enthusiastically to Fox on 20 November that "a man of a noble mind, did as good as put himself in a loving way to get thy liberty. He prevailed with the k[ing] for a pardon, but that we rejected." Undaunted, this man[45] then "pressed for a more noble release that better answered Truth," and in fact secured such a release from the king. However, Lord Keeper Finch balked at executing it. Consequently, added Penn, "we have & do use what interest we can." For at least ten days, Friends had been also seeking a writ of error, "well nigh resolving to be as sure as we can," but a writ of *habeas corpus* was to go out that night.[46]

The following day, however, Penn wrote another letter indicating that Edmund Saunders, a future chief justice of King's Bench, on the advice of Thomas Rudyard, had moved the judges of King's Bench for a writ of error, but Justice Wylde remarked that "to jaunt thee up & down, without any certainty, would be at this time very serious." Wylde decided that "first of all they will have a copy of the judgment, & it shall be considered at Westminster, before any *habeas corpus* be granted. If there be a cause then would be time enough; so said the rest." That, Penn added, would unfortunately mean waiting another law term, because the writ of error had to be accepted at Worcester quarter sessions by the clerk of the peace, who was at present in London. The clerk would then need to certify the record of the judgment to the judges in London. All that would take time. As for "the other business, or way of doing of it, [it] is not quite despaired of." Here Penn was referring to the outright release granted by the king.[47] Fox had already responded to Penn's letter of 20 November, and indicated that he again hoped to make use of influence at court. "Here was a Friend of Banbury with me that said if the matter stick[s] with the [lord] keeper he could improve some interest by some friends of his to remove that obstacle." The Friend, Edward Vivers, was willing either to go to London or to contact his friends there. Fox was puzzled over Finch's resistance. "What reason doth he pretend for it, for if the king hath granted such a thing, there needs no more than a warrant to the sheriff to set me at liberty." Enclosed with this letter was another from Margaret Fox to Penn offering to come up to London herself if it "be thought convenient & requisite."[48]

There is no indication that Vivers was put to use, as Penn continued to persist in London. On 1 December he wrote that he was "yet resolved to make one push more about it, so that I cannot write a positive and conclusive account till next seventh or second day, by which time I hope to have an answer of this great man. His uncle lately died, and left him £3000 per annum and [he] just married, which did divert the matter."[49] Penn again explained the lengthy procedure involved with a writ of error, but if it appeared that there were grounds for such a contention, then a *habeas corpus* was also necessary. "The king knows not that thou refusest a pardon, only that we choose rather a more clear and suitable way to thy innocency."[50]

Apparently Penn's efforts were fruitless. Margaret Fox was now called upon. She went to London and saw Charles who, in turn, told her to speak with Lord Keeper Finch. On 25 December she wrote to Finch about the case, but he replied that legally the king could release Fox only by a pardon. In fact, Charles had tried to convince Thomas Moore that Fox should not scruple at accepting a pardon, "for many a man that was as innocent as a child had had a pardon granted him." Nonetheless, Fox continued to oppose a pardon. He finally insisted, after consulting with attorney Thomas Corbett, on a trial of the errors. Writs of error and of *habeas corpus* were therefore obtained and Fox was again to come to London.[51] However, he was unable to meet the specified return date of the writ, thus necessitating further fees and delays. Just before leaving Worcester, he responded to an angry letter from his wife, who was upset over the delays, over fees to be paid to the sheriff, and over disparaging remarks by Fox's attorney in Worcester about Friends' shortsightedness in acceding to such an early return date for the writ of *habeas corpus*. Fox chided her for suggesting that he could have come to London earlier by means of the stage coach, having told her before that it "was fully taken up for two weeks." As for "all those mistakes and neglects at London, they must be looked over, which cannot be helped now they are past." Matters at Worcester had been handled with as much diligence as possible, for Thomas Lower had gone with an attorney on a Friday to speak with the sheriff, "though it was rainy and blustering weather." Unfortunately the sheriff was then executing a commission in the country, but the following day Lower served him with the *habeas corpus*. The sheriff, however, noted that he was required by the writ to certify the entire cause of Fox's imprisonment: that would take time and could not be done until Monday. Lower, upset, insisted that the information had already been certified by the clerk of the peace upon the writ of error. Quite properly, the sheriff countered that that was irrevelent, for he was to do as this writ required. But if Lower would enter into a bond of £1000, an outrageous sum, to bring Fox to London within the time required in the writ, he would allow him to act as Fox's keeper. Lower complained that Fox was as yet in no condition to ride, but the sheriff pointed out that that was the fault of those in London who had "not made the return more large," thus giving Fox more time. Responding to Margaret's annoyance, Fox added:

> & therefore now judge how was it possible, my present condition considered, that I could have come up within the time, for if you did look into the writ you might have seen the writ did require the ground & cause of my imprisonment to be certified, & . . . as for *pro rege & ad subjiciendum*, it was sufficiently understood, both the one & the other, but as the attorney says, though the writ

be *pro rege*, yet the sheriff ought to be paid for his certificate & return, which the court would allow him though for the king. But the attorney was grieved upon my account & that made him express himself so as he did, that things were not managed as they might have been, nor that my condition was not considered, how I was.

Fox added that Thomas Lower had partly engaged for them to come up by coach on Wednesday, 3 February, and that he intended to speak with the sheriff "tomorrow." In what was becoming a veritable farce, Thomas Lower added a postscript defending his own actions, and explaining that Fox and the sheriff would be in London by the end of the week. They could not come up by horseback, but were forced to wait for the stage, "for if the sheriff had been never so ready & all things done to our minds, without a coach my father could not have travelled without hazard of his life, that is tired with walking a little in the garden. But I am better satisfied he is here & pretty well than to have him upon the road, sick & in danger of a relapse, which such a sudden push might have cast him into."[52]

Finally, on 4 February, the undersheriff, clerk of the peace, George Fox, and others set off for London, reaching it on 8 February, near the end of Hilary term. Three days later Fox was brought before the judges in King's Bench. Sir Matthew Hale presided, Thomas Corbett pleaded for Fox, and Thomas Walcot, a future justice of King's Bench, acted for Parker. Corbett surprised the court by ignoring the writ of error, and arguing instead that it was illegal to imprison upon a *praemunire*. Hale correctly retorted that the counselor should have brought this matter up at the beginning of the term, to which Corbett countered that they had been unable at that time to procure a copy of the return and of the indictment. After some more bantering, the matter was deferred until the following day.[53] That evening Richard Davies, a Welsh Friend, acting on Corbett's request, brought him another copy of the indictment. After writing something in the margin in French, Corbett had Davies deliver it to Thomas Rudyard, who in turn delivered it to Hale. Corbett meanwhile delivered his own copy to Judge Wylde. It appears that Corbett, perhaps feeling he had gone too far, suggested that the court first consider the errors before debating the issue of imprisonment.[54] In the event, the errors were considered and allowed, and Fox was ordered to be discharged. Hale turned down Walcot's request that the court re-tender the oath to Fox, who was thereupon officially discharged "without receiving any pardon or coming under any obligation or engagement at all."[55]

Thomas Lower, writing to Margaret Fox from Swarthmoor on 18 February 1675 summed up what had been a most frustrating ordeal. He believed that the Quaker leader "could not have been more nobly released & his adversaries & malicious persecutors less gratified, than by this way & manner of discharge which was always unto me the most probable way to be effected in, & I think my father's mind mostly inclined that way also, though by some . . . it was obstructed, but in that it is at last effected we do rejoice."[56] Although Corbett, when questioned by Friends, reaffirmed his belief that imprisonment on a *praemunire* was illegal and gave legal grounding for his opinion,[57] it does not appear that this defense was used again by Friends or that the authorities gave any credence to it.

This lengthy, frustrating, and convoluted case, involving as it did an extremely important Quaker leader, indicated the necessity for a centralized and coordinated approach to prosecutions. Part of the problem, of course, lay in Fox's principled refusal to accept a pardon, a scruple not adhered to by many other Friends who had shown a willingness to accept the Declaration of Indulgence of 1672. Fox had placed Friends in the untenable position of turning down offers from the crown predicated either on sureties or on willingness to be pardoned. He also put Charles II in an awkward position, since the king did not wish to appear too severe towards the Quakers and yet needed to be wary of parliamentary and local anger at unwonted interference in the legal process. However, as advised by his lord keeper, the king could not, after conviction, grant an unconditional release which implied no wrongdoing. Fox either had to accept a pardon or use the courts to overturn the conviction. As we have seen, he ultimately chose the latter.[58] Nonetheless, without realizing Fox's scruples until late in his imprisonment, Friends had demonstrated an inability to fully cooperate with one another, and had been seriously confused over what type of release was appropriate for a Quaker. Fox was undoubtedly also alarmed by the obviously frayed tempers of his wife and his brethren. However, his imprisonment had revealed an increasing willingness to employ legal counsel, to pay the fees necessary for copies of indictments, mittimuses, and writs, and to combat the law with legal tactics. While this was not completely new, the imprisonment of George Fox, more than any other case, focused Quaker attention dramatically on the need to provide access to legal counsel for those Friends who wished to utilize it, and to coordinate lobbying activities. It is to the credit of the Quakers that they recognized the need for such a legal defense committee, rapidly put it together, and made substantial use of it.

Fox was released in February 1675. Yearly Meeting on 4 June 1675 wrote to provincial Friends asking every quarterly meeting to send a representative to London on 18 October to discuss the best method for easing the sufferings of Friends "by such lawful and just means as may be found out and made use of." It was hoped that this proposed meeting for sufferings would enable provincial Quakers to "obtain such a general understanding of proceedings both in city and country about sufferings" that they would be capable of assisting one another.[59] Although the first officially minuted Meeting for Sufferings did not take place until 22 June 1676, and initially had few cases, it would soon be swamped with enquiries and would develop into a sophisticated legal defense organization which would play a strategic role in the survival of Quakerism into the Age of Toleration.

NOTES

Unless otherwise stated, manuscript sources are located in the library of the Society of Friends, London. At the risk of losing some of the flavor of seventeenth-century prose, but for ease of comprehension, all manuscript and primary printed quotations have been modernized in punctuation, capitalization, and spelling. The only exceptions are archaic words or awkward tenses, e.g. doth, shouldst, believeth.

1. See Anne Audland, *A True Declaration of the Suffering of the Innocent* (London, 1655), p. 4; John Camm, *Some Particulars Concerning the Law, Sent to Oliver Cromwell* (London, 1654), pp. 4–5; Anthony Pearson, *The Great Case of Tythes Truly Stated* (London, 1657), p. 23; Joseph Besse, *Collection of the Sufferings of the People Called Quakers*, 2 vols. (London, 1753), 1:46–47.

2. This is not intended to overlook the continuing contribution of older Friends, particularly George Fox, whose organizational skills and symbolic role as "founder" of the Children of Light were still essential (see below). Yet many early Quaker leaders were dead or were spending most of their time traveling in the ministry. See, for example, John Blaykling to George Fox, 29.xi [January]. 1687/8, Draw-Well (A.R.B. MSS, fol. 139); Barry Reay, *The Quakers and the English Revolution* (New York, 1985), p. 127, although some of those he cites as influential Quakers are highly questionable.

3. MS Book of Cases, 1:3.

4. See, for example, George Fox, *The Law of God the Rule of Law-makers* (London, 1658), pp. 4, 25–26.

5. *Journal of George Fox*, John Nickalls, ed. (London, 1975), pp. 670–71.

6. Spence MSS, 2:397. For the mittimus, see 2:394–95.

7. T. Lower to Mary Lower, 7.xi [January].1673/4 (Abraham MSS, fol. 17).

8. Thomas Moore to James Parke and George Fox, 14.xi [January].1673/4

(Spence MSS, 3:169–70); Ellis Hookes to Margaret Fox, 9.xi [January].1673/4 (Swarthmore MSS, 1:58); see also Spence MSS, 3:169–70.

9. Hookes to M. Fox (Swarthmore MSS, 1:58). Hookes had hoped to obtain a writ of *habeas corpus* to bring Fox and Lower to London, but he had been advised by legal counsel that it was "contrary to practice to grant any habeas corpus to remove any prisoners on the Crown side, but motion in court in the term time."

10. T. Lower to Mary Lower, 7.xi [January].1673/4, Worcester gaol (Abraham MSS, fol. 17).

11. Fox to Whitehead, Ellis Hookes, and Thomas Moore, 17.xi [January].1673/4, Worcester gaol (Spence MSS, 2:398); George Fox, *A Journal*, Thomas Ellwood, ed. (London, 1694), p. 391. Although staying with Fox, Lower had been technically discharged (*Journal*, Nickalls, p. 677).

12. Fox to Whitehead, Hookes, and Moore (Spence MSS, 2:398). Italics are those of Fox.

13. G. Fox to M. Fox, 21.xi [January].1673/4, Worcester gaol (*Journal of the Friends Historical Society* [hereafter *JFHS*], 11 [1914]:98); E. Mann to M. Fox, 23.xi [January].1673/4, London (Spence MSS, 2:400); John Rous to Margaret Fox, 24.xi [January].1673/4, Kingston Upon Thames (Spence MSS, 3:172–73).

14. G. Fox to M. Fox, 8.xii [February].1673/4 (Abraham MSS, fol. 18). Part of this passage was subsequently crossed through, probably by Fox, but is legible.

15. *Journal*, Nickalls, p. 682. The four judges of King's Bench were Chief Justice Matthew Hale, and puisne justices Richard Rainsford, William Wylde, and Thomas Twisden. Apparently, either Twisden or Rainsford was not present.

16. *Journal*, Nickalls, pp. 682–83.

17. Fox to Charles II and his Council (Spence MSS, 2:399); George Fox to Margaret Fox, 6.i [March].1673/4, London (*Journal*, Nickalls, p. 684). In fact, since Fox had not yet been convicted, Charles could have granted a *nolle prosequi*, thus superceding the prosecution. He chose to ignore this option.

18. M. Rous to Margaret Fox, 21.i [March].1673/4, Kingston Upon Thames (Spence MSS, 3:178–79).

19. W. Penn to M. Fox, 16. i [March].1673/4 (*Friends Miscellany*, 5 (1834): 228).

20. George Fox to Margaret Fox, 4.ii [April].1674 (*Journal*, Nickalls, pp. 686–87); see also *JFHS*, 11 (1914):100–1. Turner, of course, could have actively supported Parker and those justices anxious to *praemunire* Fox, by re-tendering the oath. Like the king, however, he chose not to intervene.

21. The Quakers were often confused as to whether traversing was consistent with their principles. For more on this and other legal issues Friends encountered, and their response, see Craig W. Horle, "Partridges Upon the Mountains: The Quakers and the English Legal System, 1660–1688," Ph.D diss., University of Maryland, 1985.

22. *Journal*, Nickalls, pp. 689–92.

23. G. Fox to M. Fox, 4.iii [May].1674 (Gibson MSS, 1:123).

24. George Fox to Margaret Fox, 17.iii [May].1674 (A. Midgeley Cash Collec-

tion, unpaginated, in envelope endorsed "Original Letters written by George Fox, (Admiral) W. Penn, Benjn. Holme").

25. For the paper presented by Fox, see Spence MSS, 2:387.

26. G. Fox to M. Fox, 9.iv [June].1674, London (Portfolio 36:35).

27. *Journal*, Nickalls, pp. 694–98; *The Journal of George Fox*, Norman Penney, ed., 2 vols. (Cambridge, 1911), 2:288–89; see also Spence MSS, 2:401.

28. *Journal*, Nickalls, pp. 696–97; *Journal*, Penney, 2:290–93.

29. *Journal*, Nickalls, pp. 697–98.

30. Ellis Hookes to Margaret Fox, 15.v. [July].1674, London (Spence MSS, 2:401); E. Hookes to M. Fox, 23.v [July].1674 (Spence MSS, 2:406); *Journal*, Nickalls, p. 699.

31. *Journal*, Nickalls, pp. 699–700.

32. T. Moore to G. Fox, 7.vi [August].1674 (Spence MSS, 2:415). Meade had been William Penn's co-defendant in the landmark 1670 trial. In 1681 he would marry Sarah Fell, one of the daughters of Margaret Fox, and would become an increasingly prominent member of the London executive meetings.

33. Sir Henry Bennet, earl of Arlington, secretary of state.

34. T. Moore to G. Fox, 14.vi [August].1674 (Spence MSS, 2:417–18).

35. Gilbert Latey to George Fox, 15.vi [August].1674 (Spence MSS, 2:390–91).

36. E. Hookes to G. Fox, 27.vi [August].1674 (Spence MSS, 2:392).

37. G. Fox and T. Lower to W. Penn, 28.vi [August].1674 (Historical Society of Pennsylvania: Penn-Forbes Papers, 2:49).

38. T. Moore to G. Fox, 3.vii [September].1674 (Spence MSS, 2:393).

39. W. Penn to G. Fox, 5.vii [September].1674 (Penn MSS, fol. 131).

40. *The Papers of William Penn*, Richard and Mary Maples Dunn, eds. (Philadelphia, 1981), 1:292–93n.

41. E. Hookes to Margaret Fox, 8.vii [September].1674, Southwark (Spence MSS, 2:419); T. Moore to G. Fox, 24.vii [September].1674 (Spence MSS, 3:171).

42. H. Parker to John Harris, 8 October 1674 (*Journal*, Nickalls, p. 701).

43. G. Fox and Thomas Lower to W. Penn, 10.viii [October].1674 (HSP: Penn-Forbes Papers, 2:50). Italics are mine.

44. T. Moore to G. Fox, 21.viii [October].1674 (Dix MSS, Z2).

45. Charles Sackville, earl of Middlesex.

46. W. Penn to G. Fox, 20.ix [November].1674 (Friends Historical Library, Swarthmore College, Small Collections, Penn).

47. W. Penn to G. Fox, 21.ix [November].1674 (Friends Historical Library, Swarthmore College, Small Collections, Penn). Because of the substantial likelihood of error in most indictments, a writ of error was issued only by grace of the court of King's Bench, and required a fiat from the attorney general.

48. G. Fox and M. Fox to W. Penn, 25.ix [November].1674 (HSP: Penn-Forbes Papers, 2:51).

49. Charles Sackville's (see n. 45, above) uncle was Lionel Cranfield, earl of Middlesex, who died on 26 October 1674; his new wife, whom he married in June 1674, was Mary, widow of Charles Berkeley, earl of Falmouth (*Papers of William Penn*, R. and M. Dunn, 1:293n).

50. W. Penn to George Fox, 1.x [December].1674 (Gibson MSS, 2:39).

51. M. Fox to Heneage Finch, 25.x [December].1674 (Spence MSS, 3:129); *Journal*, Nickalls, pp. 701-2.

52. G. Fox and T. Lower to M. Fox, 30.xi [January].1674/5 (Spence MSS, 3:167-68); see also *Journal*, Nickalls, pp. 702-3. The writ of *habeas corpus ad subjiciendum* ordered the sheriff to produce the body of the prisoner, with the day and cause of his arrest and detention, to submit to and receive whatever the court awarding the writ should decide. Its purpose was to rectify illegal imprisonment.

53. *Journal*, Nickalls, pp. 703-4.

54. Richard Davies, *An Account of the Convincements, Exercises, Services and Travels of . . . Richard Davies*, 6th ed. (London, 1825), pp. 104-5; Alfred Braithwaite, "Imprisonment upon a Praemunire: George Fox's Last Trial," *JFHS*, 50 (1962-64):42n.

55. Davies, *Account of Convincements*, p. 104; *Journal*, Nickalls, p. 705.

56. T. Lower to M. Fox, 18.xii [February].1674/5, Swarthmore (Spence MSS, 2:420).

57. Corbett's opinion can be found in MS Book of Cases, 1:17, and has been modernized and printed (with some minor inaccuracies) in Braithwaite, "Imprisonment upon a Praemunire," p. 41.

58. For more on this question of a pardon, see Alfred W. Braithwaite, "George Fox's Last Imprisonment," *JFHS*, 51 (1965-67):165-66.

59. MS minutes of London Yearly Meeting, 1:22-24.

Quaker Prophetesses and Mothers in Israel

To write about early Quaker women in an age of great modern women scholars should evoke modesty in any man who can aspire to that virtue. Antonia Fraser and others have made vivid to us the dramatic lives of all manner of seventeenth-century women. Quakers can gain insights from the works of Mabel Brailsford, Auguste Jorns, Elfrida Vipont Foulds, Emily Manners and Emelia Fogelklou Norlind on early Friends in general, and specifically from Maria Webb and Isabel Ross on Margaret Fell, and Mary Maples Dunn on early Quaker women.[1] Elizabeth Gray Vining has pointed out that Quakerism gained strength from its start by treating women not as a special group, nor even as mere equals, but simply as people.[2] My concern here is with two specific roles played by early Quaker women, which continued in later times and affect Quaker women ministering today. Both roles are named from the description in Judges of Deborah as prophetess and nurturer in the Wars of the Lord.

Early women Friends spoke of themselves as prophetesses, divinely led and given a message to write, preach and speak in meetings for worship and in missions throughout the world. Margaret Fell and others were called Mothers in Israel, as they counseled each other and younger Friends in spiritual crises, visited the sick, prisoners and poor Friends, managed their households, and organized the Women's Meetings. If we divide these two roles into the sacred and the secular, this would be our distinction, not theirs; they had placed all of life under the testing and leading of the Light. Neither their prophetic nor motherly roles implied at first any new status within the family, nor in the economic market nor on the social ladder. New forms of Quaker women's organization changed men's ideas of women only slowly.

Friends were not always the pioneers. It is important to notice the roles of non-Quaker women and the respect they were given for practical, if not always for spiritual, achievements. In the Puritan environment in England and its colonies, the place of women can easily be portrayed too

darkly or else too glowingly. Puritan men gave women more companionship and respect and allowed them more integrity than men in most
previous ages. The "Dame school" and the parsonage school, where
women learned to read, write and keep accounts, even if not much more,
were crucial in Puritan England and New England.[3] Calvinist doctrines
of the weakness of Eve's causing original sin remained as a mark against
women. Puritans had no patience with either courtiers or courtesans, nor
hence with women's leading roles later in Baroque drama, society, and
the arts. A community like Massachusetts that ignored noble rank had
also little place for scholarly patronesses like Lady Conway or Princess
Elizabeth of the Palatinate, whose roles combined high rank and
spiritual depth.[4] But on the farm or in the workshop, Puritan husbands
and wives shared spinning, weaving and tilling in every household. The
medieval tradition that work was shared by men and women had seldom
extended to giving women guild membership. Thus a fuller family part-
nership probably resulted in the seventeenth-century when guilds and
town-wide communities lost their hold on individuals.[5]

In Puritan churches a polity without nuns created no roles for women
even as deaconesses. Even in his own family the father was expected to
lead worship.[6] The general ridicule of the home worship led by Ann
Hutchinson and the few Baptist preacheresses underlined the usual
norms. Yet Roland Bainton has shown that Luther and the Puritans saw
the home replacing the convent as the "school of Christ" based on the
"counsels of perfection": humility and selfless love. Here male and
female shared a calling both earthly and spiritual, and made daily home
worship a substitute for the monastic hours. Puritan diaries and death
memorials show the same sharing of deep purposes between husbands
and wives, even when physically separated, as do early Quaker journals.[7]

In early Quakers' marriages, the experience of positive companionship
in faith and worship paralleled the Puritans'. A large part of the journal
of John Banks consists of his letters to and from his wife. Banks was a
Cumberland farm boy of only local education and meager religious background before his convincement as a Friend in 1653. Fifteen years later
he felt called to travel in ministry. On his first journey he wrote back:

Dear wife,
   In that love that lasteth and still endureth, remaineth and increaseth in my
heart to thee is it wherein I read and feel thee; the farther I am separated from
thee, the nearer thou art unto me, even in that which length of time nor
distance of place shall never be able to wear out or bring a decay upon; feel the
reach of my love in thy heart.

Ann Banks' replies were in the same spirit:

> My dear and well beloved husband, unto whom my love reacheth, though separated in body for a season, according to the good pleasure of the Lord, . . . I dearly salute thee, in a measure of that . . . Truth that is our Life, our unity and fellowship. . . . Dear Husband, by this thou mayst understand that I and all our dear children with the rest of the family are all well, and as truly willing and content to give thee up to do service for the Lord, being satisfied it is in answer to his requiring that thou art separated from us.[8]

Francis Howgill's last letter to his daughter Abigail reflects the same spirit, as does Margaret Fell's one surviving letter to her non-Quaker husband (in which she also instructed the Judge about some Quaker publishing): "Dear Heart, mind the Lord above all, . . . to keep thee pure and clear and single before him, without self-end whatsoever."[9] One should not assume that all early Quaker itinerants' marriages were sunny or spiritual. Miles Halhead's wife complained: "I would to God I had married a drunkard, I might have found him in the Alehouse," and Halhead told her their son's death was God's judgment for her rebellious spirit.[10] Early Friends' openness to travel probably had multiple motives.

Thomas Edwards' *Gangraena* and an act of Parliament of 1646 attacked women preachers among the Dutch and English separatists in Holland, the "Brownist" congregations in southeastern England, and the General Baptists of Coleman Street in London. Katherine Chidley, already suspect as a Leveller, gathered her own Brownist group in Bury St. Edmunds. Antonia Fraser says that

> in contrast to the 'preacheress', the prophetess had always been treated with a certain nervous respect by society . . . Jane Hawkins, 'a poor woman (and she but a pedlar)' . . . in 1629 had for a period [of weeks] prophesied before 200 people. Claiming direct inspiration from God, the prophetess might challenge accepted notions concerning religion and society but she did not necessarily in her own person challenge the accepted order. [The parallel may be with spiritualist mediums today.] What differentiated the Civil War period was the substantial increase in the number of prophetesses. . . . In this time of hopes and dreams and visions the attitude of authority itself—the Army, Council, new Parliament, new rulers such as Cromwell—was equally more responsive.[11]

The Army Council heard and discussed the prophecy of Elizabeth Poole encouraging its power, and Mary Pope wrote on *Magistracy*, "God having made me a Mother in Israel." Individual women claiming direct divine inspiration later led the Shakers, the Amana Inspirationists, Christian Scientists and Jemima Wilkinson's community of the Public Universal Friend, just as Antoinette Bourignon was "Light of the World" to her own Dutch sect in Fox's day. All these women shared with early Friends a millennial trust that with their movement a new "Age of the Spirit" had begun, justifying new ways of life for both genders.[12] The eccentric lives of Eleanor Davies and the antinomian morals of Anna Trapnel, however, made Puritans suspect most prophetesses. Mrs. Attoway rejected her "unsanctified" husband. In any case, Friends did not distinguish prophetesses from other preachers.

The prophetic call to speak came to most early men Friends first in the setting of their own meeting, followed months or years later by a call to carry a message further afield. We must assume a similar sequence for women Friends: the first surviving records of their experiences, in the relative absence of journals, are often tracts telling of their journeys.

Quaker women's journeys took place disproportionately within the first eight years after the religious awakening on Firbank Fell, the period of "the Lamb's War" when the Spirit of the Lord seemed to be conquering the English Northwest and then the whole nation and the world. Puritans noted the prominence of Quaker women preachers, usually traveling in pairs. Women were the first Friends at London, Oxford, and Cambridge. Twelve of the twenty-two Quaker challengers from England to Massachusetts before 1660 were women, though only fourteen out of sixty-eight in the next forty years. Data from both Philadelphia and Wales show this proportion of one in five was fairly stable thereafter.[13]

Most of those who went to judge New England had already traveled widely to preach within England. The women traveled more often than men did to far and dramatic places. Elizabeth Harris did the pioneer work in Maryland. The journeys of Mary Fisher, Katherine Evans and Sarah Cheevers in the eastern Mediterranean in 1659–60 became famous, but Beatrice Beckley, Mary Prince and Elizabeth Cowart also reached "papist" Italy. Along with the hanged Mary Dyer and flogged Elizabeth Hooton, Quaker martyrology should include Mary Clark and Mary Weatherhead who were lost at sea, and Sarah Gibbons drowned in a canoe as she landed in Rhode Island. Even more than Quaker men the women seem to have felt called to confront hostile environments. Since most women then were identified by the names of their husbands, the lack of clues about most women itinerants suggests that many of them were unmarried, widowed, or out of sympathy with their husbands.[14] Some were restless at home. It is astonishing how many women married and settled far from their childhood homes: Ann Clayton and Mary Dyer in Rhode Island; Mary Fisher in Carolina.

We may remember that these women were ready psychologically for such exotic missions, as we consider specific prophetic "leadings" of early Quaker women. Friends were pioneers in expecting divine "openings" to come to all their members, women and men alike. Key Quaker Bible texts about their own movement included Joel 2:28 and its fulfilment at Pentecost, when God's Spirit is poured out on all flesh so that both sons and daughters shall prophesy. Those verses grace the title page of Margaret Fell's tract, *Women's Speaking* (1666), perhaps the first book by a woman on this subject. As Quakers' experience of moral purification implied the restoring of Eden, she gave priority to the first two chapters of Genesis, where God blessed male and female equally and Eve was Adam's helpmeet, rather than Chapter 3 where Paradise was lost. Margaret Fell played with Paul's phrases about Christ as the Seed of Woman and the Church as his bride. She omitted the bloodthirsty "Song of Deborah" but otherwise outlined the succession of prophetesses, from Miriam through Hannah and Huldah to the New Testament Anna and Mary Magdalene, the first person to see the Risen Christ. Since Puritans constantly quoted Paul's ban on women's speaking in Church, Margaret Fell made clear, as had Fox and Samuel Fisher before her, that Paul had said nothing against the Holy Spirit speaking through women.

"Leadings" to give a message were normally received during a silent gathering "in the Spirit" at a meeting for worship, but many came at home or at night. The phrases most often used, "it was said to me," "I was commanded," "it came to me," avoided identifying the divine speaker as one Person of the Trinity, leaving moderns free to wrestle with relevant issues of faith and insights of psychology. Early Friends themselves knew that such impulses might be premature or "mixed" in origin. George Fox, for instance, gave no encouragement in response to a widowed schoolteacher, Barbara Blaugdone, who wrote him a few weeks after her convincement,[15] and a bit later carried out an effective prophetic mission to Dublin. Fox also ignored her letter two years later:

George: I had these words rose in me: "Wo be to that nation whose teachers are fools and princes are children, that hew unto themselves broken cisterns that will hold no water; therefore everyone to your tents, return unto your habitations, even to the Light which Christ Jesus hath enlightened you withal. [cf. Isa. 3:4; Jer. 2:13; 1 Kings 12:16.] For as ye take counsel of the mouth of the Lord, even so shall your work prosper." This rose in me the first day the [1656] Parliament sat; but I was then in prison [in Marlborough?], and I knew not whether that might be shown to me which was done by another to them in a steeple-house. If it hath not been done, and thou see the work be mine, I desire a line from thee the second or first post. . . . If I hear not from thee, I shall abide here till the understanding of those I writ to thee of be opened, that should go with me to Jerusalem; they have all been very sick. . . .

Barbara Blaugdone

Since that, I saw Christopher Burket, Sara Smitten and Margaret Thomas should pass to Jerusalem; but the time I knew not, nor of those I writ to thee of before.[16]

Barbara Blaugdone treated her "leadings" not as "experiences" but as objective messages to be delivered by any or many Friends interchangeably. There was always a "truth-content" to a Quaker leading.[17]

Women Friends were as likely as men therefore to try to put into print messages they had been given. At a period when books by women were rare and few women intended to be known as authors,[18] Quaker women wrote 220 tracts of the 3853 which Friends are known to have published before 1700. Eighty-two of the 650 early Quaker authors were women, though 48 of them published only one tract each. Most used an educated or at least a biblical vocabulary, but their handwriting and spelling in letters home varied from neat to childish.[19] Of all the Quaker women's publications, nine to twelve were partially autobiographical accounts, but they were shorter and simpler than the men's journals. None except Margaret Fell had her written works reprinted as a collection. Eight other Quaker women had five or more tracts published: Sarah Blackberry, Hester Biddle, Ann Dockwra, Dorcas Dole, Abigail Fisher, Rebekah Travers, Dorothy White and Joan Whitrowe. None was a well known leader or preacher. Of their tracts, apart from joint petitions, 36% represent prophetic messages of about eight pages, and 16% exhortations to those in political power, doubling in both areas the corresponding percentages of tracts by men. By contrast theological tracts debating against Puritans and other Churchmen were only 8% of the women's titles, against 21% for the men's; if the ratio is based on numbers of pages the disproportion is much higher.[20]

When a Quaker woman spoke, the message was more often moral than doctrinal, expressing a judgment against injustice; a modern writer may see this pattern as affirming women's identity.[21] Often a warning was given face-to-face to a non-Quaker priest, ruler or judge, so that emotional intensity and intuitions of God's prompting were appropriate. The message and the messenger could ignore social courtesies and class conventions.

The right of God's Spirit to transcend ordinary social mores had been invoked not only by Quakers, but by women halfway to Ranterism, such as Anna Trapnel and Nayler's friends Dorcas Erbury, Martha Simmonds and Hannah Stranger. Friends then as now knew some were psychotic;

indeed the conflict of Fox and Nayler concerned whether their duty was to foster or to judge "leadings" in other Quakers which might be delusions. In the public mind these women's lives discredited the claims of all who felt prophetically led. "Leadings of the Spirit" might represent the surfacing of impulses, healthy or not, that neither men nor women normally let themselves express, or perhaps even feel, in respectable society. The antinomian Mary Gadbury had been deserted by her husband. She encouraged her lover William Franklin's claims to be Christ reincarnate; she was shattered when during his trial he renounced them.[22]

Yet Friends as sober as Robert Barclay sometimes felt the call to "go naked for a sign." A Quaker reader of Isaiah 20, where the prophet stripped himself like a prisoner of war to warn Hebrews of the results of rebellion against Assyria, might feel an impulse to do likewise. The shock of resistance in his or her ego would then seem like pride that must be yielded to the Spirit. No women Friends felt this burden laid upon them as regularly as did William Simpson, Richard Robinson, Samuel Cater of Ely and Solomon Eccles; two Massachusetts women Friends along with three Englishwomen did so once.[23] Women less often made predictive prophecies, whether they were fulfilled like Humphrey Smith's, or "deluded" like James Milner's.[24]

A commoner ploughing up of the psychic depths came through dreams and visions, which were not limited to old and young men as in Joel 2:28. Mary Penington's, though preceding her Quaker "convincement" (which in her mind it forecast) and hidden for a century in a letter to her daughter, has become famous:

My mind being thus almost continuously exercised, I dreamed that I was sitting alone, retired and sad; and . . . heard . . . shrieking, yelling and roaring, . . . in a way of triumph and joy. . . It was manifested to me that . . . "Christ is come indeed, and is in the next room; and with him is the bride, the Lamb's wife [the true Church]." At this my heart secretly leaped within me, and I was ready to get up to go and express my love to him; . . . but something within me stopped me and bade me not to be hasty, . . . for it was said unto me: "Stay and see whether he will own thee. . . ." So I stood still . . . at the lower end of the hall, and Christ was at the upper end, whose appearance was that of a fresh lovely youth, clad in gray cloth, very plain and neat (at this time I had never heard of the Quakers or their habit) I saw him embrace several poor, old, simple people, whose appearance was very contemptible and mean, without wisdom or beauty. . . . At last he beckoned me to come near him, of which I was very glad. . . .

After a little while it was said: "the Lamb's wife is also come"; at which I beheld a beautiful young woman, slender, modest and grave, in plain garments.[25]

Much less well-known is a letter from Susanna Arnold to Fox, who dated it 1657:

Dear ffrend:

I am moued to declare unto thee how it hath bene with me since I sawe thy face in the flesh. Upon the seaventh day, when I departed from the, being come about five miles, I sait me downe to rest, & sitting upon the ground a while, I [was as(?)] if I had bene taken out of the body, being not sensable where [I was in the outward] but after a while [(words torn out and blotted make the next two lines nearly illegible)] In Spirit and upon the f[our]th day after, I dreamed that I was carried into a p[leasa]nt garden where [(illegible)] the weeds the ground brought forth & as I came from the garden there stood in the way many outward p[(?)]s & I was maid to stand [(word lost)] when I came at them & they was very viseius, but after awhile I was maid to come bouldly through the midst of them, declareing and spreading forth my hands at them, and they was all put to silence & then I was brought to my outward being, and when I came there: there was a taall child brought unto me which were clothed in whit Raiment and where soever I went It with me, & the next day after, being the fift day of the weeke, wee had a meting at my outward being. As I was wating upon the Lord in silence, it came: "the manhood of Christ is witnessed." Upon the third day of the weke after, there was at the next house to ours a company of proud men & some of them they call gentlemen which did hiely dishonor the Lord in drinking & vaine pastime which I was much burthened with all, but at that preasant I had nothing given from the Lord & so I was willing to be silent; but in the neight they was set in my vewe and how it was with them, so I was wakened by the mighty Power of the Lord working in me & I was commanded to write, & in obedience to the Lord I was said to rise out of bed in the night & writ unto them, & in obeying I had s[weet] peace; and upone the seventh day after, it came in great power: "heatherto I have wrought, and worke thou"; and it continued with me all the day. & upon the secant day of the weke after, in the morning, I was at our fire & it came unto me in great power: "I have chosen thee into [(word blotted)]." And so I Rest wating upon the Lord & desireing the [(blotted)] of the Lord to pray for me, that I may be kept faitul & obedient unto the Lord iesus Christ.

Susanna Arnold[26]

Friends commonly felt intense emotions upon first convincement. Fox crossed out phrases in other letters of intense affection to himself. Even Margaret Fell had signed with the whole Swarthmoor household one such rhapsodic letter in 1652, whose postscript seems to be in her handwriting:

Thee knows that wee have recived thee into our hearts, & shall live with thee eternally, & it is our life & ioy to be with thee. And soe my Dear heart, let not the power of darknesse separate thy bodyly presence from us, which will be A greefe & trouble to us.[27]

Considering the intensity of feelings stirred up by early Quaker experience, it may bring comfort to note that Christopher Atkinson was the only early Quaker preacher charged publically with a sexual offence.[28] Outbursts of joy and mutual affection easily overwhelmed newly convinced Friends because they had sat for agonizing weeks of bitter self-discovery under the searching Light. Their torments and their breaking through were described in Banks's, Crisp's, Burnyeat's and many other journals and Hubberthorne's letters.[29] Their pilgrimage through self-judgment and inner purgation made them need to check their impatience for the dawn of joy, making doubly intense the moments when a gathered Quaker meeting experienced love or surrender. Drastic changes in the self and in human habits aroused intense feelings. However dangerous, the process was known and was as intentional among Friends as later among Wesleyan revivalists. Quaker women were as sober and wise in handling such emotions in themselves and each other as were the men, often indeed showing more maturity.

The role of spiritual counselor, for which Quaker women were noted, bridges any gap we might make between the inward and outward, the roles of prophetess and "Mother in Israel." Many Friends recorded in their journals that early in their inner struggle "a Friend . . . being touched with a sense of my Condition, was made willing to [speak words, or] read a paper in the Meeting which was suitable to my Condition."[30] Often it is not clear whether the helper was man or woman. Later, men were encouraged to help men, and women women, and the formal title of Elder was recognized among Friends,[31] though the practice was as old as medieval nuns or hermitesses. Some early letters survive whereby men Friends sent women to Margaret Fell for guidance. Nayler wrote in 1653:

> As for Ellen Parr, I hear that she is come towards thee; inquire and send for her, if she be not come to thee. Judge the death, but save the little thing which I have seen moving in her. Let her stay a while with thee, and show her the way of love, which is much lost in the height.[32]

Cases of such counseling by Margaret Fell, Ann Downer, Mary Penington, and other Quaker women can be found in the journals of Thomas Ellwood, and are implied in many letters to Swarthmoor which closed by asking for prayer for the writers. Letters of spiritual counsel, like those later written by Isaac Penington and Fox, or those between Robert Barclay and Princess Elizabeth of the Palatinate, seem less common from Quaker women, though many have been lost.[33]

Quaker women had also much experience in providing practical help. Friends' country homes, shops and farms had been kept solvent, and open to Quaker visitors, by women like Margaret Fell, Ann Banks, Ann

Nayler, Ann Camm and Loveday Hambly whose husbands were away on the road. Quaker matrons in England and New Jersey shared in a tradition running from the Crusaders' widows to the redoubtable Victorian lady missionaries for "coping" with the management of a big household. A study found 12.9% of sixteenth century English households headed by widows, who by law could inherit as freeholders at least a third of the husband's estate, quite apart from those whose husband was regularly away as a trader or at war.[34] The English Civil War made heroines on both sides who led the defense of their homes as castles under many months of siege, or made repeated hard journeys to London to petition for their imprisoned husbands' freedom or their legal rights to sequestered estates. Most married women had young children, (though Quakers had fewer and later than the population at large)[35] and no alternative to staying home.

Most unmarried women of all classes spent at least their teen years on the staff of a large household, often not under their mother but at a king's court, a nobleman's estate or a merchant's or farmer's homestead. Marriage gave them a home to manage themselves.

Wives in Puritan homes had shared in daily home worship and had led it when their husbands were away. Those who headed a "house" or manor had usually held responsibility for the parish:

> [Margaret Fell had been] inquiring after the way of the Lord, and went often to hear the best ministers that came into our parts, . . . whom we often entertained at our house, . . . and had often prayers and religious exercise in our family.[36]

Wives of tradesmen and craftsmen were even more likely to have taken part in the life of congregations outside the Church of England parishes, like the women to whom John Bunyan ascribed his conversion in *Grace Abounding.* In London the organizational role of Isabel Buttery, Ruth Brown and Ann Downer in setting up the first Quaker meetings has been described. From 1653 also, Quaker women seem to have worked with Amor Stoddard and the Drings to oversee Quaker publications through the London printers. Martha Simmonds, whom Quakers know mainly as James Nayler's adoring follower, may have played a wider intellectual role. Perhaps partly responding to her interests, her brother Giles Calvert and husband and brother-in-law Thomas and Matthew Simmonds, all printers, began from 1648 onward to reprint English editions of the tracts of the continental mystics Jakob Boehme and Henrik Niclaes, whose sects had virtually died out, as well as most of the Quakers' early writings.

London Quaker women organized too to meet Friends' physical needs,

50

William Crouch reported that "some ancient women Friends did meet together . . . to inspect the circumstance and condition of such who were imprisoned on Truth's account, and to provide things needful to supply their wants."[37] Upon their work, Fox established about 1659 the weekly "Box Meeting," the women's "Two Weeks Meeting," and a decade later the "Meeting for Sufferings," which took over the roles that Margaret Fell's "Kendal Fund" in the Northwest had played in gathering information and collecting and distributing funds for all Quakers in prison or suffering economic hardship everywhere. The practical results of the women's care for prisoners can be seen in Thomas Ellwood's accounts of the crowded Quaker groups in Newgate and Bridewell jails in 1662, to whom the women brought not only food and bedding but tools to work at their trade. Elizabeth Lilburne and Mary Overton became famous for their visits and jailings with their Leveller husbands, and the biggest, most-signed petition of the era was by women on their behalf.[38] Prisoners' wives or lovers usually brought their meals and jailer's fees, but the early Quaker women cared more equally and efficiently in each prison for all male and female Friends, whose suffering was part of their common campaign, "the Lamb's War." In 1656 Ann Downer walked 200 miles to Cornwall where Fox was in Doomsdale dungeon; Ann Nayler came the next year from Yorkshire to nurse her husband in the Tower of London; and Margaret Fell traveled the length of England repeatedly to try to persuade the London authorities to liberate Fox. Quaker women too were imprisoned. Margaret Fell and the Boston prisoners are famous, but nearly every traveling preacher spent nights or months in jail; by day they could often join the men prisoners for meals or in meetings for worship.

Some of the practical services done by early Quaker women were not unique to Friends, being substitutes for the welfare services intended by the medieval Church and the Church of England parishes under the Elizabethan "Poor Law." These included care for orphans and for those too old to support themselves. Some of the poor, both Friends and non-Quakers, needed to be fed. Yet the main difference between Quaker women of all classes and the most charitable gentlewomen was probably the intensely religious spirit in which each meeting's members felt called to help.

Margaret Fell's letters asking money for the "Kendal Fund" for prisoners and their families in 1654–58 expressed this spirit:

> You may know the mystery of the Fellowship, and be in that Mystery, in Unity with the Brethren: that so you may come to be with them in their Sufferings, in their Tryals, Travels [travails], Troubles, Sufferings, Whippings, Stockings, Prisonings.[39]

After the Conventicle Act of the 1660s had jailed and caused the death of most of the Quaker leaders, closed channels like the Kendal Fund, and driven all the local meetings back upon their own resources, Fox proposed in 1671 a nationwide system of parallel men's and women's monthly meetings for business. Some jobs tended to be the men's meetings' responsibilities: teen-agers needed to be formally apprenticed in a craftman's home and shop to learn a trade, tools or materials loaned even for adult craftsmen, and graveyards bought and maintained. Farmers who had lost their cattle and barns by fires or by sheriff's fines were given emergency help. Other needs came under the women's meetings for example, registration of births and care of the sick, cripples and elderly. The women's money might come from their own household funds or from the men's meetings: the basic social and economic pattern of the wider society was little changed. Women's meetings caused ardent polarization among Friends, however, when they were asked to approve separately all prospective marriages.[40]

Quaker marriages combined a traditional English pattern with a prophetic Quaker "Testimony," in this case against the parish clergy. Friends felt an intense religious responsibility for individuals and families. Oliver Cromwell's Civil Registration of Marriages gave status after 1653 to some common law marriages, and to North-of-England "handfast marriages" before lay witnesses. For the sake of the legitimacy and property rights of children, Fox worked to legalize Quaker marriages, especially after new marriage laws in 1655 and at the Restoration. For moral reasons, to protect against men or women running away from a prior engagement or a marriage in a Baptist or sectarian group, and to ensure the approval of parents, the engaged Quaker couple had to show their "clearness" before both the men's and women's meetings. Women were more likely to know and to be able to guide the prospective bride. The special strain which Quaker life put onto both individuals and families needed the mutual support of a couple who shared a commitment to Quakerism, and of families who knew all about their fellow members in the meeting.

The newly formalized responsibilities required techniques of presiding and record-keeping which some Quaker women had yet to learn. Handmade copies have recently been found of an "epistle" sent out by the Lancaster Quarterly Women's Meeting some time between 1675 and 1681, to "Women's Meetings Everywhere."[41] It was written by Margaret Fell's daughter Sarah, whose careful account books of Swarthmoor Hall for the 1670s have also been published.

Any uniform, centralized pattern always draws fire from some Friends.

Fox found that those who stood against the independent, separate and almost equal status of women's meetings were often the weightiest male Friends in little local meetings. Their protest upset Fox, since they accused him of seeking undue authority as a "Quaker Pope," whereas there is some evidence that he wanted to devolve authority from himself and all weighty Friends upon the Quaker community as an organized whole.[42]

The *Minute Book of the Men's Meeting of . . . Friends in Bristol, 1667–1686* preserves a lively debate between the men and the women:

27th 9ber [November, old-style] 1671
Dennis Hollister, Thomas Gouldney, Wm. Ford, Charles Harford, Miles Dixon, Wm. Rogers, or any foure of them, are appointed to goe to the next weomens meetings, and there to know ye ground wherefore Margaret Hale & Jone Hiley publisht a womens monethly meeting & likewise to know how & on what account that monethly womens meeting was first sett up; & to give an account to this next meeting, WR
The 11th of the 10th moneth 1671
[The men] went to the weomens fourtnights meeting, and the accowmpt that they retorne to the mens meeting, . . . is to this effect.
To the first Question. That Margaret Heale of her self, and not by order of any meeting, published the weomens monethly meeting in the publique meeting house.
To the second Question. That a letter of George Fox's, dillivered & read in the weomens meeting as sent from the mens meeting was the ground which occationed the proposing & concluding of the weomens monethly meeting.
[Fox's letter about Women's Meetings became confused with a] paper recommended by the mens meetinge . . . against vanity & excess.
[The women, not coming] to unity amongst them selves . . . a agreed to reffer it to the wisdome of god in the friends of the mens meeting.
Upon weighty consideration of the matter friends of the mens meeting, haveing a deepe sense upon their spirrits that tis their duty to mind only those things that tend to peace . . . doe with one accord conclude that . . . to desire the weomen Friends to forbeare the said Monethly meeting untill such tyme they have unity among them selves & with the mens meeting conserneing the same.[43]

Russell Mortimer interprets this as referring to the setting up of a women's monthly meeting for discipline, since there had long been a joint men's & women's meeting, in addition to the fortnightly separate women's meeting since before 1667, with which the men's meeting had worked at least fifteen times:

[An orphan was] maintain'd by freinds out of the publique stock for . . . the father was understood to bee a freind of truth, and dyed in the faith, and that the women freinds doe according to the accustom'd manner take the care of the child. [Margin:] The child is dead & was buryed 17th 9th mo 1667.

That the summe of five Pounds bee disbursed out of the Publique stock to the Women at their Meeting, as they shall desire towards a provision of coales & cheese for the poor this winter; & other occasions for the poor as they shall think fit.

6th of 2d month 1668

That six pounds bee paid unto the women freinds out of the publicke stocke for the use of Sarah Graves widow, . . . on the presentment of her condition by Bethshua Speed, Ann Jones, & Mary North who were appointed at the women's meeting to inspect the necessities of her condition.

21th of 8th month 1669

The women freinds att a mens meeting this day assented & agreed to take care that the births of freinds children may for the future bee brought to this meeting to ye entent that all births may bee duly kept [Fox had requested Friends to do this in 1656.][44]

Tis agreed that subscribed forme of
CERTIFICATE for mariages bee used for the future and that all persons marryinge have recourse to Francis Rogers to give forth certificates as occasion offers.

Also that for the future, the copyes of every certificate bee entered into the booke for mariages, & that the partyes marryed & (at least) twelve of the wittnesses present doe thereunto sett their handes. . . . The forme of the above mentioned Certificate: [the classic Quaker formulae, including:] Wee therefore whose names are hereunto subscribed are wittnesses that the said A did in the presence of the Lord & us all take the said B to bee his wife and that the said B did take the said A to bee her husband & that they did mutually promise each to other to live together as man & wife in love and faithfullnes according to Gods ordinance . . .and herunto with us putt their hands.

17th of 8ber 1670

Whereas it hath been the approved practice of freinds to cause all marriages to bee publisht at their publick assemblies, & whereas also freinds are at this time forcibly kept out of their publick meetinge houses, it is therefore agreed that for the future the intentions of all mariages among freinds bee publisht in their mens and womens meetings usually held once every fortnight on the second dayes of the weekes until such time as that they have admittance into their publique meetinge houses againe.

31 of 8 month 1670

Joel Gilson beinge at the last meeting permitted to cause his intentions of mariage to bee publisht was this day againe before freinds & denyed to have the same publisht in the Mens meeting untill from the womens meetinge they shall be atisfied that all thinges are cleare; from some objections raysed concerninge his freing Jane Fletcher.[45]

54

But already on 18th 8th month 1669 the combined men and women had met together to approve the marriage of George Fox and Margaret Fell.

The upholding of the authority of meetings over members could claim religious validity only if the sense of the meeting could claim the same divine leading and truth as had been felt by prophetic individuals. Establishing of women's meetings also rested on the experience that women were as truly led as men. As late as 1680, in one of the first of Fox's sermons to be taken down in shorthand, he was still stressing that authority was to be shared equally between men and women. In the day of creation,

> God placed man in a blessed habitation, . . . and set him in domination over all the works of his hands. . . . God said to them "have domination," he did not say to them, "do thou have dominion without thy wife," but said to *them*, "have domination," . . . man was blessed and so was woman, and all things blessed unto them.[46]

Then Fox went on through the same cycle of texts Margaret Fell had used, from Huldah to Mary Magdalene, but now included Deborah.

Fox's sense of a divine calling to set up the women's meetings, and the women's own prophetic leadings, transformed the other aspects of Quaker women's work and lifted them beyond either biblical legalism or mutual aid. He did not make social conventions, or women's rights as such, key issues. The old pattern curbed the Spirit of God, not the freedom of women. Sarah Fell's epistle from Lancaster Women's Meeting also began biblically, with Christ as the Seed of the Woman, thereby adopted as the Seed of Abraham:

> So here is the blessed image of the living God restored againe, in which he made them male and female in the beginning, . . . so that you may be helps meet in the Restoration and Resurrection of the body of Christ, which is his Church.[47]

Along with Miriam, and Hannah, who brought a bullock to sacrifice in the Temple, Sarah Fell was willing to notice the worldly women whom the Hebrew prophets condemned, and the women of Canaan and Samaria whom Jesus enlightened, going on to the women who announced to the men Christ's resurrection. Then the Epistle turned to the duties of women's meetings:

> Where the mens monthly meetings is established, let the women likewise of every monthly meeting meet together to wait upon the lord, and to hearken what the lord will say unto them, . . . and answer him in evey motion of his eternal spirit and power. And also to make inquiry, . . . If there be any that walks disorderly, . . . to Admonish and exhort them, and to bring them to

Judge and Condemn what hath been by them done or acted contrary to the truth, [notably] if there be any that goes out to Marry with the priests, or joineth in Marriage with the world.

The women's meetings were also to oversee joint testimony statements against tithes, affirming each woman's own clearness from paying any. Sarah Fell concluded as her mother's tract had begun a decade before, with the reminder that women's character as the "weaker sex" is the kind of weakness which by God's strength is made perfect, as his wisdom is made perfect in what seems human foolishness. The openness of Mary at the Annunciation is the model for all Quaker experience.

NOTES

This paper was first presented in briefer form as part of the symposium: "American Quaker Women as Shapers of Human Space" at Guilford College, North Carolina, on 16 March 1979. Since it was given, three major studies of seventeenth-century women have been written: Antonia Fraser, *The Weaker Vessel: Woman's Lot in Seventeenth-Century England* (New York, 1984); Helga Moebius, *Woman of the Baroque Age*, Barbara Chrucik Beedham, trans. (Montclair, N. J., 1984), and Jeanette Gadt, "Women and Protestant Culture," Ph. D. diss., University of California, 1974). My attention has also been called to Elaine C. Huber, "'A Woman Must Not Speak': Quaker Women in the English Left Wing," in *Women of Spirit*, Rosemary Ruether and Eleanor McLaughlin, eds. (New York, 1979), pp. 153–182; and Mary Maples Dunn, "Women of Light," in *Women of America: A History*, Carol Ruth Berkin and Mary Beth Norton, eds. (Boston, 1979), pp. 114–138.

1. On Quaker women, see esp. Mabel R. Brailsford, *Quaker Women, 1650–1690* (London, 1915); Emily Manners, *Elizabeth Hooton, First Quaker Woman Preacher* (London, 1914); Isabel Ross, *Margaret Fell, Mother of Quakerism* (London, 1949). We may also here record the debt of Quaker history in general to Caroline Fox and Caroline Stephen in the last century and in our own to Margaret Hope Bacon, Elizabeth Brockbank, Elizabeth Isichei, Mary Hoxie Jones, Isabel Grubb, Amelia Gummere, Margaret Hirst and Lucy Hodgkin, to the biographies by Janet Whitney and Elizabeth Vining and the novels of Jessamyn West, Daisy Newman and Elisabeth Hering. Has any religious movement been as well served by its women historians as have the Quakers?

2. Elizabeth Gray Vining, "Women in the Society of Friends," the Ward Lecture at Guilford College, 11 November 1955.

3. Roland Bainton, *Women of the Reformation in France and England* (Minneapolis, 1973), p. 7; Edmund S. Morgan, *The Puritan Family: Religion and*

Domestic Relations in Seventeenth-Century New England (Westport, Conn., 1944, 1980); George H. Tavard, *Woman in Christian Tradition* (London, 1973); *Women of America*, Berkin and Norton, Introduction, p. 18. Good grammar schools like Banbury admitted girls only to age nine; neither Comenius nor Locke included post-primary girls in their educational schemes. Women who could read and write Latin and Greek, like Lucy Hutchinson, Lady Jane Grey and Queen Elizabeth, became famous; English Catholic families sent their daughters to continental convents for schooling, but most gentry settled for arithmetic, music, singing, needlework and French. See Fraser, *The Weaker Vessel*, pp. 125-137; Moebius, *Baroque Women*, 93-96, chap. 4.

4. Bainton, *Women of the Reformation* describes in England only ladies of the royal nobility, except for "Foxe's martyrs" under "Bloody Mary" Tudor. Moebius, *Baroque Women* tells of Protestant and Catholic witches, but under saints and pious women only of Catholic gentlewomen. See Fraser, *The Weaker Vessel*, on Ann Finch, Lady Conway, whose household and guest list were full of Quakers, pp. 345-351.

5. Morgan, *The Puritan Family*; Christopher Hill, *Pelican Economic History of Britain, vol. II: Reformation to Industrial Revolution* (Harmondsworth Middlesex, 1969), p. 83; Carl Bridenbaugh, *Vexed and Troubled Englishmen, 1590-1642* (New York, 1968), pp. 169-170. On Baroque women see Pat Rogers, *The Augustan Vision* (New York, 1978), chap. 9.

6. See Owen Watkins, *The Puritan Experience: Studies in Spiritual Autobiography* (New York, 1952); and William Haller, *The Rise of Puritanism* (New York, 1938).

7. Cf. Bridenbaugh, *Vexed Englishmen*, p. 7.

8. John Banks, *Journal* (London, 1712), pp. 22, 56-57.

9. Abraham MS #1, correcting from microfilm Ross, p. 119. Howgill's letter now prefaces the 1696 edition of his *Works*.

10. Sources cited in Hugh Barbour and Arthur O. Roberts, *Early Quaker Writings* (Grand Rapids, 1973), p. 595.

11. Fraser, *The Weaker Vessel*, pp. 249, 250. See also p. 155 on Jane Hawkins, pp. 155-156 and 250-251 on Lady Eleanor Douglas, p. 253 on Elizabeth Poole, p. 255 on Mary Pope and pp. 254-263 on Anna Trapnel.

12. On Bourignon, see J. G. Riewald, *Reynier Jansen of Philadelphia* (Groningen, 1970), chap. 4.

13. Combining data from Rufus Jones, *Quakers in the American Colonies* (2d ed. (New York, 1966) with George A. Selleck, *Quakers in Boston* (Cambridge, 1978) and G. J. Willauer, Jr., "First Publishers of Truth in New England, 1656-1775" in *Quaker History, 65,* #1 (Spring, 1976) pp. 35-44. Dunn, "Women of Light," p. 120, notes that 26 out of the 59 Quaker preachers who came to America in 1656-63 were women. Elizabeth Vining reckons 22 women out of the 66 "First Publishers of Truth," and 32 of the 112 overseas visitors to Philadelphia Friends before 1773. The Lloyds of Dolobran in Wales recorded 36 women out of the 174 traveling ministers visiting there around 1700: see Arnold Lloyd, *Quaker Social History: 1669-1738* (Westport, Conn., 1950, 1979), p. 126.

14. Dorothy Benson, like Margaret Fell, was supported in her missions by her justice husband, and Elizabeth Hooton's Quaker husband came to her trial on her early York mission (he died before her American journey). Ann Audland and Margaret and Joan Killam preached with their husbands, and Elizabeth Leavens married her preaching partner Thomas Holme. Yet Mary Dyer's husband William was a friend of Roger Williams and Samuel Clarke (as Mary was of Ann Hutchinson) but when she became a Friend (apparently during a three-year stay in England without him) William did not, and he or their son William later tried to persuade the Boston authorities to send her home to Rhode Island in his care. Mary Askew, Anne Clayton and Dorothy and Jane Waugh were still unmarried servants at Swarthmoor Hall, and Mary Fisher in the Tomlinson's Yorkshire home, when they went out to preach. Dorcas Erbury and Ann Downer were parsons' daughters, and the Fell sisters, Elizabeth Fletcher and Elizabeth Smith were maidens from good families. Barbara Blaugdone may have been a widow before she became a Friend (so may several others). But Sarah Cheevers and Katherine Evans were married when they set out alone for Malta, and Ann Austin and Mary Clark when they sailed for America. About the marital status of Sarah Blackborow, Sarah Gibbons, Anne Gould, Mary Prince, Joan Vokins, Mary Weatherhead and Anne Wilson I have no information (data from Barbour and Roberts, *Early Quaker Writings*, Biographical Appendix; see also Fraser, *The Weaker Vessel*, pp. 357–376; Ross, *Margaret Fell*).

15. Swarthmore MS 1:155: "i have seene i have seene i have seene thy beautie and tasted a little of thy power praisis glory eternal prayses be to our god . . . I should have come to thee long since When thou bid me come i shall."

16. Swarthmore MS 3:194 (October, 1656). Geoffrey Nuttall, *Early Quaker Letters from the Swarthmore MSS to 1660* (London, 1952), suggested that the prophetic message "done by another" might be Samuel Fisher's protest at the door of Parliament in September, 1656. Barbara Blaugdone never went to Jerusalem, presumably because her friends never received a parallel leading.

17. See James Childress, "Answering That of God in Every Man: an Interpretation of Fox's Ethics," in *Quaker Religious Thought, 15, #3* (1974).

18. See appendix by David Runyon to Barbour and Roberts, *Early Quaker Writings*.

19. 30 of the 144 writers of surviving letters to Swarthmoor Hall were women, though 22 wrote only one letter each. Elizabeth Hooton's letter to "Mayor Bullock" of Derby is the only document I know which Fox recopied to improve the spelling.

20. Data, augmented, from Joseph Smith, *Descriptive Catalogue of Friends Books* (London, 1867).

21. Huber, "Woman Not Speak"; see Gerda Lerner, *The Female Experience: An American Documentary* (New York, 1979) on Mary Dyer, and a spate of recent writings on Lucretia Mott.

22. Her story was first explored by Allen Hole of Earlham College. On similar cases see G. F. S. Ellens, "The Ranters Ranting" in *Church History, 40* (1971), pp. 91–107; and Christopher Hill, *The World Turned Upside Down* (New York,

1984). See also A. L. Morton, *World of the Ranters: Religious Radicalism in the English Revolution* (Atlantic Highlands N.J., 1979); B. S. Capp, *The Fifth Monarchy Men* (London, 1972); and Keith Thomas, *Religion and the Decline of Magic* (New York, 1975) who all, like Hill, try to show Ranters as a proletarian counter-culture.

23. Kenneth Carroll, "Early Quakers and 'Going Naked as a Sign' in *Quaker History, 67,#2* (Autumn, 1978), pp. 69–78, names Lydia Wardel of Hampton and Deborah Wilson of Salem, along with Elizabeth Fletcher (who went topless through Oxford), Elizabeth Milner and Edward Adlington's wife, all of Kendal, Westmorland. See also Geoffrey Nuttall, *James Nayler, a Fresh Approach* (London, 1954). The tract of the briefly Quaker John Gilpin, *The Quakers Shaken* (London, 1655) tells his own and other lurid stories, eight of which from the Kendal area had been printed in Thomas Welde, *A Further Discovery of that generation of men called Quakers* (Gateside, 1654).

24. Kenneth Carroll, "A Look at James Milner and his 'False Prophecy'" in *Quaker History, 74, #1* (Spring, 1985), pp. 18–26.

25. *Some account of Circumstances in the Life of Mary Penington* (London, 1821), pp. 22–24.

26. Swarthmore Manuscript 4:37; punctuation modernized.

27. Swarthmore Manuscript 3:24–26, see Ross, *Margaret Fell*, p. 37. This postscript includes Margaret Fell's regret that Fox "shaked the dust of thy feet at him who would not receive thee, nor is worthy of thee; which shall be a testimony against him for ever." Was this Henry Fell or the Judge himself? Fox added later a note that "he . . . was not long after convinced."

28. Agnes Wilkinson was disciplined privately, and Friends warned Elizabeth Fletcher and Elizabeth Williams who traveled incautiously with only a male companion.

29. Hugh Barbour, *The Quakers in Puritan England* (Richmond, Ind., 1985), chap. 4; and Documents in Barbour & Roberts, *Early Quaker Writings*, Part II. The Swarthmore Letters show that neither the intensity of the experience nor the biblical language from Job & Jeremiah used to describe it, resulted from Quaker norms nor later reflection.

30. Banks, *Journal*, p. 5.

31. Lloyd, *Quaker Social History*, pp. 2, 128, dates Quaker Overseers from the Balby General Meeting of 1656, but describes Elders as meeting regularly with Quaker Ministers only from about 1698. There is little data on early women Elders.

32. Swarthmore MS 3:3, 26 July [1653], to Swarthmoor from Sedbergh. On the longer and harsher letter of Thomas Aldam to Margaret Fell about Agnes Wilkinson, asking her to combine counsel with discipline and exclusion from the Quaker fellowship, see Swarthmore MS 4:89 (Barbour and Roberts, *Early Quaker Writings*, pp. 471–473).

33. Margaret Fell, *Works: A Brief Collection of Remarkable Passages* (London, 1710), include one to Howgill and Nayler (with his name omitted) in Appleby jail in 1653; Ross, *Margaret Fell*, preserves one to Anthony Pearson (p. 58),

and one to Caton and Stubbs as they returned to Holland (p. 70).

34. Peter Laslett and R. Wall, eds., *Household and Family in Past Time* (Cambridge, 1972), p. 147, cited by Elise Boulding, *The Underside of History: A View of Women Through Time* (Boulder, Colo., 1976), p. 554. See Fraser, *The Weaker Vessel*, pp. 5, 231, on the rights of widows, including the seldom used right to vote.

35. See David Eversley and Richard Vann, *The Demography of the British Quakers* (still in press). I am grateful to have seen their manuscript with very detailed data on ages at marriage (the median for Quakers married 1675-99 was 27.3 for men and 24.0 for women) and also on the spacing of later children in an early-married couple's home.

36. Fell, "A Relation," prefacing *Works*.

37. William Crouch, *Posthuma Christiana* (London, 1712) section III; see also full quotations in William C. Brathwaite, *The Beginnings of Quakerism* (London 1912), p. 341; Brailsford, *Quaker Women*, p. 271; Lloyd, *Quaker Social History*, p. 109.

38. Thomas Ellwood, *History of the Life of Thomas Ellwood* (London, 1714), pp. 188-189. See Fraser, *The Weaker Vessel*, pp. 226-228 on a seemingly Royalist women's Peace Petition of 1643, and on women's riots against enclosures, fen drainage and (pp. 239f) on the Lilburne petition.

39. Fell, *Works*, p. 97. See Ross, *Margaret Fell*, p. 63; and Spence MS III:10 and Swarthmore MS 1:210-212, 236-240 for reports concerning the "Kendal Fund."

40. The best studies seem to remain Lloyd, *Quaker Social History*, pp. 177-179; and Richard Vann, *The Social Development of English Quakerism* (Cambridge, Mass., 1969), p. 103; though there is much new data in Eversley and Vann, *Demography*.

41. Isabel Ross found a copy at Nottingham, and, more recently, Milton Speizman and Jane C. Kronick, of Bryn Mawr, published a copy found in Philadelphia in *Signs: Journal of Women in Culture and Society*, 1 (Autumn, 1975), p. 235. See also Huber, "Woman Not Speak," p. 176.

42. See Emilia Fogelklou-Norlind, *The Atonement of George Fox* (Wallingford, Pa., 1969). Both William Penn and Robert Barclay nevertheless at this time wrote books supporting Fox's unique authority.

43. Russell Mortimer, ed., *Minute Book of the Men's Meeting* (Bristol Record Society, 1971), pp. 54-55 from pp. 30-30a in the original.

44. See Eversley & Vann, *Demography*, introduction.

45. *Men's Meeting in Bristol*, Mortimer, pp. 4, 9, 14, 26-27, 34.

46. Fox, "Sermon at Wheeler Street," 1st of 4th Month, 1680, in Barbour and Roberts, *Early Quaker Writings,* pp. 502ff.

47. See Speizman & Kronick, *Signs*, pp. 236, 237, 241.

Thomas Loe, Friend of William Penn and Apostle to Ireland

Thomas Loe was the first Quaker William Penn ever encountered. Likewise, some years later, he was responsible for Penn's convincement. So close were they that Penn was present at the time of Loe's death, leaving a rather full account of that development. Thomas Loe was quite active in the struggle against John Perrot's schismatic activities, as well as vigorously denying the "false pretensions" of Lodowick Muggleton. Fourteen years of intense laboring in the ministry made him one of the outstanding leaders of the early Quaker movement, both in England and Ireland. Truly he was, to use the language of a recent TV commercial, a "real work-horse of a man." Yet, he is almost unknown today—for no study of the man and his work has ever been made.

Loe's background remains virtually unknown, for all that we are told is that he was an Oxford tradesman connected in some way with the university.[1] No real information about the year of his birth is available, although M. R. Brailsford hints at a date of about 1633.[2] Likewise, very little is known about his pre-Quaker life, except that he was married and that his wife's sister was wed to Silas Norton.[3]

The preaching of John Camm in Oxford convinced Thomas Loe in 1654.[4] Shortly after his convincement Loe appeared "in a testimony" and rapidly became a "very servisable man" as the "Lord . . . made [him] a Minister of his Everlasting Truth."[5] His wife, Mary, must have been drawn into Quakerism at about the same time as Thomas, for both of them are listed as Quaker sufferers shortly thereafter. In 1654 Thomas Loe was arrested for speaking to the priest and the people in "Martin's Masshouse" and suffered a three months' Oxfordshire imprisonment as a result. In the same year Mary Loe was twice imprisoned for speaking to the priest and the people, first at All Hallows and then at "Martin's Masshouse".[6]

Thomas Loe's long relationship with Ireland began in the late summer of 1655. Shortly after his release from prison in Oxford,[7] Loe went on to Ireland after some brief activity in Gloucestershire. On the 6th of 7th Month [September], 1655, John Camm—whose early preaching had convinced Loe—wrote to Margaret Fell that three Friends had lately "gone from these parts to Ireland, one man [Thomas Loe] from Oxford that is a precious hart and two women [Elizabeth Fletcher and Elizabeth Smith] that have been much in service in threshing the priests."[8] Before long Loe was hard at work in Ireland, so that Edward Burrough (writing to Margaret Fell from Dublin) reported "here is a friend come from England since I wrott thee, from Oxford, which saith he was moved to come & I believe itt, I am refreshed by him."[9] Loe also appears to have labored in other parts of Ireland during this 1655 and early 1656 visit, especially in Limerick, Cork, and Youghal.[10] In Youghal he, with several Irish Friends, was taken from a meeting at the Widow Jones' house and committed to prison.[11] It is not known whether or not this was his earliest Irish imprisonment, but there were many more to follow.

Loe's whereabouts and activities for most of 1656 are unknown. By 1657, however, he was back in Ireland once more, starting his work in Dublin where he is reported to have preached "through the Dublin streets from St. James' Gate to Stephen Rich's house, that is from the extreme west of the city to the extreme east."[12] He was also active in Carlow (with Robert Roper and William Waller),[13] and County Tipperary—where he and some other Friends were thrust outside the gates of Cashel as night drew close (a very dangerous time for Englishmen to be outside the city walls.)[14] It was during this 1657 visit to the south of Ireland, while Loe was directing his ministry towards the Cork area, that William Penn, aged thirteen, first heard Loe preach. Many years later Penn reported this event to Thomas Harvey (who later related it to the unknown author of the "Convincement of William Penn" manuscript):

> While he was but a child living at Cork with his Father Thos. Low [Loe] coming thither, his Father proposed to some others (when it was rumour'd A Quaker was come from England) to be like ye Noble Berean's to hear them before they Judg'd 'em and sent to T. L. to come to his House where he had a meeting in ye family, and tho' W. P. was very young yet [he] observed what effect T. L.'s Doctrine had on ye Hearers so that a Black of his Fathers could not contain himself from weeping aloud & he looking on his Father saw ye Tears Running down his Cheeks also; he thought in himself w[ha]t If they should all be Quakers [   ] opportunity he never forgot.[15]

Toward the end of 1657 Loe moved towards the north of Ireland, going from Dublin to Armagh to address a meeting attended by Archibald Bell and a number of others. Shortly after this Bell was convinced and entered into a deep discussion with Loe about Bell's doubts about "water baptism" and "the [Lord's] Supper." It is recorded that Thomas Loe "who was a man largely endued with heavenly wisdom and discretion did not enter into a disquisition tending to foster a spirit of reasoning or argument but tenderly instructed him saying that as he looked to the Lord he would see over those things: for the redemption of the soul was an inward work."[16]

This second visit to Ireland continued well into 1658, with Loe being at Dublin early in May, at Mallow late in May, and back at Dublin at the beginning of July. It was during this 1657–1658 period that Loe began to pen some of his "prophetic" utterances that are still extant. At the end of 1657 he sent out his "Thus Sayth the Lord unto all the Called & chosen of himself," calling people to be subject to God in all things and to stand in his "Councell." From Mallow he issued his "To all the Wicked in the World," and from Dublin his "To friends in & about Catherlagh."[17]

In 1659 Loe was in England for a time, proclaiming the "Truth" at Witney with his companion Richard Greenaway.[18] Soon, however, he was back in Ireland once more, for Thomas Morford in May 1659 wrote to George Fox that Thomas Loe who had come "from the West" [Munster] had briefly joined Morford in Waterford but would soon be heading toward Dublin and the north.[19]

Loe's 1660 activity also was in both Ireland and England. While at Tallow in County Cork Loe was hauled from a meeting for worship, taken before a court, and imprisoned. Early in June a meeting at Waterford was broken up; Loe and some others were taken out forcibly, and they were threatened with being turned out of town.[20] Later that summer, from the north of Ireland, Loe wrote to Fox:

> I came lately out of the west from Cork, Bandon, Lim[e]rick, & those parts wher[e] persecution hath been great since these chainges, prisons dayly attending us hailling out of their towns & breaking Meetings, & blows & threats & many other sufferings friends have sustained by them, whole meetings have been carried to prisons in several places: & at Lim[e]rick they have kept friends near 4 weeks together & at Dublin the greatest part of a quarter of A yeare & at Corke they have several times don[e] the same. I was there a littell while since at a monthly meeting & neare the end of our meeting they Came with a guard of souldiers & carried away all the men friends to prison, & soe about Waterford they have don[e] the same & allmost in all parts of the nation.

At the end of this letter Loe reports that he has been in prison "divers" times but feels that he must stay with Irish Friends and suffer with them, in spite of the many threats against him.[21]

Loe was back and actively preaching in England before the end of

1660. On 13 January 1661 Loe, who had been proclaiming the Quaker message in London, reached the Oxford area and continued his work there until he and a number of other Friends were arrested at meetings at Banbury, Milton, and Brisnorton (at the height of the Fifth Monarchy scare). The Great Book of Sufferings records an exchange which took place between Loe and the judge, in which Loe (who answered that he was now in his "native place"), when asked what he would promise the king, responded "To live God-likely and righteously in this present world, & peaceably with all men, yielding all due obedience to his just Commands & Allegiance as a faithful subject, provided nothing was imposed upon his Conscience, as touching the worship of God."[22] Loe refused to accept the title "head" of the Quaker movement, as the judge sought to fasten it upon him, and also rejected the oath which was tendered him. He was, therefore, committed to prison until the next assizes. From prison Loe wrote to Thomas Ellwood (who had been arrested as a "dangerous person" for attempting "to gather a Concourse of People together, in such a Juncture" and was then committed as a prisoner in the home of the city marshall at Oxford when he refused to take an oath):

> a Time of Tryal God hath permitted to come upon us, to try our Faith and Love to Him: and this will work for the good of them that through Patience endure to the End. And I believe God will be glorified through our Sufferings, and His name will be exalted in the Patience and Long-suffering of his Chosen. When I heard that thou wast called into this Tryal, with the Servants of the Most High, to give thy Testimony to the Truth of what we have believed; it came into my Heart to write unto thee, and to greet thee with the Embrace of the Power of an Endless Life: where our Faith stands, and unity is felt with the Saints forever. Well, my dear Friend, let us live in the pure Counsel of the Lord, and dwell in his Strength; which gives us Power and Sufficiency to endure all things, for his Name's sake: and then our Crown and Reward will be with the Lord for ever."[23]

Loe was still a prisoner in Oxford Castle in March 1661.[24] Before long, however, he was released and soon returned to Ireland once more, proclaiming the Truth and suffering imprisonments there. Sometime in 1661 he was taken from a meeting for worship in Limerick and given four weeks in prison simply for being at the meeting.[25] The same treatment was experienced in Cork, when Loe and sixteen other Friends were kept prisoners for several weeks for attending a meeting for worship.[26] In 1662 Mary Loe (whose whereabouts are something of a mystery for the 1655–1661 period) was with her husband Thomas in County Wexford, Ireland, and both of these Friends were detained for visiting Quakers in Wexford prison — with Thomas being kept there until the next Sessions.[27]

64

There is a void in our knowledge of Thomas Loe's activities for the 1663–1665 period. If Loe continued to suffer imprisonments during this period, either in Ireland or England, they seem to have gone unrecorded. One is simply left to guess that, unless his deteriorating health hampered him, Loe continued with his ministry, both in Ireland and England. One is also tempted to conjecture that Mary Loe died during these "years of silence" for no further mention of her has been found.

Only in 1665 does Thomas Loe surface once more, this time in England and in connection with the great crisis stirred up by John Perrot. John Perrot had sent a letter from Jamaica to England dated 12th of 4th Month [June], 1665. This produced a response from Richard Farnworth, who penned his last tract to answer Perrot: *Truth Vindicated, or an Answer to a Letter sent by John Perrot out of Jamaica into England, &c* (London, 1665). Thomas Loe and ten other Friends signed this attack on Perrot.[28] In May 1666 Loe and ten other outstanding Quaker ministers gathered in London and issued "A Testimony from the Brethren who were met together at London in the 3d Mon[th] 1666 to be commended to faithful friends & elders in the Country."[29] This document helped stem the tide of the Perrotonian movement in England and also marked a very important stage in Quaker history, as Quakerism became less of a movement and more of a denomination.[30]

Sometime later in 1666 Loe was back in Ireland once more, especially active in the Cork area.[31] Loe's Irish work continued well into 1667, with the most notable development being his convincement of William Penn who was managing his father's estate in County Cork. As Penn later told Thomas Harvey, when he had returned to Cork he felt the need of some "Cloaths" and went to the shop of a woman Quaker whom he "had knowledge of" about the time he had first heard Thomas Loe. Penn reminded the woman of the meeting which had been held at his father's house and told her that he would never forget it. He then said that if he knew where Loe was he would go hear him again, even though it might be one hundred miles away. Her response was that he need not go so far, for Loe had only lately come into the area and would be at a meeting the following day. Penn went to that meeting, reporting later that:

> another appearing first [in the ministry] he was not Effected with his Testimony but when T. L. [Thomas Loe] stood up [Penn] was exceedingly reach'd so that he wept much and it seemed to him as if a Voice sayd stand on thy feet, How dost [thou] know but somebody may be reach'd by thy tears so he stood up that he might be seen. After the Meeting some friends took notice of him and he went to a friend['s] house with T. L. in discourse T. L. was saying he should want a horse either being without one or his own being not fit to travell. W. P. offer'd him his Sumture horse he had brought from France but T. L.

65

said he was not willing to take his, which made W. P. think he was not friend enough to have his horse accepted.[32]

Irish Friends had a deep appreciation of Loe and his ministry, so that they later reported that he was:

a man of an Excellent Gift, Sound and cleare in his Ministry. Much people flocked after him and thronged the Meetings where hee would bee. And many friends up and down this Nations Received their Convincement by him, and many [were] confirmed in the Truth that had received their Convincement before him. . . . He was an able Minister of the Gospell, powerfull in Preaching, Ellegant in Speech, Sharp and quick in the understanding, and his Testimony very convinceing to the Stopping of the mouths of Gainsayers, many a time being often Engaged in Meetings by Opposers and sometimes by Priests in all which Exercises and Labours the Lord made him as a Sharp threshing Instrument in his hand — to confound the Adversaries of Truth.[33]

Loe is reported to have been "weak and consumptive" for a number of years. Irish Friends remembered that "it was very apparent his outward man was much impaired in his last visit from England."[34] Yet he still possessed a great deal of vigor as he approached the end of his life. Shortly before his final departure from Ireland he summoned Joan Pildren, with whom he had labored for some time, to appear before him.[35] When she did not come, Loe wrote her a letter so that she might know that she:

grieves the holy Spirit of the pure God with thy wicked Imaginations which thou brings forth in the strength of darkness and blackness in contempt of the Truth, And to the great dishonour of God, in the Assemblies of his people, And Thy outward and Beastlike Cover [of white frieze], which thou indiscreetly and unwisely wears in the meeting of God's people, is a figure to thy own Blackness and darkness that is over thy head, and by which thou art wholly swallowed up . . . , And this is a warning to thee from the Lord God to Repent and Cease from thy Imaginations and deceit, least God smite thee in his wrath, and Chastise thee in his sore displeasure, and thou find no way to Escape.

I have borne with thee long Expecting thy Amendment but finding thee still to persist in this Rebellion and stiffe neckedness, it lyes upon me to Cleare my Conscience to thee, And if thou still continue in thy folly Remember thou art warned by a Servant of the Lord, who is a Lover of the souls of all. But an Enemy to all deceit, Imagination, and unrighteousness.[36]

It was this same calling to be "an Enemy to all deceit, Imagination, and unrighteousness" which led Thomas Loe — perhaps while still in Ireland but more probably just after his return to England in 1668 — to denounce Lodowick Muggleton and the Muggletonians. It may well be that Loe's ire was roused by the fact that a few Irish Quakers were in the process of being drawn toward Muggletonianism. Whatever the reason for Loe's writing, his paper persuaded Muggleton to put a curse on Loe and even to take credit for Loe's later death.[37]

Loe continued to be active in England until the autumn of 1668. Together with William Penn and George Whitehead, Loe visited the Duke of Buckingham (who had a great influence on Charles II) "in relation with Friends' liberty."[38] About this very time Loe became suddenly and violently ill and withdrew to the house of Ann Cullen, a Friend who lived quite near. Three hours later Penn and Whitehead, when they had finished at the Duke of Buckingham's house, found Loe to be "by excessive reaching [retching] very feavourish." That evening he was transferred to Ann Greenhill's house where he remained for about a week, quite ill much of the time. The noise to which her home was exposed made it impossible for him to rest, so that Loe was finally removed to the home of Edward Mann, where he had a very quiet room in which to lie. Although at first there was hope for his speedy recovery, Loe's body—never very strong and gradually weakened by all the years of suffering and imprisonment in both England and Ireland—proved to be too weak to withstand the ravages of his "infirm inside and an extraordinary feaver." Gradually, over the next ten days, he decreased in strength, so that a number of people expected his death at almost anytime, although some few had not given up hope of his recovery.

William Penn, who himself had fallen ill, when he learned that Loe was near death, left his own sick bed "though still in a sweat" and hastened to Loe's bedside where he found him:

> in a sweet readiness to be gone. . . . several heavenly expressions fell from his mouth, & so shook was he by the power of the Lord & overcome by the ravishing glory of his presence, that it was wonderful to all friends; whose testimony concerning his departure was, that they judged it impossible for any to have layn so long, with more patience, resignation, & lamb-like innocency, than he did, yet truly bold & courageous.[39]

To Penn, whose convincement at the hands of Loe had taken place only a year or two earlier, Thomas Loe said, "Dear Heart, bear thy cross, stand faithfull for God & bear thy testimony in thy days & generation, & God will give thee an eternal crown of glory that none shall ever take from thee: there is not another way, this is the way the holy men of old walked in, & it shall prosper."[40]

Loe seemed so enlivened by his speaking to Penn and the others at his bedside, that he arose from his bed and walked around a bit. Then he lay down once again, with death coming upon him rather rapidly. His death occurred on the 5th of the 8th Month, 1668, with burial taking place the next day in Checker Alley.[41]

NOTES

1. C. E. Gillette, "The Early Quakers in Oxford," *The Oxford Review*, June 12, 1902 (Friends House Library, London, BB. 135). Gillette speculates that Loe may have been the son of George Lowe of St. Aldates by his first wife.

2. Mabel Richmond Brailsford, *The Making of William Penn* (London, 1930), p. 235, says that Loe died before his thirty-fifth birthday but gives no source for this information which may well be apocryphal.

3. Thomas Ellwood, *The History of the Life of Thomas Ellwood*, S. Graveson, ed. (London, 1714), p. 118. Gillette, "The Quakers in Oxford," reports that Silas Norton's daughter Elizabeth married William Penn's brother-in-law William Penington (druggist of Newgate, London) under the care of Oxford Monthly Meeting in 1689.

4. Norman Penney, ed., *The First Publishers of Truth* (London, 1907), p. 212.

5. Penney, *First Publishers*, pp. 212, 216.

6. Great Book of Sufferings, I, 1. This manuscript collection of sufferings is found in Friends House Library, London. Cf. Joseph Besse, *A Collection of the Sufferings of the People Called Quakers* (London, 1753), I, 563.

7. A. R. Barclay MSS, LVIII (Friends House Library, London), where John Audland reports in a 2nd of 5th Month 1655 letter that Thomas Loe was in prison at Oxford and "is keepe [kept] in wisdom."

8. Caton MSS, III, 154 (Friends House Library, London). This note gives us our only known reference to Loe's 1655 English activities, as it was written from "Kendelshire in Gloucestershire."

9. Swarthmore MSS, III, 17 (Tr. I, 297), (Friends House Library, London).

10. Thomas Wight and John Rutty, *A History of the Rise and Progress of the People Called Quakers, in Ireland, from the Year 1653 to 1700* (London, 1800), p. 86; Henry J. Cadbury, "More First Publishers of Truth," *Journal of Friends Historical Society*, LII (1968–1971), 163.

11. Swarthmore MSS, VI, 18 (Tr. VII, 499). This letter is undated but appears to be quite early. There is no mention of this episode in Besse, *Sufferings*, but it does appear in National Sufferings, I (1655–1693), 5, found in Friends Historical Library, Eustace Street, Dublin.

12. Olive C. Goodbody, "Irish History and the Earliest Irish Friends," *Journal of Friends Historical Society*, XLIX (1959–1961), 193.

13. Wight and Rutty, *Quaker Irish History*, p. 105.

14. National Sufferings, I, 8.

15. "The Convincement of William Penn," manuscript found in MS Box 10, item 12, Friends House Library, London. This manuscript has been printed in *Journal of Friends Historical Society*, XXXII (1935), 22-26.

16. George Chapman, "Archibald Bell, 1620-1707," unpublished typescript in Friends Historical Library, Dublin.

17. Swarthmore MSS, V, 28 (Tr. VII, 127), and VI, 45-46 (Tr. VII, 585, 587).

18. Penney, *Early Publishers*, p. 206; Ellwood, *Thomas Ellwood*, p. 345.

19. Swarthmore MSS, I, 26 (Tr. II, 781).

20. National Sufferings, I, 23, 24.

21. Swarthmore MSS, IV, 238 (Tr. IV, 249). Note the mention of a *monthly meeting*, something which developed in some parts of England and Ireland quite early. Loe may have meant the "three weeks" or "six weeks" meetings found in early Irish Quakerism. He reports that Friends have come through this suffering fairly well and that he believes many of them are "freely given up to suffer" and to bear "all things for truths sake." This letter is dated in August 1660.

22. Great Book of Sufferings, II, Oxfordshire section, pp. 7-8.

23. Ellwood, *Thomas Ellwood*, pp. 118-119. Perhaps Thomas Ellwood's letter to Loe (whom Ellwood later calls a "faithful and diligent Labourer . . . in the work of the Lord; and an excellent Ministerial Gift he had") attempting to set up a meeting for Loe to address Ellwood's neighbors was the reason they saw Loe as a leader or "head." His natural ability also thrust him into the upper echelons of Quaker leadership. See pp. 106-114, for this episode and especially pp. 107-108 concerning the difficult times Quakers experienced at the time of the Fifth Monarchy uprising. Ellwood later visited Loe and the forty or more Friends who were being held at Oxford Castle, see pp. 122-123.

24. Swarthmore MSS, VI, 55 (Tr. VII, 613). Probably this letter, dated 16th of 1st Month, 1661, is March 1661 rather than 1662.

25. National Sufferings, I, 27.

26. Great Book of Sufferings, II, Munster Province section (no page number). Cf. Thomas Holme and Abraham Fuller, *A Brief Relation of some part of the Sufferings of the True Christians, The People of God (in Scorn called Quakers) in Ireland . . . from 1660-1671* (London, 1672), p. 18.

27. Great Book of Sufferings, II, Ireland sufferings, County Wexford section; Cf. Besse, *Sufferings*, II, 472.

28. Richard Farnworth, *Truth Vindicated, or an Answer to a Letter sent by John Perrot out of Jamaica into England, &c* (London, 1665). In addition to Farnworth, the other signers were Morgan Watkins, Solomon Eccles, Thomas Loe, Stephen Crisp, John Elson, Josiah Coale, Samuel Newton, Gerrard Roberts. Thomas Green, Amor Stoddard, and Gilbert Latey.

29. Penington MSS, IV, 43-44 (Friends House Library, London). Other signers were Richard Farnworth, Alexander Parker, George Whitehead, Josiah Coale, John Whitehead, Stephen Crisp, Thomas Green, John Moon, Thomas Briggs, and James Parke. Cf. Samuel M. Janney, *History of the Religious Society of Friends, From Its Rise to the Year 1828* (Philadelphia, 1860), II, 213-214.

30. Cf. Kenneth L. Carroll, *John Perrot, Early Quaker Schismatic* (London, 1971), pp. 91–92.

31. Cf. Limerick Monthly Meeting Family Lists, p. 3 (Friends Historical Library, Dublin), where Loe is listed as being present at the marriage of James Craven and Dorothy Aldworth.

32. "The Convincement of William Penn," MS. See fn. 16.

33. Testimonies from 1661, p. 16a. This manuscript volume is found in Friends Historical Library, Dublin.

34. Testimonies from 1661, p. 17a.

35. Was she one of his earlier converts? Was she one who had been influenced by John Perrot's teachings and embraced "signs and wonders" at the time that the Society of Friends was moving away from that approach? We know very little about her except that she and her companion Alice Sanderson were testified against by Dublin Friends in December 1669.

36. Dublin Testimonies (MMII, Fl), pp. 6–7, Friends Historical Library, Dublin. Cf. p. 7 for the testimony of Dublin Friends against Pildren and her companion Alice Sanderson. Concerning "signs," "figures,' and "wonders," see Kenneth L. Carroll, "Sackcloth and Ashes and Other Signs and Wonders," *Journal of Friends Historical Society*, LXII (1975), 314–325; "Quaker Attitudes Toward Signs and Wonders," *JFHS*, LIV (1977), 70–84.

37. William Penn, *The New Witnesses Proved Old Heretics* (London, 1672), p. 40; Kenneth L. Carroll, "Quakers and Muggletonians in Seventeenth Century Ireland," *A Quaker Miscellany for Edward H. Milligan*, David Blamires, ed. (England, 1985), pp. 49–57. The work by Loe does not appear to be extant. Cf. Christopher Hill, Barry Reay, and William Lamont, *The World of the Muggletonians* (London, 1983), p. 75.

38. Penington MSS, IV, 6. This Letter from Penn to Isaac Penington is dated 17th of 8th Month, 1668. Brailsford, *Making of Wm. Penn*, reports that Josiah Coale was also present.

39. Penington MSS, IV, 7.

40. Penington MSS, IV, 7.

41. Penington MSS, IV, 7, lists his death as taking place on the 5th, with burial the following day. London and Middlesex Digest of Burials (1661–1699), Friends House Library, London, reports that Loe, whose residence was Oxford, "Died of a Fever, at Edward Man's a Hosier, in Bishopgate within."

PART TWO

Colonial America

Toleration Comes to Sandwich

When in 1657 Massachusetts expelled Nicholas Upshall for being sympathetic to Friends, it was no accident that he went to Sandwich in Plymouth Colony, or that English Quaker missionaries visited Sandwich. While the majority of Sandwich residents did not become convinced Friends, at least twenty per cent of the townsfolk did, thereby defying Plymouth's General Court and establishing their town as one of the prime centers sympathetic to Quakerism.[1]

Equally important for the survival of Sandwich Quakerism was the willingness of other town residents to accept the Quaker presence. Like the towns north of Boston on which Jonathan Chu has reported, there was enough support within the town for Sandwich Friends to challenge successfully Plymouth Colony's leaders. What was true for Kittery in Maine was also true for Sandwich. Sandwich's civil authorities were unequal and probably unwilling to undertake the task of suppressing Quakers. In 1658 the colony's solution was to appoint its own officer, Marshal George Barlow, to impose its authority on the recalcitrant town. Sandwich Friends resisted his efforts and their publicists in England reported in distressing detail the numerous fines, imprisonments, and physical punishments inflicted on resident and missionary Friends because of his zeal. Less obvious at that time and since was the occasional help given Friends by their neighbors either directly or indirectly. Some residents refused to help Barlow's enforcement efforts. Friends survived in Sandwich with their lands intact and few of them fled the town. Local and perhaps even colony officials, after the initial furor died down, connived at these laxities by not collecting all fines, much as other localities spared their Quaker neighbors to the north.[2]

After 1660, Plymouth Colony apparently decided to let Friends alone, although there was no effort immediately to repeal punitive legislation. While some instances of petty harassment by individuals may have occurred, active official persecution ended. For Sandwich Friends life must have returned to normal. Although only one of their number, William Allen, achieved minor elective office in this decade, Friends had good reason to expect that the time would soon come when they could resume political activity and share in the distribution of land.[3]

There matters rested until the 1670s when deteriorating relations between Indians and colonists and the creation of the formal Quaker business meeting structure led to changes. Apparently because Friends got along well with Indians, the town appointed Friends Edward Perry and Joseph Holaway to advise Richard Bourne, a town official, regarding Indian testimony. More important was the campaign that the two-year-old Sandwich Monthly Meeting began in 1674 for reenfranchisement and restoration of benefits for Sandwich Friends. The meeting instructed William Newland to search town records for signs of Friends as townsmen. When he found none, it appointed him and Edward Perry to see if John Smith, the teaching minister at Sandwich, could offer redress for disfranchised Friends. After several approaches to Smith, the monthly meeting followed Smith's advice and made a direct approach to the General Court to see if it would grant relief. According to monthly meeting records, William Allen, Ralph Allen, and William Newland attempted to obtain satisfaction from both the General Court and Governor Josiah Winslow over the next few months. No trace survives in colony records that they succeeded in obtaining a hearing, and so they sought relief from the town, perhaps with the encouragement of town leaders.[4]

Ignoring the colony, the town reacted favorably. The town meeting decided on 25 April 1675 to record all the names of those who "have and can make apeare theare just righte and title to the privileges of the Town." Names of ninety-six men appear on that list, thirteen of them Friends (Friends' numbers had declined by this time to twelve per cent from the twenty per cent originally). Thus the town continued its earlier policy of moderation towards Quakers, in effect annulling locally the colony laws that had disfranchised Friends. Apparently, both town and colony were content to permit this local solution to the Quaker problem now that Friends had become less threatening and less like the feared enthusiasts who had run amuck since the beginning of the Protestant Reformation.[5]

Even before the town decided to readmit Friends to the franchise, the town meeting had elected Quakers to minor posts like surveyor of highways. Now with Friends' names on an electoral list, the town meeting responded by electing them to minor offices in greater numbers. In 1675 King Philip's War broke out. It was a war that severely strained resources of both town and colony and a war that Plymouth Colony Friends, true to their developing pacifism, refused to fight. During war years, despite the Quaker refusal to take up arms, leading Friends Edward Perry and William Newland were elected as rate makers, major offices, given the current crisis, and offices that reflected the trust placed in some Friends

by the town as a whole. While effectively excluded from the top town offices of selectman and representative to the General Court, Friends continued to serve in some offices and on committees like the boundary
commission with neighboring Barnstable that included Edward Perry
among its members.[6]

The accommodation was clearly not acceptable to many in the town.
Willing as they might have been to let Friends settle boundaries, survey
highways, and set town tax rates, many town residents were angered by
the Quaker refusal to take up arms in King Philip's War. A smaller number were upset at Quaker resistance to support of a minister and the up-
keep of the meeting house. They were happy to be able to take advantage
of wartime passions to reverse the recent favor to their Quaker
neighbors. In 1678, the group filed a petition to the General Court alleg-
ing many Quaker missteps. Some charges were as old as the Quaker
presence in the colony: Friends had a turbulent spirit, circulated Quaker
books, and were abusive towards their neighbors. Other complaints were
of a more recent vintage and reflected recent quarrels in the town:
Friends refused to support a clergyman for the town and, of greater significance, had failed to "preserve his mjesties interest their Neighbours,
& their owne." That is, Friends had refused to fight in the recent war.
The petitioners managed to restrict Friends by invoking an often-used
measure (in Plymouth and elsewhere) to limit Quaker privileges: requiring that everyone take an oath before participating in town affairs.
Friends refused, as apparently did fifty others who sympathized with
them. The design of the oath is apparent from the protest filed the next
day by Friends Peter Gaunt, William Newland, and John Jenkins. They
opposed the town's "disposing of any privileges that belong to them as
Townsmen (of lands)." Friends also hastened to reply to the town's official petition to the General Court with one of their own that denied all
charges. Concerning their alleged failure to support the Crown, Friends
suggested that the original petitioners were more guilty than they, a view
that would have found considerable support among Crown officials in
London who had found entirely too much independence in all New England colonies.[7]

The town had granted relief to Friends before 1675, and would again
by exempting them from taxes for church maintenance, but now Friends
had to turn for a longer-range remedy to the General Court, keeping in
reserve the strong likelihood that the Crown would interfere. Edward
Randolph's criticism of persecution of dissenters in Massachusetts could
also be used against Plymouth, and its leaders, with less constitutional
security than those of Massachusetts, knew it. Early in 1680 Sandwich

Monthly Meeting appointed William Newland and Edward Perry to write Governor Josiah Winslow about Plymouth's "Prohibiting of friends by their Laws from our Common Rites & Priveleges as voate in towne meetings."[8]

Any answer to Quaker concerns had to come from the legislature, not the governor, and Plymouth General Court was at first not forthcoming. Friends were not prepared to continue to submit quietly to what they viewed as manifest injustice. In 1681, they tried again. This time the monthly meeting stressed Friends peaceable nature. None of the stridency of the earlier petition was in this petition, although Edward Perry delivered just as strong a condemnation of persecution to the General Court as in times past. The monthly meeting made it plain to Plymouth authorities that in England the king had indulged those who could not take an oath. Clearly if the king could grant an indulgence to Friends, should not Plymouth also relent, for its continued existence depended on royal indulgence? Friends threatened to petition the king if their petition were not successful. The colony got the message—Friends should get the vote in the town.[9]

William Newland took the petition to the General Court in July, and the court responded favorably this time. Friends who had lived in Sandwich for many years and had bought lands there could "voate in the dispossall of such lands, and shall have liberty to voate for the choise of rators, and shalbe capeable of makeing rates if legally chosen thereunto by the towne and psons aforesaid soe long as they carry ciuilly and not abuse their libertie."[10]

Plymouth had finally restored many of the liberties taken from Sandwich Friends a quarter of a century earlier. Bidden by the colony, Sandwich hastily added the Friends' names to the town list. Friends could now legally continue to serve in minor offices, but not in major offices, for Plymouth law required an oath for positions like selectmen and representative to the General Court.[11]

Successful in their campaign to regain the local franchise, Sandwich Friends also managed to avoid paying church taxes. Laws of 1655, 1657, and 1670 called in various ways for public support of the clergy. Plymouth towns, however, honored these laws as much in the breach as in the observance. Even the town of Plymouth was without a minister from 1654 to 1666, not an auspicious example for other towns. Gradually most towns came into compliance in the 1670s, but not Sandwich. The complaint about the Quaker refusal to support the local church in 1678 was probably a minority view unleashed only because of resentments generated by King Philip's War. By 1682 the town was collecting taxes for the support of a minister, but Friends do not seem to have been assessed as they neither complained about suffering for the support of the local church nor resigned from elected posts as raters, something such stormy petrels as Edward Perry would have done had Friends been so taxed. An informal agreement to exempt Friends apparently existed. Formal action to remit Quaker church taxes came in 1695, confirming previous practices. Sandwich in this way set a precedent that the colony of Massachusetts would follow over three decades later.[12]

Quakers were always a minority in Sandwich, but a strong enough minority from the beginning to obtain support from other townsfolk. Thus they escaped the worst of the persecution dealt to other Friends in Plymouth and Massachusetts. By the 1670s old passions had cooled, and Friends no longer seemed the threat they had been. And so first the town and then the colony proceeded to accommodate Friends even as their share of the town's population shrank from roughly twenty per cent in the 1650s, to twelve per cent in 1680, to under ten per cent early in the eighteenth century. By that time new Quaker centers had developed, like Dartmouth, where they and their Baptist allies controlled the government, and Rhode Island where enterprising young Friends found economic as well as political opportunity.[13]

NOTES

1. Arthur J. Worrall, *Quakers in the Colonial Northeast* (Hanover, N.H., 1980), p. 16. I derived my estimate for Quaker numbers by using names in Sandwich Proprietors' Records of those who had lands in 1657 and 1658, adding names of others from Sandwich town records, 1652–1692, pp. 24, 25, and developing a list of Quaker residents from *Records of the Colony of Plymouth in New England*, David Pulsifer, ed., 12 vols. (Boston, 1855–61), 3. Estimates for Friends are probably on the low side.

2. Jonathan M. Chu, *Neighbors, Friends, or Madmen: The Puritan Adjustment to Quakerism in Seventeenth-Century Massachusetts* (Westport, Conn., 1985). *Plymouth Records*, Pulsifer, 3:140–141, 173, 178–179. In 1659 Edmond Freeman, Jr. and Thomas Burgis, Jr. refused to help George Barlow and for that were fined ten shillings each.

3. Sandwich town records, 1652–1692, p. 87.

4. Ibid., p. 106; Sandwich Monthly Meeting, 3/V/1674, 7/VI/1674, 4/VII/1674, 2/VIII/1674, 6/IX/1674, 5/XII/1674.

5. Sandwich town records 1652–1692, p. 198. For the perception of seventeenth-century Friends as enthusiasts see David S. Lovejoy, *Religious Enthusiasm*

in the New World: Heresy to Revolution (Cambridge, Mass., 1985), chaps. 5 and 6. Estimates of Quaker numbers in 1680 came from the lists in Sandwich town records 1652–1692, pp. 198–203 compared to a list of Quaker names derived from Sandwich Monthly Meeting minutes.

6. Sandwich town records, 1652–1692, pp. 106, 110, 113, 124, 125, 178. Friends did not fight in this war although some leading Friends in Rhode Island helped direct defensive preparations.

7. Sandwich town records 1652–1692, pp. 202–203; Sandwich Monthly Meeting 4/V/1678.

8. Michael Garibaldi Hall, *Edward Randolph and the American Colonies 1676–1703* (Chapel Hill, N.C., 1960), chaps. 2, 3. Sandwich Monthly Meeting, 7/III/1680, 2/V/1680, 6/VI/1680. Unlike Massachusetts, Plymouth did not have a charter.

9. Sandwich Monthly Meeting, 3/IV/1681, I/V/1681.

10. Pulsifer, *Plymouth Records*, 6:71; Edward Perry, "To the Court of Plymouth" in *A Memorable Account . . . of Edward Perry* (Philadelphia, 1729), pp. 79–84.

11. Sandwich town records 1652–1692, p. 200.

12. George D. Langdon, Jr., *Pilgrim Colony: A History of New Plymouth 1620–1691* (New Haven, 1966), pp. 76–77, 117–125; William G. McLoughlin, *New England Dissent, 1630–1833: The Baptists and the Separation of Church and State*, 2 vols. (Cambridge, Mass., 1971), 1:119; J. M. Bumsted, "A Well-Bounded Toleration: Church and State in Plymouth Colony," *A Journal of Church and State*, 10 (1968); Sandwich town records 1652–1692, pp. 215, 236; Sandwich town records 1692–1767, p. 17. Sandwich remitted church taxes. It could not exempt Quakers from Massachusetts law.

13. See notes 1 and 5 for population estimates in the seventeenth century. For the early eighteenth century I compared names of inhabitants in Sandwich town records 1692–1767, p. 44, to a list of names derived from Sandwich Monthly Meeting records. For population movement in southeastern Massachusetts see Thomas R. Cole, "Family Settlement, and Migration in Southeastern Massachusetts 1650–1805: The Case for Regional Analysis," *New England Historical and Genealogical Register*, 132 (1978), pp. 171–185. For the less hospitable area in Salem and Gloucester see Christine Leigh Heyrman, *Commerce and Culture: The Maritime Communities of Colonial Massachusetts 1690–1750* (New York, 1984).

JACK D. MARIETTA

The Growth of Quaker Self-Consciousness in Pennsylvania, 1720–1748

P ennsylvania early acquired the reputation of being the Quaker colony because of the prominence of William Penn, the predominance of Quakers in the colony's population (until approximately 1710) and government, and the colony's sectarian religious atmosphere. The reputation can be misleading, however, and a possible misconception is that Quaker features of Pennsylvania such as these meant that unity and harmony characterized the Quaker population of Pennsylvania from the start. Actually, at least forty-two years passed before Quaker leaders and legislators quit struggling among themselves and cooperated from a concern for their religious body. Fifty-eight years passed before Friends became consistently conscious of their Quakerism and consistently cooperated in its behalf. Not until the 1720s did Friends come to appreciate their common interest and react to the dangers to it. Only in the 1740s did they organize, collaborate, and advance policies that were popularly identified with Quakerism—this novel collaboration marking the advent of the famous "Quaker Party." The purpose of this article is to describe these events, explain when and how Quaker self-consciousness and unity appeared in Pennsylvania's history, and when Quaker leaders and office-holders behaved from considerations that were conspicuously Quaker.

A salient feature of Pennsylvania's politics from 1682 to 1710 was its disharmony, although a large majority of the participants in the province's earliest political history were Friends. Even when the provincial government was taken from William Penn between 1692 and 1694, the charter suspended, and royal government imposed, Friends did not unite. Their superiority in the Pennsylvania population may have afforded them the security of mind to continue fighting among themselves. The internecine fighting lapsed in 1710 when Philadelphia Yearly Meeting intervened in an unprecedented way to urge that the members cast their ballots on behalf of peace and unity.[1]

By 1721 rancor in public life and divisions among Friends had returned, yet with a difference. In the 1720s Friends noticed that they had become a minority in Pennsylvania, and some Friends, mostly city people and political activists, disliked their new neighbors. When divisions and political parties revived, immigrants to the province dismayed some Quaker politicians who found these new people allied with their rivals. This unfamiliar quality about Pennsylvania alerted Quaker leaders to their exposure when they were weakened by internal quarrels. Pennsylvania Friends had earlier known the hostility of the English government, the Church of England, and a few local minions of both. A sizable, growing, suspect, domestic enemy, however, was new.

The first surge of the "new" immigration of Palatine Germans and Scotch-Irish occurred in 1717.[2] Two years later some Friends began to complain about crime and disorder in the province and the degeneration of morals. Neither immigration nor complaints about it would stop in the next two decades. When Isaac Norris, clerk of Philadelphia Yearly Meeting and prominent officeholder, learned in November 1719 that someone had burglarized Jonathan Dickinson's home and taken £500, he generalized that "many Robberies are committed Such as never heretofore known in the Country. The people who were never before under apprehensions of the kind are now afraid of travelling the Roads."[3] In Norris's view the city did not become any safer in the following years; in 1728 he lamented that "in my memory we could Safely go to bed with our doors open but now Robberies, housebreaking, Rapes & other crimes are become Common." James Logan sounded the same lament: "We were happy formerly while the ancient Friends and first settlers lived not broke in upon. Now the Case quite altered by the licentious Youth, Strangers, Love of Spirits, Morals debauched. . . ." Between 1710 and 1730 the city had grown from 2,400 inhabitants to 7,000.[4]

Friends in the city meetings and Philadelphia Yearly Meeting displayed similar anxiety about the changing province. Anxiety appeared as concern to preserve Quaker children from the "rudeness," "intemperance," and alien behavior which the elders observed in the city streets and elsewhere. Quaker complaints and cautions climaxed with the "multitudes of people coming in from Ireland" and "the vast number of Palatines" immigrating in the early 1730s.[5] Friends, at this juncture, refused to separate their apprehensions about public life from the fact of immigration, and did not refrain from comparing themselves favorably with the new people. In 1730 Philadelphia Monthly Meeting sent Isaac Norris, Samuel Preston, and Israel Pemberton, Sr., to complain to Governor Patrick Gordon about the "dangerous consequence" of St. Patrick's Day "revellings" — a custom so alien to "this country which was chiefly settled by sober people." Gordon had no remedy for them. They next sought relief from the general disorder in the city through a memorial to the mayor and aldermen of the city (who were largely Friends) in which they doubly emphasized Pennsylvania's Quaker patrimony. "The people called Quakers who (by far) were the greatest part of the early adventurers with our first proprietor (of the same persuasion) in the settlement of this colony, had chiefly in view a quiet, moral, and religious life which by the blessing of God many enjoyed for several years, to their own comfort and the reputation of the country. But now for some time past . . . vice and immorality greatly abounds. . . ."[6] Philadelphia Yearly Meeting in 1733 wrote to London Friends that "Greater circumspection appears the more necessary by the increase of people, not only of those born among us, but other of divers nations, customs and manners, which of late years have flow'd in upon us, so that with grief we observe vice and immorality to increase."[7]

The aliens educated, married, and buried differently. They also danced, fiddled, sang, reveled, raced horses, gambled, got drunk and fought, celebrated St. Patrick's Day and shot off guns on New Year's Eve. The Society did not always make its point politely. Philadelphia Monthly Meeting published a broadside in 1732 which observed that "Remarkable and grievous is the Depravity of Manners so observable in our Streets; sorrowful enough is it to see the great Encrease of Prophaneness and Lewdness . . . much owing to the Importation of great Numbers of the vicious and scandalous Refuse of other Countries." In their private correspondence, Norris and Logan vented this kind of prejudice, especially upon the Ulster Scots, or Scotch-Irish, "among whom a great part seem to be ye very Scum of mankind," wrote Norris. "Pray think what Condition we are like to be in," Logan rhetorically asked John Penn, "with those additions [of more Scotch-Irish] to ye Poyson in our Bowels. . . ." Logan wrote that he felt ashamed that he was a Scotsman.[8]

The addition of newcomers to the Quaker founders affected the politics of the province after 1720. By 1722 a depression had settled into Pennsylvania to stay throughout the decade. The immigrants, poor and in debt, joined older residents in urging the government to relieve their plight. Sir William Keith, deputy governor of the province from 1717 to 1726, helped to awaken them as much as the depression itself. He explained the causes of their troubles, advanced remedies, and in populist language unprecedented in early Pennsylvania, castigated his opponents. Because his performance from 1717 to 1722 had pleased both proprietor and colonists and because of his knighthood, he appeared unlikely to fashion a party of anti-proprietary, low-class upstarts and strangers and to harangue like a nineteenth-century demagogue.[9] In 1721 the always-cautious Logan believed that Keith had established "a perfect peace" in Pennsylvania. The next year Keith threw over the consensus by publicly taunting "the Great, the Rich," and "the Learned" of the province while congratulating "the poor laborious and industrious Part of Mankind." Logan later admitted that by confiding in Keith he had made the most serious error of his political life (*V*, II, 1459–60).[10]

In Philadelphia, the depression had by 1722 divided the wealthier merchants, many of whom were Quakers and friends of the Penn family, from the poor and debtors, who, in the city, were often immigrants and other newer people. Keith pressed the Assembly to stay the prosecution of debtors and to issue paper money in order to relieve the scarcity of coin in the province. Both remedies won the gratitude of most Pennsylvanians — in the countryside, where most Friends lived, as well as the city. Both offended the proprietary party, whose leaders candidly styled themselves the wealthy and wise, and thereby enhanced the ombudsman's role that Keith assumed for the people.[11]

In order to cultivate further the awakening electors and to increase their numbers, Keith espoused liberalized naturalization laws, illegally opened new lands for settlement, and organized his people into political clubs which took to the streets, paraded, and rallied. From Isaac Norris's point of view, Keith was organizing "the mob." Keith ignored Logan, the Council, the Commissioners of Property, and whenever possible he replaced the Penns' appointees with his own favorites. When the Penns commanded him to desist, he publicly flaunted their commands and won still more of the populace to his party. After six years of this prodromal democracy, Norris revised Logan's optimistic 1721 assessment of Keith: "He [Keith] found us an United peaceable people & left us by his wicked politicks & Artifice Divided & in partys."[12]

Despite Keith's currying favor with country people, and the new Germans especially, his political constituency remained in the city. His economic remedies and opposition to proprietary power attracted support throughout the province, but his personal political credit did not grow apace. The countryside had its own favorite, the Quaker David Lloyd. Since the mid-1690s, Lloyd had been one of the two or three central personalities in Pennsylvania's politics, and leader of the anti-proprietary forces. Without naming him, it was Lloyd especially whom the Yearly Meeting wished to stymie in 1710 when it urged Friends to choose more irenic politics and legislators. In 1718 Lloyd retired from politics, but had returned by 1722. Now he supported the same economic remedies that Keith did, but with less bluster. And much more so than Keith, he fashioned legislation that brought about actual changes. He also penned the constitutional attacks upon proprietary power in Pennsylvania. By 1725, Keith and Lloyd had concocted an alliance or party. To an amalgam of Scotch-Irish, Germans, debtors, plus ambitious Anglicans and nondescript Pennsylvanians, Quaker David Lloyd brought a large contingent of his brethren. Because Lloyd's Quakers, who were perhaps a majority of the Friends who voted, supported his party, the Society of Friends again divided itself between two parties, as it had from 1692 to 1710. That, however, was the last time the Society would do so.

For the first time these Quaker followers of David Lloyd shared their party and the politics of the province with a mass of non-Quakers, and Lloyd shared the leadership with a non-Quaker who was more partisan than himself. Never again could Quaker politicians overlook the non-Quaker voters. The province had become sufficiently open and cosmopolitan to preclude any retreat to the more exclusive Quaker past.

As Keith's biographer, Thomas Wendel, remarks, the Keith-Lloyd alliance was "a marriage of convenience." In pursuing his fortunes as governor, Keith needed the assistance of the Assembly which Lloyd led. Lloyd needed the governor's assent to legislation. In a curious episode in 1725 Keith discovered how easily he could raise the anger of his putative allies if he ignored their Quaker sensibilities. He insisted that John Kinsey, Jr., who later became clerk of Philadelphia Yearly Meeting, remove his hat at Chancery Court. The order aroused Quaker zealots who got Keith to apologize. Isaac Norris remarked that he had never seen anything exact such speedy submission from Keith as "this famous hatt." Norris understood that Lloyd disliked much of Keith's behavior, even while Lloyd cooperated with him.[13] Before the depression ended, the alliance dissolved. Hannah Penn dismissed Keith as governor in 1726 and Keith audaciously planned to get elected to the Assembly and oust Lloyd from the speaker's chair. He did not doubt that he would do it.[14]

Before Lloyd and his Quaker followers discovered the enemy in Keith, Logan had warned that Keith endangered the Society of Friends in Pennsylvania. "The Quaker Countrey, as this is called abroad, is become a scene of the vilest, most extravagant Licentiousness by the management of those who cannot but radically either hate or despise all dissenters, and who may, one day, derive a merit from exposing them. Yet, instead of cherishing of Love & Peace, & strengthening ourselves in unity, too many hug their own shame, & are fond of their disgrace and confusion."[15]

In the election campaign of 1726 Keith's partisans showed Logan "licentiousness" such as he had never before witnessed in Pennsylvania. Keith's city constituents took to the streets in unprecedented numbers; they climaxed their raucous behavior at the October election by burning down the pillory and stocks and some butchers' stalls. Whether or not Keith could run the politics of the province, he could disrupt it and the public peace.[16]

Earlier, in the spring, Logan had so abused Lloyd in a pamphlet entitled *The Antidote* that Philadelphia Monthly Meeting, never a stronghold of Lloyd's friends, disciplined Logan. Despite Logan's abuse of Lloyd, only four months later he was campaigning for Lloyd in the hope of forestalling the greatest evil of all, the election of Keith to the speakership. The danger to the peace was extreme, according to Logan; Keith had long intended to throw the province into chaos and return to preeminence under some new regime. Logan urged Friends in Chester County to take the utmost care to elect moderate, peaceful assemblymen, Lloyd among them. Bucks County was safe from Keith's influence and, were Chester to return wise men, Keith would be thwarted. By August, Lloyd himself was extremely angry with Keith, either out of knowledge that Keith envied him or from disillusionment with the chaos Keith incited, or both.[17]

In September, on the eve of the Assembly election, Philadelphia Yearly Meeting advised the members about provincial politics for the first time since 1710. The Meeting appointed Lloyd, Caleb Pusey, Samuel Preston, and Thomas Chalkley to draft the message—a mixture of conservatives and radicals which indicated that an irenic spirit was stirring within the Society. The authors revealed Friends' common anxiety about immigrants, immorality, and Quaker security. Of "the great increase of People," it read, "many . . . among them, do appear regardless of religion, Probity, and Virtue. . . ." They "seem to Combine in uncommon manner, to rush into Immoralities and tumultuous Practices, using many artful ways, to draw others to fall in with them. . . ." "Since they cannot persecute them [Friends] as in Time past," the enemies of the Society have entered politics in order "to give them [Friends] Disturbance and Trouble of Another Sort." The Meeting instructed Friends not to countenance in the least these machinations of the enemy, but to oppose them insofar as they could.[18]

In the October election, voting against Keith did not entail voting against depression remedies that Keith had advanced, especially paper money. Lloyd had originated them and engineered their enactment into law. The newly appointed deputy governor, Patrick Gordon, also adopted the paper money remedy. In the 1726 election, the poor, wherever they lived, were left to choose between candidates or parties mostly on other grounds than depression remedies. Lloyd and the Quakers won Bucks County and pivotal Chester County, whereas the Keithians won Philadelphia city and County. At the convening of the House, Keith, now a representative from Philadelphia County, challenged Lloyd for the speakership, still believing that he would win the chair. He lost.[19]

Keith and Lloyd became completely alienated. The new House, dominated by Lloyd's friends, passed a law regulating elections.[20] The design of the House was especially to inspect the voters in the city and prevent the unqualified from voting. Presumably, newcomers to the province and other constituents of Keith would be the ones culled from the ranks of the enfranchised. The act provoked a very wordy war in which Keith and the clerk of Yearly Meeting, Isaac Norris, were most often belligerents.[21]

In the spring of 1728 Keith left Pennsylvania. Nevertheless, in subsequent elections the Quakers could not dislodge from office the now leaderless Keithians from Philadelphia despite advice from Yearly Meeting that Friends "unite, and be strong in the Lord, against all our Adversaries" and more campaigning by Logan. Meanwhile, Chester and Bucks counties remained securely Quaker in politics.[22]

As early as the October 1726 election, some Pennsylvanians apparently understood that Keith hoped ultimately to disrupt politics, trammel the governor who had replaced him, and harass the proprietors until in despair they would sell the proprietary to the Crown. Thereupon he, Keith, would become the royal governor of the province. The tale was credible because Keith had already been at work to free the Lower Counties from the Penns' proprietorship and had employed Colonel Alexander Spotswood of Virginia in his machinations. That was public knowledge.[23] Few Friends could imagine any prospect worth forfeiting Pennsylvania's charter, which secured their religious and political liberties. Keith's legislative palliatives for the depression and other considerations could not reconcile Quakers to him, for with them he would bring royal government. To Friends he was the enemy.

After Keith disappeared, the raucous city people continued to worry Friends. More immigrants compounded the political problem, or the Keithians compounded the problem of the immigrants, or both. Twelve hundred Palatines arrived in the first nine months of 1727. In the spring of 1728 the Quaker Assembly begged the new governor, Patrick Gordon, to do whatever was necessary for the security of the citizens. The assemblymen suggested that immigration be terminated completely because the pacifist Quakers of the province could do little to prevent the disorder the immigrants brought with them.[24] Then, in the fall of 1728 when the Quakers came down to Philadelphia for the Assembly session, rioters assaulted them. The Assembly quickly moved to petition Governor Gordon to appoint a location other than Philadelphia for the subsequent sitting of the House. The assemblymen rehearsed to the governor the history of Pennsylvania: The province had been settled by a "sober and orderly People" who forsook the use of arms and for decades lived peaceably and quietly. But "great Numbers of dissolute and disorderly Persons" entered the province and by their evil dispositions or the connivance of dissatisfied, older residents, the strangers threatened the peace. Gordon sympathized with the assemblymen, offered his help, and suggested they help themselves. And they did help themselves; to keep the peace they passed a bill which duplicated the Riot Act of England. Then, in the same session, they passed a duty upon foreigners, Irish servants, and Negroes. Later, they added a duty upon felons. As late as 1728, Lloyd, a progressive jurist and chief justice of Pennsylvania, had urged that a convicted murderer be treated leniently. In 1730 he urged that a burglar deserved to die because of the ill effect that sparing him would have upon public order.[25]

For the first time in Pennsylvania's history the conditions of the 1720s had caused Friends to close ranks and to regret their differences. Immigrants, protesting debtors, non-Quaker political interlopers all troubled the Quaker politicians. And because the leadership of the Society so often duplicated the political leadership, it was no surprise that the Society expressed the same anxiety.

While immigration to Pennsylvania continued, the other conditions that had stimulated Friends' self-consciousness did not outlast the decade: Keith left the province in 1728, the depression disappeared about 1730, and Lloyd died in 1731. A more peaceful atmosphere appeared within Pennsylvania and its government, and stayed for some ten years.[26]

The greatest causes of Quaker anxiety and unity in the 1720s were immigration and economics; the causes in the 1740s were war and Quaker pacifism. Surprisingly, while Friends identified new dangers to themselves and the Quaker province in the 1740s, they found their security in the immigrants. Friends remained a distinct minority and their political hegemony was envied by non-Friends who depreciated their minorityhood, their religious ethics, their patriotism, and their presumption about the peculiarly Quaker character of Pennsylvania. In responding to the new and the old in the 1740s, Friends displayed such unity in public life as they never before had done—and would not again do until the American Revolution.

The respite from rancorous public life that the 1730s afforded Pennsylvanians ended with the outbreak of war with Spain in 1739. It was not necessary that any war in which the British engaged would have that effect. The dynastic nature of the wars before the French Revolution assured that they would have limited consequences for much of the British population and that the political leaders of Britain's provinces could satisfy the Crown's demands for their collaboration by contributing money or material. Friends' ethics permitted that collaboration, as we will later see. A crucial factor was the presence in Pennsylvania of dissident peoples and proprietary officials, jealous of Quaker power and presumptions, who expected to profit from renewed war, to make Friends obnoxious to their constituents and the Crown, and finally, to change the governance of Pennsylvania by barring Quaker politicians from office. The parties to the peace of the 1730s had lived together assuming that some kindred outlook united them. But war disclosed how incompatible the several parties were.

The deputy governor of Pennsylvania after 1738 was Colonel George Thomas, an ex-military officer as bellicose as any English patriot might desire. Beginning in 1739, for at least the first four years of war, Thomas was in the vanguard of the fight against Spain and France and against local pacifists who refused, in his opinion, to prosecute adequately the war. Thomas found that he had a vocal band of local well-wishers and collaborators. Unlike earlier nemeses of the Society in Pennsylvania, they were not transient officials of the English government or the Church of England, nor were they debtors or recent immigrants. Thomas's allies were natives, many the proud sons and grandsons of Pennsylvanians who expected the provincial government to respect their rank and protect their considerable property from foreign enemies. Most importantly, they stoutly denied the presumption that Pennsylvania had a peculiar relation to the Society of Friends.[27]

The enlistment of indentured servants by Governor Thomas in 1740 without compensating their owners has figured most prominently in the explanations of these acrimonious years. The enlistment did deeply offend Pennsylvanians' esteem for the security of private property. Friends were at least as much affected by the loss of this property as any other Pennsylvanians. Quakers were not singled out for loss, nor was there anything discriminatory in the causes of the losses. The distinctly religious feature of this acrimonious era was that Friends' rivals intended to exclude all Friends from public office only because of their religious profession. It was Friends' pacifism, the rivals insisted, that justified such a sweeping prohibition and the end of the Holy Experiment. Yet the significance of Quaker pacifism in the growth of Quaker self-consciousness and in the creation of a unified Quaker party in the 1740s has been largely ignored.[28]

The war with Spain provoked the most sustained debate in colonial history on the fitness of Friends to hold public office, and this was followed by an effort to eject them from provincial government. Governor Thomas initiated the debate. His obtuseness about Quaker pacifism or his perversity toward Friends embittered relations between the governor and the Quaker-dominated Assembly for at least three years. In October 1739, two months after the advent of undeclared war with Spain, Thomas asked the Assembly to prepare the defenses of the province. The Quaker-dominated Assembly presumed that Thomas might not understand how Pennsylvania stood regarding matters like defense, and so it explained the provincial charter to him. Its explanation disclosed a great many of the previously unspoken assumptions of Friends about this peculiarly Quaker colony. In the Charter of Privileges and the "Laws Agreed Upon in England," founder William Penn had granted to Pennsylvanians liberty of conscience, the assemblymen began. The parties to these agreements, being Friends, understood the meaning of that liberty and the purview of Quaker conscience. Some circumstances had changed in Pennsylvania since the founding, but the descendants of the founders continued here and had been joined by other men and women who came to Pennsylvania to enjoy that same liberty. Time had not dissolved Penn's legacy whatever the governor or his collaborators might believe or wish. Therefore, to make Friends or like-minded Pennsylvanians bear arms would be to persecute them unconstitutionally. To compel others to bear arms on Friends' and others' behalf would be to treat citizens unequally and unjustly. Instead, the assemblymen suggested, the governor ought to avail himself of that part of the proprietary charter which granted to the proprietor the military powers of Captain-General (V, III, 2512–3, 2529–31).

Thomas replied that the proprietors had explicitly instructed him never to compel Friends and other pacifists to bear arms or to be punished for refusing arms. As for the non-pacifists, a law was needed to oblige them to be equipped and trained; the governor's power of Captain-General was insufficient and could produce only "a pretty piece of Pageantry for a little time." On the other hand, the very existence of the Captain-General clause in the proprietary charter implied that Penn the Quaker had anticipated the armed defense of the province in a broader way than the assemblymen had assumed. Thomas concluded that the charter, therefore, obliged the Assembly to do its part to defend the province (*V*, III, 2535-8).

The governor then gratuitously attacked the Quaker legislators' conception of Pennsylvania's past and understanding of their own ethics. In 1711, said Thomas, the Assembly had provided Queen Anne with aid for the war with France as Friends in England always did. He expected a like response from Friends in the Assembly now. Next, he revived George Keith's criticism of 1692 that Pennsylvania Friends violated their ethics in holding civil offices: In order to protect their persons and property, Friends condemned "little Rogues to death" for housebreaking. Did Friends, he chided, merely preserve their property from thieves in order to give it to His Majesty's foreign enemies? (*V*, III, 2535-8).

Thomas attempted to discomfit the Quaker legislators and prod them out of their refusal to defend Pennsylvania in the manner he wished. His tactics were inept. He misunderstood the 1711 episode in which a Quaker legislature had given an appropriation to Queen Anne "for her use," misrepresented English Friends payment of taxes for war, and ignored the differences between ethical Quaker conduct and what he had asked from the Assembly for Pennsylvania's defense. And so his effect was to alienate Quakers, publicly expose them as a distinct group, and (by his use of Keith's criticism) even invite accusations of their hypocrisy. This first exchange between Assembly and governor anticipated the future as well as rehearsed the past. From 1739 through the American Revolution Friends would refuse the executive and others' requests for military preparations with the argument that the charter and laws of Pennsylvania protected conscience. The executive—governor, proprietors, or Crown—as well as some citizens would deny the Quaker interpretation of the charter, the purview of conscience, and the implications of the Captain-General's powers. Critics from Governor Thomas to Tom Paine would point impatiently at Quaker magistrates' use of force and to Quaker wealth. Friends hereafter had to defend publicly one part or another of their religious profession; at first they did so successfully, but later, not.

The Quaker Assembly replied to the governor's reply and brought into better focus some of its grievances—while obscuring others. The Assembly improved the focus upon Quaker ethics when it rebutted Thomas's equating the 1711 appropriation with his current request and his equating the situation of English Friends with that of Pennsylvanians. In 1711 Queen Anne had demanded Pennsylvania assist an expedition to Canada and the Assembly had replied that it could not actively engage in assisting the expedition but could pay tribute to the Queen by giving her a sum of money for her to use. That was as much as Friends' ethic permitted. But now Thomas was asking for a greater engagement on their part, a militia. As for English Friends, they paid taxes which were used for carrying on war, but that was not what Thomas was asking from Pennsylvania Friends (*V*, III, 2540–5).

Unfortunately, the assemblymen put the important matter of their ethic out of focus by gratuitously claiming that a governor of Pennsylvania had misapplied the 1711 appropriation, which, they sniped, was "no great Encouragement for future Assemblies to follow the Example" of the 1711 House. Even if Thomas's honesty had been beyond question Friends could not consistently have complied with his request. But their inability to resist demeaning him after he had demeaned them raised tempers still higher.[29]

Thomas picked up the slight on his honesty and told the Assembly he resented it. More important, Thomas said the assemblymen had not demonstrated the difference between their situation and that of English Friends. Because in fact there were several differences, Thomas's obtuseness or obstinacy began to appear. Thomas insisted that in 1711 when Governor Gookin translated a demand from the Queen into a call for the raising and supplying of soldiers, or for the equivalent in money, the Assembly gave the equivalent. Why did Thomas point out the same fact the House was calling to his attention? He attempted to argue that he and Gookin had asked for the same thing, but he did not understand the difference. In 1739 he, and not the Queen or King, requested a militia law, not the equipping or an army or its equivalent in money (*V*, III, 2547–52).

On the day the 1739 session of the House adjourned, the members sent Thomas a message almost entirely devoted to defending its slight on the character of provincial governors. We take "little Delight in Controversy," it began and it continued equally distant from the truth. Outside the House, Israel Pemberton, Jr., future clerk of Yearly Meeting and son of a leading assemblyman, said publicly what many Quaker assemblymen were thinking. "It was [Thomas's] Design or Endeavor to overturn the Constitution and reduce this to a King's Government, . . ." Pemberton was glad that his remarks reached Thomas's ears "since by this means he had heard Truths which the sycophants who kept the Governor Company would never tell him. . . ."[30] The current six months of rancor had revived the most sobering prospect in Pennsylvania's history short of revolution—that is, the threat of the loss of the charters of 1682 and 1701 and their guarantees of religious and civil liberty. For the first time since

Sir William Keith's flight in 1728, the bugaboo of royal government reentered the picture. It did not disappear thereafter.

1740 brought a call from the King for the enlistment of men for Admiral Vernon's ill-fated expedition to the West Indies. While the House took no initiatives to induce enlistments, recruiters enlisted indentured servants who were glad to escape their servitude. In July the Governor called the representatives back from their summer adjournment and laid before them the King's order to provision and transport to the West Indies the recruits from Pennsylvania. Thomas added that, lest the assemblymen suspect that he would dishonestly misapply the funds, as they had insinuated he might do, the Assembly should select commissioners to expend the money and to account to the Assembly for their performance. The Assembly's gratuitous slight on Thomas's character had gone awry. Thomas, believing that his honesty concerned them most of all, innocently invited them to violate their ethic by actually expending the money instead of giving it to him or the King. "We have ever esteemed it our Duty to pay Tribute to Caesar," the Assembly responded to his offer, "and yield Obedience to the Powers God hath set over us . . . but we cannot preserve good conscience, and come into the Levying of Money, and *appropriating* it to the Uses recommeded to us in the Governor's Speech. . . ."[31]

The point, which has escaped historians as well as the governor, is that Quaker pacifism sanctioned the payment of taxes for war; indeed, required it. That requirement followed from Friends' understanding of Jesus' reply to the Pharisees in Matthew, chapter 22: "Render therefore unto Caesar the things that are Caesar's and unto God the things that are God's." In the case of Pennsylvania, the Quaker legislators must appropriate money in response to King George's (i.e. Caesar's) demand— as they had in 1711 for Queen Anne's. But to *spend* it or do anything beyond rendering it to the Crown was to violate Quaker pacifism.

Still Thomas missed the point, probably while scrutinizing the message for more slights on his honesty. "I am not sensible that I have in the least deviated . . . from His Majesty's . . . Instruction," he fired back, thinking that the Assembly had accused him of altering the *uses* recommended by the King. The Assembly Quakers had objected to *their* using the money —for whatever warlike purpose the King or governor had recommended. Then Thomas concluded, since the House mistrusted him, "I recommend to you the Levying of Money, and *appropriating* if agreeable to that [royal] instruction" (*V*, III, 2593, 2594, emphasis added.)

Thomas must have maddened the assemblymen with that response. Or, in light of young Pemberton's comments about the governor, they might have suspected that Thomas was cannier than he made himself appear in his bewildering messages. Whatever credit Thomas retained among the assemblymen for either innocence or obtuseness disappeared two days later when he flatly accused Friends of being unfit to govern. It was unjust that one-third of the people of Pennsylvania, the Quakers, should harm the other two-thirds and refuse even "one single Act for the service of your King, or the people you represent." "This," he asserted, "is a Behaviour very different from that Spirit of Christianity you profess," and contrary to the behavior of English Quakers. "Your principles," Thomas generalized, "are inconsistent with the Ends of Government." Pennsylvania Friends deduced that Thomas was attempting to alienate non-Quaker Pennsylvanians and even their own English brethren from them, and they told him so (V, III, 2605-11, 2617-27, 2632-8).

In the meantime, the Assembly granted £3,000 to the King's use, but with the proviso that all the servants who had been enlisted earlier be returned. Thomas refused the Assembly's offer and sarcastically told the members he was glad to learn that Quakers who a month earlier could not ethically raise and appropriate money for war, could now resolve to give £3,000 to the Crown for the same use. Which is to say, Thomas still did not see the difference between Friends expending the money and their giving it to the Crown to expend. And so, once again the House repeated the distinction. (V, III, 2630-1, 2638, 2658-9). But the legislators were by now pretty well convinced that Thomas sought not to be enlightened on matters of Quaker ethics, but rather to put Quaker assemblymen in the worst possible light for the view of Crown officials and English Friends.

Both sides understood the futility of badgering the other and each appealed to superior authority in England to force its adversary to submit. The Assembly petitioned the King-in-Council to have the servants returned.[32] In October 1740, shortly after the greatest turnout of voters in Pennsylvania history sent Friends to fill twenty-five of the thirty House seats, Thomas complained to the Board of Trade. Thomas professed that he was at wit's end with the Quakers in the Assembly and he offered to resign. The only alternative, he suggested, was that the Crown recognize that the "bigotted Views of the governing Sect here" disqualified them from office in wartime.[33]

Richard Partridge, the Assembly's agent, cleverly got a copy of Thomas's letter to the Board and by the spring of 1741 Pennsylvanians had spread copies of it all over the province.[34] Friends and other constituents of the Quaker party were satisfied that Thomas plotted to exclude Friends from office and curtail their civil and religious liberties. Several months later Thomas had his revenge by dismissing John Kinsey as attorney-general of the province. Kinsey was also Speaker of the House, clerk of Yearly Meeting, putative head of the Quaker party, and one of the province's most eminent lawyers. He refused to give up the office until the Penns confirmed to him the governor's dismissal. They did, and he left office. The incredulous Kinsey had discovered for himself the truth of the breach between Friends and proprietors.[35]

Thomas and John Penn had not been indifferent toward the confrontation between Governor Thomas and the Assembly and Friends. They actively supported their appointee. Thomas Penn was in Pennsylvania at the time and had shown the Assembly that he disagreed with it. In England, concurrently, John Penn had interviewed the Duke of Newcastle, who was Secretary of State, Privy Councillors, and even some eminent London Friends in order to support Governor Thomas's enlistment of servants and his demands on the Assembly. When the Quaker Assembly shortly dismissed from the Pennsylvania agency in London Ferdinand John Paris, who was also the Penn's attorney, and hired the Quaker Richard Partridge, the Quakers and Assembly disclosed the contrariety of their interests and those of the proprietors. The harmony between colony and proprietors that had subsisted in the 1730s was gone, and the proprietors now ranked among the enemies of Pennsylvania's Quakers.[36]

The list of Friends' antagonists did not conclude with Governor Thomas and the Penns. Philadelphia city merchants had twice petitioned the Assembly to defend the province, once in the summer of 1740 and again in the summer of 1741. This second time the Assembly found the petition a "high Insult and Menace of the Assembly" and destructive of the constitution. This anti-Quaker clique—often called the proprietary party—was really intriguing to get Friends out of government, possibly even if it required a royal government in the province to do it.[37] From the increased tempo of opposition to the Quaker Assembly the assemblymen concluded that "there is a manifest design against the Liberties of the Freemen of this Province" (*V*, IV, 2752).

The rumored conspiracy against Quaker governance of Pennsylvania came to light late in 1741. The opposition prepared a petition to the King against the Quakers and sent it off with Thomas Penn when he left the province after a twelve-year stay. In February 1742 the petition with its 265 signatures of Philadelphia merchants and professional men arrived and was referred to the Board of Trade. Ferdinand John Paris, the Penns' legal counsel, was the petitioners' solicitor. The petition recounted the supine situation of Pennsylvania in the face of its foreign enemies and blamed Quaker legislators, whose religion allegedly stopped them from defending the citizens of Pennsylvania.[38] The Board of Trade sympathized with the petitioners and in July 1742, resolved the case in their favor.[39] Disappointed Friends and counsel for the Assembly appealed the Board's decision to the parent body, the Privy Council. In May 1743, the Council Committee on Plantation Affairs heard the respective arguments on the case. This time Friends were much better prepared and the Assembly's solicitor argued its case well. The Council essentially reversed the Board of Trade's judgment.[40] The Philadelphia petitioners were inconsolable in defeat. Thomas Penn asserted that had the Philadelphians been less motivated by hatred of Friends they would be better able to understand the reasons for their loss.[41]

Before the issue of the petition had been completely decided in England, the provincial opponents of the Quakers mounted a second challenge. In the 1741–1742 House these opponents of the Quaker party had not a single loyal informant to report on the House's machinations; in face of wild rumors the proprietary party scrambled for reliable news. In the summer of 1742, with the favorable Board of Trade report in hand, they were emboldened to battle the Quakers at the polls. Too, the Penns had published a letter to the Quaker assemblymen in which they advised that as "Men of Honour and Conscience" the Quakers ought to have resigned their seats in the House. William Allen, the leader of the party, vowed that in this election they would give the Quakers "a warm one."[42]

In Philadelphia the 1742 election was warm; it turned into a riot. Witnesses disagreed upon who was to blame for the riot, but no one disagreed about its effects: the opponents of the Quaker party lost their momentum, their prestige, and the election. The Quakers gained all three.[43] All the previous assemblymen were returned, among whom there was not a single adherent of the proprietary party. The election victory was the best evidence to that date of the unity of Friends in Pennsylvania politics and of the popularity of Quaker leadership in the province. In the history of the province there had never been such an obvious, widespread, and concerted effort against Quaker governance, one which called into question presumptions about the nature of the province Penn had established. The 1742 election was something of a referendum on Quaker leadership and the character of the province, and a very successful one for Friends.

The Quaker party's awesome victory was due in part to its success at winning the support of the German voters. The Quaker party retained the loyalty of most ethnic groups in Pennsylvania but, in view of Friends' anxieties over the Germans in the 1720s, their later affinity for them needs some explanation.

Friends' anxieties at the end of the 1720s were premature. The Germans had not been in Pennsylvania long enough to prove their loyalty to any party before the Quakers began to fret. Granted that William Keith's courtship of the Germans with land and camaraderie had given Friends reason to pause and think about a possible menace, Keith had not the power to continue that largesse for long.[44]

The political union of Quakers and Germans appears predetermined, for the German sectarians and pietists shared many ethical tenets with Friends or else sympathized with Quaker politics for expediency's sake. Either way the Germans did not like oaths, militias or military service, and the taxation which came with wars and a military establishment. Some had come to Pennsylvania from the Palatinate explicitly to escape these burdens. And so, when confronted with the choice between Friends and anyone else, they understood immediately that their security lay with Friends. Friends had little to do to capture these people's votes. In the hotly contested election of 1742 one of the simple measures the Quakers had to take in order to keep the Germans' votes was to circulate the militia law just then passed in the Lower Counties (Delaware).[45] The opponents of the Quaker party were at that very time championing the same kind of law for Pennsylvania. Only an immediate danger to the life and property of the Germans would cause Friends to lose their loyalty.

When, in 1743, war with France appeared certain, Governor Thomas revived his demand for a militia law in Pennsylvania, as though he had learned nothing from his past confrontation with the Quaker Assembly. Isaac Norris, future speaker of the House, thought he detected in Thomas's sally upon the assemblymen's ethics the continued "bold attempt which has been so artfully made upon our religious and civil liberties."[46] While the foreign war — King George's — was real, a revival of war between the branches of Pennsylvania's government did not get beyond preview. On the other hand, the discontent and envy of the Pennsylvanians who had earlier petitioned the Board of Trade against Friends was not as easily contained.[47]

In November 1744 the erstwhile petitioners went on the offensive with a new edition of their old stratagem to get Friends out of government. The outbreak of war with France in the summer of 1744 supplied the occasion, because for the first time since Queen Anne's War, the Delaware River Valley and its commerce were threatened by privateers and possibly warships. The conflict with the Spanish, 1739-1744, had been, at least locally, something of a lark. Spanish seapower had posed no great threat to the Delaware. Meanwhile, the Philadelphians fitted out privateers to prey upon the Spanish. Thomas Penn had engaged in the business and Governor Thomas owned one or more shares in every privateer sailing from Philadelphia. And all the "principal gentlemen" were determined to "engage deeply in privateering."[48]

The lark ended only months after France entered the war. French privateers cavalierly stationed themselves in Delaware Bay to overhaul the coming and going merchantmen. Rumor spread that the French would attack the city itself and in the fall of 1744 some easily frightened souls talked of moving from the city to the safer countryside.[49] With good reason the Assembly discounted the rumor and belittled the danger. A letter discovered in the mail pouch of a captured French merchantman described a projected attack upon Philadelphia. The letter proved to be a forgery concocted by Benjamin Franklin and Tench Francis. William Allen was furious that the fraud had been discovered; the mail pouch had first been taken to Allen's house where its contents were inspected and the alleged letter discovered.[50]

Allen and his confidants, finding that too few people feared any French danger to support a popular movement against Quaker government, arranged to get the Philadelphia city government (which was much their own clique) to protest. Late in 1744 the agreeable councilmen and aldermen met to draft a petition to the Crown, and the remainder, such as Friends Israel Pemberton, Sr. and John Dilwyn, were kept uninformed of the meeting. Their petition claimed that Philadelphia lay undefended because the Quaker Assembly found all warlike preparations against its principles. The petitioners asked the King to take appropriate action.[51]

The Assembly discovered this machination and informed agent Richard Partridge of the danger. Philadelphia Quarterly Meeting similarly informed London Meeting for Sufferings. American Friends had nothing to fear, their London brethren replied. The invasion of Charles Stuart and the Scots was distracting the government and most of Britain.[52] The Privy Councillors did not consider the petition or hear Richard Partridge on behalf of the Assembly until March 1746. As in the earlier petition, counsel for the petitioners pleaded that Quakers had to be ousted from the Assembly. Partridge in his turn repeated the Quaker interpretation of the Charter of Liberties of 1701 regarding its protection of conscience. The Council did nothing; the petition languished. The danger from Whitehall had passed—until the next war.[53]

Pennsylvania's closest brush with the enemy in King George's War came in 1747. In the summer of 1747 reports reached Philadelphia that privateers were active in Delaware Bay and had even come ashore in

Newcastle County and plundered two towns. Some of the reports were false; but anxiety got the better of skepticism, and "Many hard speeches [were] made against the poor Quakers for their harmless principles." The fall brought more captures of merchantmen, more importuning of the Assembly.[54]

The enemy provocations tested the pacifism of some prominent city Friends and their pacifism gave way. Robert Strettell and his son Amos, Reese Meredith, and William Coleman, all merchants, members of the City Corporation, and Councillors, joined in fitting out a privateer to protect commerce and pursue the French. They were meanwhile "pressing with all their might a Petition to the Assembly for Money to put the town in a posture of Defense & to protect the trade of the Province." All of them defended their behavior when the Society disciplined them. Robert Strettell accused the Society of "persecution for conscience sake." Eventually all were disowned.[55]

The disownments raised what Richard Peters called "an Universal Odium" toward the Society of Friends—some of the public apparently believing that the Quakers, though a private, voluntary association, infringed on public policy when it enforced its regulations. "Ben. Franklin, observing this Turn in the Peoples minds, thought he cou'd by some well wrote Papers improve this opportunity, take an advantage of their Fears & spirit them to an Association for their Defense." Here was a new stratagem as clever as the reputation of Franklin promised. Franklin would use the press and public opinion to embarrass Friends and change public policy in Pennsylvania. Franklin would probably have been satisfied had only the policy changed, but the stature of the Society of Friends and future of Quaker governance might easily have been jeopardized by his machinations. In any case, consulting his old collaborator and friend, Tench Francis, plus William Coleman and Thomas Hopkinson, Franklin schemed to assume in print "the Character of a Tradesman, to fall foul of the Quakers & their opposers equally, as People from whom no good cou'd be expected, and by this Artifice to animate all the middling Persons to undertake their own Defense in opposition to the Quakers & the Gentlemen." If the scheme succeeded, the rivals of the Quakers, as planned, would first disingenuously defend their own behavior, then looking chastened, become reconciled to the projected volunteer defense association.[56]

Meanwhile, Franklin published a pamphlet, *Plain Truth*, according to plan. It was a skillful piece of demagoguery aimed at the "middling persons." In order "To take advantage of their Fears," Franklin forecast "Sacking," "Burning," at the hands of "licentious Privateers," and if that were not enough, "Rage, Rapine and Lust, of Negroes, Molattoes, and others." Then came the ruse. Franklin doing their reasoning for these middling folk, told them that they and not the rich—Quaker or non-Quaker—would suffer the cruelties of the French and blacks. "Tis true . . . the Rich may shift for themselves. The Means of speedy Flight are ready in their Hands; and with some previous Care to lodge Money and Effects in distant and secure Places . . . enough may be left them, and to spare." "That wealthy and powerful Body of People," the Quakers, would not defend the people nor shoulder the expense of others doing the job. The Quaker Assembly while squandering money to oppose the petitions against its supine policy, refused to grant money for local defense. And to appear nonpartisan, Franklin claimed that the gentlemen would rather "Let the Trade perish, and the City burn," than lift a finger to defend, even coincidentally, a Quaker's property. Finally, Franklin suggested that the Quaker legislators in wartime "might retire, relinquish their Power for a Season, quit the Helm to freer Hands during the present Tempest. . . ."[57]

Friends were sufficiently disturbed by Franklin's exposing them to public debate that an eminent member, Samuel Smith, published a rejoinder. The New Light Presbyterian, the Rev. Gilbert Tennent, then entered the fray with a theological piece on the lawfulness of war. Smith's brother John replied to Tennent and Tennent in turn wrote a two-hundred page reply to John Smith. Two other authors defended the Quaker side. In this wordy war, it was alleged that Tennent, Franklin, and others' purpose was really to change the governance of the province rather than to defend it. Considering the recent petitions, the election, and some rumors of royal government, Quaker skeptics did not need to recall much political history to corroborate that allegation. Only the authors, Franklin and Tennent, were new.[58] In the French and Indian War the notion of a withdrawal was revived and forced upon Friends, perhaps in part from someone's recollection of *Plain Truth.*

Quaker assemblymen barely disguised their impatience for the October election in 1748, once again to trounce their disparagers and rivals, and reconfirm for all the popularity and success of Quaker leadership of Pennsylvania.[59] The election fulfilled all their expectations; the Quakers won without opposition, and even if there had been a contest, Peters lamented, "there cou'd be no hopes of Success." The Quakers, it developed, were firmer than ever and could not be removed unless they divided among themselves. Moreover, when Quaker candidates and legislators strayed from party policy, they were replaced. Samuel Levis and Peter Dicks of Chester County espoused yielding to the request of the Governor's Council to fit out a warship and they lost their seats. "What made it appear worse," commented Israel Pemberton, Jr., "was that they were such as have for many years appeared in public testimony in our meetings." King George's War, however, did not discover many defectors from the Quaker line; only a dozen Friends in the city took up arms under the Association.[60]

The war ended in 1748 and also the exposure of Quaker governance to accusations of incompetence, misguided religion, and callousness. It is doubtful that jealousy of Friends' power and status likewise ended, although its effects disappeared. The efforts of Friends' detractors availed nothing in the decade. Quaker politicians defied every assault by their enemies. The fullness of Friends' victory appeared almost everywhere—in the Privy Council, in the acquiescence of Governor Thomas, in the disarray and dispiritedness of their opponents, and in every election to the Assembly in the decade. Quakers' political strength and their presumptions about Pennsylvania's character had been tested and had unquestionably triumphed. Equally clear, the victory had not come without Friends' conscious effort and unparalleled cooperation among themselves. Their motive, as they said, was the anxiety that their religious and civil liberties, as well as their power, were endangered. Perhaps, ironically, their strength was greater before 1720 when, less troubled by critics and rivals, they could indulge in intramural contests. Unity at its best may be the product of insecurity. In any case, that unity appeared by reasons of apprehensions. It would not long endure—at least not in its present character. In the next decade, reformist Friends would question the reasons for such unity and the whole historical role of the Society in Pennsylvania.[61] In 1748, however, while enjoying their triumph, very few Friends forsaw that future.

NOTES

HSP	Historical Society of Pennsylvania
LLB	James Logan Letter Book
NLB	Isaac Norris Letter Book, 1719–1756
PemP	Pemberton Papers
PMHB	*Pennsylvania Magazine of History and Biography*
PnLB	Penn Letter Book
PPOC	Penn Papers Official Correspondence
PtLB	Peters Letter Book

1. For the early history of the province and political divisions see Edwin B. Bronner, *William Penn's "Holy Experiment." The Founding of Pennsylvania, 1681–1701* (New York, 1962); Gary B. Nash, *Quakers and Politics. Pennsylvania, 1681–1726* (Princeton, 1968), esp. 309–310; Philadelphia Yearly Meeting minutes, 17 to 20-7 month-1710; *Friendly Advice to the Inhabitants of Pennsylvania* (Philadelphia, 1710); Isaac Norris to William Penn, 29-2 month-1710, Edward Armstrong, ed., *Correspondence between William Penn and James Logan and Others, 1700–1750* (Philadelphia, 1872), II, 436.

2. W. F. Dunaway, "English Settlers of Pennsylvania," *PMHB*, LII (1928), 324; *The Scotch-Irish of Colonial Pennsylvania* (Chapel Hill, N.C., 1944), 50–51; Ralph B. Strassburger, *Pennsylvania German Pioneers* (Norristown, Pa., 1934), I, xvii–xix.

3. Isaac Norris to Henry Goldney, 25-9 month-1719, NLB, 214, HSP. Jonathan Dickinson was a wealthy Quaker merchant of Philadelphia who came to Pennsylvania in 1696. He was a Provincial Councillor, judge of the Supreme Court, and in 1718 Speaker of the Assembly. He died in 1722. Robert Proud, *The History of Pennsylvania* (Philadelphia, 1798), II, 118–119.

4. Isaac Norris to Joseph Pike, 28-8 month-1728, NLB, 515–516; James Logan to James Hoop, 15-3 month-1729, LLB, III, 235–236, HSP; Gary B. Nash and Billy G. Smith, "The Population of Eighteenth-Century Philadelphia," *PMHB*, XCIX (1975), 366.

5. Philadelphia Monthly Meeting minutes, 26-1 month-1725, 31-5 month-1730, 25-1 month-1737; The Rev. Jedediah Andrews to the Rev. Price, 14 August 1730, in Samuel Hazard, ed., *Register of Pennsylvania* (Philadelphia, 1835), XV, 257.

6. Philadelphia Monthly Meeting minutes, 21-1 month-1730, 29-3 month-1730, 31-6 month-1733, 28-7 month-1733.

7. Philadelphia Yearly Meeting minutes, 17-7 month-1733.

8. *Advice and Caution from our Monthly Meeting in Philadelphia* (Philadelphia, 1732); Isaac Norris to Joseph Pike, 28-8 month-1728, NLB, 515–516; James Logan to John Penn, 14 May 1729, LLB, II, 299; Logan to Joseph Howston, 14 April 1730, LLB, III, 150–151.

9. For the depression and its effect upon Philadelphia's artisans and laborers, see Gary B. Nash, *The Urban Crucible: Social Change, Political Consciousness, and the Origins of the American Revolution* (Cambridge, Mass., 1979), 119–120. The fullest treatment of the politics of the 1720s is by Thomas Wendel, "The Keith-Lloyd Alliance: Factional and Coalition Politics in Colonial Pennsylvania," *PMHB*, XCII (July 1968), 289–305; and Wendel, "The Life and Writings of Sir William Keith, Lieutenant-Governor of Pennsylvania and the Three Lower Counties, 1717–1726," (Ph.D. diss., U. of Washington, 1964).

10. Ibid., 538. Gertrude Mackinney and Charles F. Hoban, eds., *Votes and Proceedings of the House of Representatives of the Province of Pennsylvania, 1682–1776. Pennsylvania Archives, Eighth Series* (Harrisburg, 1931–35), II, 1459–1460. This work will be cited in the text, abbreviated as *V*.

11. Wendel, "Keith-Lloyd Alliance," 296–297, 299; James Logan, *The Charge*

Delivered from the Bench to the Grand Jury, at the Court of Quarter Sessions, held for the County of Philadelphia, the 2nd day of September 1723. Published at the desire of the said Grand Jury Together with their Address. (Philadelphia, 1723); Nash, *Urban Crucible*, 149-151.

12. Nash, *Urban Crucible*, 152-154; Wendel, "Keith-Lloyd Alliance," 298-300; Isaac Norris to Joseph Pike, 28-8 month-1728, NLB, 515-516; Mackinney and Hoban, *Votes*, II, 1608, 1620-1643, 1655.

13. Wendel, "Keith-Lloyd Alliance," 302; Isaac Norris to Clement Plumstead, and Isaac Norris to "Respected Friend," 30-2 month-1725, NLB, 429, 423.

14. Mackinney and Hoban, *Votes*, III, 1895-1896; Roy N. Lokken, *David Lloyd, Colonial Lawmaker* (Seattle, 1959), 226, 228.

15. Logan was ranting; yet the danger to Quakerism was real. Keith, as explained below, intended to make a royal colony of Pennsylvania, and this would likely bring with it an established Anglican Church and threaten Friends' liberties — such as their freedom from tithes. James Logan to John Wright, 25-11 month-1725/26, Samuel Hazard and others, eds., *Pennsylvania Archives*, 2nd series (Harrisburg, 1852-1935), VII, 88.

16. Wendel, "Keith-Lloyd Alliance," 301; James Logan to John Penn, 17 October 1726, PPOC, I, 237, HSP; Patrick Gordon to John Penn, 22 October 1726, PPOC, I, 247. Some Friends or persons "who had been educated among us [Friends]" were among the rioters, according to Philadelphia Monthly Meeting, "to the reproach of our peaceable profession." The Meeting had Richard Hill censure them or their behavior in the meeting for worship. Philadelphia Monthly Meeting minutes, 28-8 month-1726.

17. Philadelphia Monthly Meeting minutes, 29-2 month-1726, undated-3 month-1726; James Logan to John Wright, 25-11 month-1725/26 and 22-6 month-1726, and James Logan to H. Taylor, 22 August 1726 and 9 September 1726, Hazard, et al., *Pa. Archives*, VII, 88-91.

18. Philadelphia Yearly Meeting minutes, 17 to 21-7 month-1726.

19. James Logan to John Penn, 17 October 1726, and Patrick Gordon to John Penn, 17 October 1726, PPOC, I, 237, 247; Mackinney and Hoban, *Votes*, III, 1787.

20. Mackinney and Hoban, *Votes*, III, 1798, 1799, 1809-1810, 1834, 1845-1848, 1851.

21. *Advice and Information to the Freeholders and Freemen of the Province of Pensilvania* (Philadelphia, 1727); *Remarks upon the Advice of the Freeholders, &c Paragraph by Paragraph* (Philadelphia, 1727); Isaac Norris, *The Speech Delivered from the Bench in the Court of Common Pleas held for the City and County of Philadelphia, the 11 Day of September, 1727* (Philadelphia, 1727); William Keith, *A Modest Reply to the Speech of Isaac Norris* (Philadelphia, 1727); Isaac Norris, *A Confutation of the Reply to the Speech, &c* (Philadelphia, 1727); *To the Freeholders & Freemen: A Further Information* (Philadelphia, 1727).

22. Philadelphia Yearly Meeting minutes, 16 to 20-7 month-1727; Patrick Gordon to John Penn, 25 October 1727, PPOC, I, 297; James Logan to John Penn, 8

October 1728, LLB, II, 274.

23. Frederick B. Tolles, *James Logan and the Culture of Provincial Pennsylvania* (Boston, 1957), 132, 143, 144; Andrew Hamilton, *The Case of the Heir at Law and Executrix of the Late Proprietor of Pensilvania in Relation to the Removal of Sir William Keith* (Philadelphia, 1726); Mackinney and Hoban, *Votes*, III, 1895–1896; *Depositions laid before the House, 9 August, 1728* (Philadelphia, 1728); James Logan to Joshua Gee, 8 October 1724, PPOC, I, 169, 171.

24. James Logan to John Penn, October 22, 1727, LLB, IV, 145–150; Mackinney and Hoban, *Votes*, II, 1877.

25. Mackinney and Hoban, *Votes*, III, 1908, 1939–1940, 1961–1962, 1983–1984, 1988; *Colonial Records of Pennsylvania*, T. Fenn (Harrisburg, Pa., 1851–1853), 16 vols., III, 340–343; Lokken, *Lloyd*, 233–234, 237.

26. The political peace of the 1730s and its causes are best explained by Alan Tully, *William Penn's Legacy: Politics and Social Structure in Provincial Pennsylvania, 1726–1755* (Baltimore, 1977), 3–22.

27. They included William Allen, Joseph Turner, James Hamilton, Thomas Lawrence, William Till, Abraham Taylor, and Thomas Willing. Also, there were some former Quakers or Quaker defectors-to-be like Robert and Amos Strettell, Benjamin Chew, Samuel Powell, Dr. Thomas Cadwalader, Jeremiah Langhorne, Lawrence Growdon, and Clement Plumstead.

28. See Tully, *Penn's Legacy*, 25–26. Tully denies that Quaker conscience operated in the deadlock between Quaker Assembly and the governor.

29. Governor Keith had misapplied the money, but his dishonesty was no reason to make an innuendo about Thomas. Mackinney and Hoban, *Votes*, III, 2540–2545.

30. Mackinney and Hoban, *Votes*, III, 2555–2557; *Col. Rec.*, IV, 389–394; Charles P. Keith, *Chronicles of Pennsylvania* (Philadelphia, 1917), III, 799–801.

31. *Col. Rec.*, IV, 395–398; MacKinney and Hoban, *Votes*, III, 2588–2593, emphasis added.

32. Mackinney and Hoban, *Votes*, III, 2616, 2627, 2629–2631, 2660; Richard Peters to Proprietors, 30 August 1740, PtLB, HSP; John Penn to Thomas Penn, 20 November 1740, PnLB, I, 339, HSP; and to George Thomas, 26 November 1740, PnLB, I, 343; *Col. Rec.*, IV, 592.

33. Richard Partridge to John Kinsey and others, 7–11 month-1740, PemP, III, 38, HSP; Board of Trade Papers, Proprietaries, 1697–1776, Bundle T, no. 42, Public Records Office (London).

34. Board of Trade Papers, Proprietaries, 1697–1776, Bundle T, 51, 54.

35. Richard Peters to John Penn, 20 October 1741, Peters to Thomas Penn, 24 October 1741, Peters to Proprietors, 27 October 1741, and Peters to F. John Paris, 8 December 1741, PtLB.

36. Richard Peters to Proprietors, 30 August 1740, PtLB; John Penn to Thomas Penn, 20 November 1740, PnLB, I, 339, and to George Thomas, 26 November 1740, PnLB, I, 343; *Col. Rec.*, IV, 592.

37. *Votes*, Mackinney and Hoban, III, 2616, 2680–2684; Isaac Norris II to ?,

12 May 1741, NLB, 8–9; Richard Peters to John Penn, 20 October 1741, and Peters to Thomas Penn, 14 November 1741, PtLB.

38. William Allen to Thomas Penn, 24 October 1741, PPOC, III, 201; Board of Trade Papers, Proprietaries, Bundle T, no. 57; John Fothergill to Israel Pemberton, Jr., 8-2 month-1742, PemP, II, 2.

39. Richard Peters to Proprietors, 3 June 1742, PtLB; PemP, III, 55.

40. Richard Partridge to John Kinsey, 13-3 month-1743 and 16-3 month-1743, PemP, III, 62, 65; John Fothergill to Israel Pemberton, Jr., 14-3 month-1743, PemP, XXXIV, 4.

41. William Allen to Thomas Penn, 3 October 1743, PPOC, III, 275; Richard Peters to Thomas Penn, 3 October 1743, Peters Papers, HSP; Thomas Penn to William Allen, 8 February 1743/44, PLB, II, 76–77; Thomas Penn to James Logan, 18 June 1747, PnLB, II, 204–205.

42. Richard Peters to Thomas Penn, 24 October 1741, PtLB; William Allen to Thomas Penn, 24 October 1741, PPOC, III, 201. *Pennsylvania Gazette*, 10 and 17 June 1742; William Allen to Thomas Penn, 8 July 1742 and 20 November 1742, PPOC, III, 227, 229, 247.

43. For differing accounts of the riot see Norman S. Cohen, "The Philadelphia Election Riot of 1742, *PMHB*, CXII (1968), 306–319; and William T. Parsons, "The Bloody Election of 1742," *Pennsylvania History*, XXXVI (1969), 290–306. Accounts by participants and observers are found in Mackinney and Hoban, *Votes*, IV, 2843–2850, 2877–2883, 2957–3014.

44. Alan Tully, "William Penn's Legacy," 15–31. This is the longer manuscript version of Tully's book, which contains additional information on Keith.

45. Richard Peters to Proprietors, 17 November 1742, PtLB.

46. Mackinney and Hoban, *Votes*, IV, 2901–2902, 2914–2915, 2917–2918; Richard Peters to Thomas Penn, 9 December 1743, 7 March 1743/44, PtLB; Isaac Norris to Richard Partridge, 31-5 month-1744, Wallpaper Letter Book, 1735–1755, James Logan Papers, HSP.

47. Ibid. Richard Peters to Thomas Penn, 24 May 1744, 31 May 1744, PtLB. William Allen was suing Israel Pemberton, Jr. for slander and Pemberton hired House speaker John Kinsey as his legal counsel. Then Pemberton contrived an attack upon the Philadelphia City Corporation—a stronghold of the Quakers' enemies. Kinsey, as Chief Justice, interfered in this instance, too, to protect Pemberton and the Quaker partisans from legal sanctions. Richard Peters to Thomas Penn, 21 November 1742, 4 June 1743, 5 June 1743, PtLB.

48. Thomas Penn to George Thomas, 13 May 1743, PnLB, II, 39; William Allen to Thomas Penn, 20 November 1742, PPOC, III, 247; Richard Peters to Thomas Penn, undated, but either October or November 1743, and 1 August 1744, PtLB.

49. Mackinney and Hoban, *Votes*, IV, 3017–3018; Richard Hockley to Thomas Penn, 22 December 1744, PPOC, IV, 29, 31.

50. Richard Hockley to Thomas Penn, 10 September 1744, Penn Papers Additional Miscellaneous Letters, I, 54, HSP; Thomas Penn to Richard Peters,

1 March 1744/45, PnLB, II, 113; see, in addition, William Allen to Thomas Penn, 8 July 1742, PPOC, III, 227, 229; John Penn to John Kinsey, 3 March 1741/42, PnLB, I, 372–373. Franklin was an old hand at imposture; see his "Silence Do-good Letters," Leonard W. Labaree, et al., eds., *The Papers of Benjamin Franklin* (New Haven, 1959–), I, 8–45.

51. Israel Pemberton, Jr. to Edmond Packover, 13-2 month-1745, Pemberton Family Papers, I, 148, HSP; Richard Peters to Thomas Penn, 2 November 1744, PtLB. A copy of the petition is found in the PemP, III, 152. Israel Pemberton, Jr. to John Haslam, 10-10 month-1744, PemP, III, 142.

52. Richard Partridge to John Kinsey, 11-11 month-1744, 2-12 month-1744, 30-2 month-1745, 19-5 month-1745, 19-6 month-1745, 25-10 month-1745, 8-11 month-1745, 3-12 month-1745, 12-12 month-1745/46, PemP, III, 147, 150, 160, 170, 174, and IV, 18, 21, 23.

53. Richard Partridge to John Kinsey, 8-11 month-1745, 3-12 month-1745, 28-1 month-1746, 3-8 month-1746, 20-3 month-1747, PemP, IV, 21, 24, 47, 62.

54. Mackinney and Hoban, *Votes*, IV, 3141–3142, 3146–3147; Robert L. D. Davidson, *War Comes to Quaker Pennsylvania, 1682–1756* (New York, 1957), 51–52; John Smith Diary, 13 and 14-5 month-1747, HSP; Mackinney and Hoban, *Votes*, IV, 3162–3163, 3167; Richard Peters to Thomas Penn, 28 November 1747, PtLB; Thomas Penn to Peters, 30 March 1748, PnLB, II, 224–226. In July 1748 Allen had one of his ships trading with the Spanish taken by the British sloop-of-war protecting Philadelphia, to the disgust of Allen and some merchants and the delight of others. Peters to Proprietors, 27 July 1748, PPOC, IV, 137, 139, 141.

55. John Smith Diary, 25 and 27-9 month-1747; Philadelphia Monthly Meeting minutes, 27-9 month-1747 through 29-2 month-1748.

56. Richard Peters to Proprietors, 29 November 1747, PtLB.

57. *Pennsylvania Gazette*, 5 and 19 November 1747, 3 December 1747; Labaree, et al., *Papers of Franklin*, III, 198–201.

58. Samuel Smith, *Necessary Truth* (Philadelphia, 1747); in January 1748 Tennent published *The Late Association for Defense, Encourag'd, or the Lawfulness of a Defensive War* (Philadelphia, 1748); John Smith, *The Doctrine of Christianity as held by the people called Quakers . . .* (Philadelphia, 1748); Benjamin Gilbert, *Truth Vindicated* (Philadelphia, 1748); anonymous, *A Treatise Shewing the Need we have to rely upon God as for Protector of this Province* (Philadelphia, 1748), 18.

59. Mackinney and Hoban, *Votes*, IV, 3197–3207; *Col. Rec.*, V, 277–279; Richard Peters to Proprietors, 20 October 1748, PPOC, IV, 157–158.

60. Ibid. Israel Pemberton to Samuel Hopwood, 19-8 month-1748, Pemberton Family Papers, I, 158–159; John Smith Diary, 1-11 month-1747/48.

61. Jack D. Marietta, *The Reformation of American Quakerism, 1748–1783* (Philadelphia, 1984).

Secularization in
Colonial Pennsylvania

Scholars seeking to understand the roles of religion in the Delaware River Valley in the colonial period have emphasized the development of pluralism, religious liberty, and denominationalism. These themes highlight issues of institutional adjustments in the new world and the relationships of church organizations to each other and to the state. However, an analysis of such phenomena does not help us to comprehend the importance of religious practices and beliefs for the participant in a meeting or church. Useful in assessing individual involvement in religion is revivalism whose major manifestation was the Great Awakening. Concentrating upon revivalism illuminates the history of Baptists and Presbyterians, but downplays the initial years of colonization before 1740 when there were no mass revivals, and results in treating as one phenomenon the very different emphases of George Whitefield, Henry Muhlenberg, and Count Zinzendorf.

This essay attempts to utilize secularization theory to elucidate further several features of Pennsylvania's religious life including church and state relationships, religious liberty, and revivalism. Secularization can be used as a conceptual device because it refers to something fundamental: the distinction between religion and its opposites whether indifference or antagonism. We have come to accept almost as axiomatic that western societies were very religious in medieval and reformation eras, became less so after the renaissance and the enlightenment, and were largely secular by the mid-nineteenth century. In spite of conservative reaction (as is presently happening), the declining influence of Christianity appears to follow an almost predestined course. Religious liberty, separation of church and state, and pluralism stand in retrospect as consequences, as well as facilitators, of secularization. From this perspective, one can almost say that Pennsylvania was born secular. Yet paradoxically, the adjustments that Pennsylvanians made can be seen as strengthening religion and retarding secularization. It is important to know whether the religious practices and ideals that William Penn and the Quakers brought and instituted in their "Holy Experiment" immedi-

105

ately or eventually contributed to a process of secularization that they would have abhorred. The purpose of this essay is threefold: (1) to examine the concept of secularization, (2) to see how usefully it can be applied to colonial Pennsylvania, (3) to enlarge our understanding of the variety, scope, and depth of religious commitment in early America.

Crucial before applying secularization is a definition of the term. Certain distinctions seem evident. Secularization refers to a process; secular is the condition or status which is presumably arrived at after a period of increasing secularization. The process of secularization involves emancipating certain spheres of life from ecclesiastical controls or the influence of religious dogmas or attitudes. Unfortunately, secular cannot be precisely defined without a satisfactory concept of religion and, in spite of attempts of sociologists of religion to create a neutral concept, the delineation of religion remains a theological enterprise.[1] It is not clear, for example, whether secularization is opposition to or only restriction of religion; whether both secularization and religion can flourish at the same time; whether the process of secularization is multilateral or unilineal; whether secularization is inevitable and accumulative or happenstance and reversible. Does secularization infect an entire culture all at once or does it influence a certain sphere, like money making, while leaving other aspects of life untouched? Should the historian examine daily routine, crisis events, or rites of passage to determine what is religious or secular? Finally, it remains unclear whether the strength of the institutionalization of religion has much effect on either a Christian world view or secularization.

In assessing the importance of religion and secularization in colonial Pennsylvania, a first necessity is a concept of Christianity. Christianity has an institutional component, the church; an intellectual component, theology with its interpretation of reality; a practical component, ethics and popular piety; and a social component, the interaction of people. Christianity includes public events like church-going, participation in the sacraments, and fast days as well as private events like prayer, devotions, and Bible reading. Virtually any act can be considered either Christian or secular depending upon the context and interpretation given by the participants. Trading, farming, sailing, governing, cooking, bearing and raising children, teaching school, marriage, death, and burial could be made religious acts. Each of them could also be divorced or separated from religious values, a common meaning of secularization.

A precise definition of either secularism or religion is likely either to be so restricted that it ignores the complexity of events or so broad as not to be very useful. But the terms are widely employed and the processes they refer to are fundamental. Perhaps the best way of proceeding is to use several working definitions of secularization employed by scholars and to see whether they illuminate phenomena in Pennsylvania.[2] Secularization in this paper includes the loss of public functions of religion, a decline in power of the churches over their members, and the growth of an alternative belief structure not founded on Christianity.

Sociologists of religion have found in Protestantism, particularly in Calvinism, a distrust of the physical, a separation of God from the world of nature, and an emphasis on the transcendence of God. Peter Berger argues that secularization became possible because Calvinism restricted the encounter with God to the individual experience of conversion, and thereby destroyed the "sacred canopy" of medieval Catholicism.[3] Certainly Calvinism, like renaissance humanism, marked a major disruption in the world-view of medieval Catholicism. Unfortunately, Berger might have argued with equal validity that Calvinism by fostering an intense preoccupation with religion delayed secularization. For Calvin and his Puritan followers destroying shrines, smashing stained glass windows, downplaying the role of Mary, and ending veneration of saints resulted in a sharpened focus on God's act of redemption through Christ. Knowledge of Christian doctrine, biblical literalism, moral precisionism, regular attendance of worship, preaching the Word, acceptance of the providence of God, and personal prayer characterized the Reformed Churches. Calvin and his successors created a new "sacred canopy" which endured for generations.

In Pennsylvania the Presbyterian and Reformed churches were the standard-bearers of Calvinism. Anglicans and Lutherans, though influenced by the Reformed tradition, remained closer to Catholicism in their stress upon liturgy, church calendar, sacraments, and the importance of the objective or institutional church. The Moravians placed such emphasis upon sacraments and liturgy that they were often thought to be Roman Catholics. All Protestant churches in Pennsylvania accepted the concept of calling, the priesthood of all believers, providential history, and prayer as providing access to the divine. In short, Protestant Christianity continued to surround the believer with doctrines and rites which allowed him to see the world and events as sacred.

One definition of secularism is the restriction of religion to the private realm, the loss of religious underpinnings for basic processes in the society. In England the structural linkage of church, state, and society was symbolized by the king's role in the church, the bishops' role in the state, the tithe, ecclesiastical courts, and the required prayers for the monarch in the liturgy.

If England is taken as the norm, obviously, on one level, the pattern of church and state in Pennsylvania reduced the political power of the institutionalized church and the religious power of the state. There was no formal representation of any church at any level of politics in Pennsylvania. What the institutionalized churches gained from this condition was more autonomy. When affairs of state intruded in church councils, the clergy were free to criticize the status quo. Indeed, the kind of political-religious opposition espoused by the Anglican Church from 1690 to 1720 and the Presbyterian Church after Braddock's defeat could not have occurred in England at any time after the overthrow of the Commonwealth. The removal of the formal linkage of the institutionalized church may actually have retarded secularization by making the church less passive and less obviously a tool of the government.

While in Pennsylvania the state was neutral in terms of a religious establishment, it was not neutral on the subject of religious observances. The government rested upon the virtue of subjects and religious observances remained the most effective creators of such virtue. The Pennsylvania laws reflected the Reformed, Lutheran, Puritan, and Quaker vision of the state hindering evil-doers while fostering those who did good. Penn's law code restricted service in government to those willing to make certain religious declarations, and later the English government required immigrants to prove they were Protestant as a requirement for citizenship. A variety of religious tests supported the government even during the Revolution. Throughout the eighteenth century the Assembly passed laws on marriage, lotteries, drunkenness, church property, and conscientious objection. The colony approved sending Protestant missionaries to the Indians, chartered insurance companies for ministers, and established a hospital. Magistrates refused to hinder the free exercise of religion even when, as in Ephrata and Bethlehem, the customs infringed upon supposedly sacrosanct ideas of property and marriage.[4]

In the eighteenth century, Pennsylvania was torn by competing views of the religious grounding of the colony, but the rivalry was not between religious and secular but between church and sect. The charter and early laws imposed on Pennsylvania a "sectarian" view of the state.[5] That is, the Assembly accepted as legal practice what the sects saw as matters of conscience while refraining from legislating on matters established churches saw as essential. In some ways a sectarian and secular view of the state are compatible in that many of the same actions are deemed preferable. But in Pennsylvania the motivation and defense of the pattern of religion was based upon sectarian ideals. Freedom of religion meant that the state would not restrict the activities of God as perceived by the faithful. Liberty of conscience, failure to create a militia, acceptance of affirmations instead of oaths for legal and commercial transactions, numerical listing of months and days of the week were tenets of Quaker belief, and of other sects as well.

The opposing or "church" view of Pennsylvania was held by some at every period, but appeared with more regularity after war broke out in 1739. Governor Thomas's long theological debate with the Assembly over the colony's refusal to provide for defense shows the different religious suppositions operating.[6] Quakers regarded the French and Indian War as God's punishment upon Friends for weakness in the faith and for the colony's betrayal of the Indians. Presbyterians and Anglicans saw the war as a defense of Protestantism against Catholicism, freedom against tyranny, reason against superstition. Quakers looked at Pennsylvania's significance in isolation, but William Smith, Gilbert Tennent, and Benjamin Franklin saw British America as the crucial unit.[7] When William Smith advocated freedom of religion, he meant freedom as it was defined in England. The alliance he posited between Lutherans and Anglicans was intended to create the church basis for affirming the religious underpinnings of a Protestant state.

An alternate paradigm of secularization is the loss of power by the institutional church over the lives of members. The first requisite here is to distinguish between adjustments made by the sects and those of the churches. If the churches felt uncomfortable with the pattern of the colony, the sects were pleased. They also enjoyed more power in the general society and more authority over their members. In England, Quakers were a minority scorned by an Anglican church and government which did not bother to hide their contempt. The rights Friends received were bestowed as privileges for which the meeting did not fail to thank the authorities. Every belief Quakers thought important had to compete against an alternative majority viewpoint. The situation was reversed in early Pennsylvania. Now every other church was a minority, for which the Quakers did not bother to hide their contempt. The culture was supportive of the meeting and vice versa. Not just William Penn, but Friends saw themselves as the proprietors of Pennsylvania, responsible for establishing and maintaining a distinctive way of life.

The meeting gained power in Pennsylvania members could not have dreamed of possessing in England. At first in Philadelphia there was no alternative form of worship. One either went to Friends' meeting or stayed home. In many rural areas of Bucks and Chester counties that pattern persisted until the Revolution.[8] The Society of Friends transferred from England to Pennsylvania an institutional framework which endures to this day. The hierarchy of meetings functioned effectively without a clearly written division of power. Ministers, women and men recognized as speaking the will of and fostering the presence of God, originated in the laity of the meeting. Their qualifications were spiritual, not education or wealth. Friends pioneered a method of making decisions which managed to forestall an aggrieved minority. The system of containing disputes broke down only once in the colonial period, during the Keithian controversy, but even this did not change the basic structure of meetings in England or America. Perhaps the most notable accomplishment of Quakers throughout the eighteenth century was their ability to stay together. In the early eighteenth century, Friends managed to contain the political divisions among the adherents of David Lloyd and James Logan. Later on they included pro- and antislavery advocates, tax resisters and taxers, Tories and patriots. While Presbyterian, Baptist, Lutheran, Reformed, and Anglican churches quarreled over responses to the Great Awakening, the Moravians, and clerical factionalism, the Society of Friends remained intact and powerful.

Trauma for Friends came from the growth in strength of religious alternatives which made the Quaker view of reality less compelling. The visible signs of this erosion of power are the growth in marriage out of unity and the revival of discipline after the 1750s. The debate within the Society of Friends was between those who wished to preserve the meeting by dominating the culture of Pennsylvania and those who wished to purify the meeting by withdrawing from the general society.[9] Until the Revolution, Friends did not have to opt for either alternative.

The events that threatened Friends also struck at the Amish, Mennonites, Brethren and, to a lesser extent, the Moravians. The early migration and political activity of the sectarians had strengthened the pattern of religion in Pennsylvania.[10] These groups agreed with Quaker attitudes in restricting the power of the state over religious activities, endorsed a refusal to take oaths, supported a pacifist state, and feared the imposition of tithes. The German religious groups who created distinctive communities supported the Quaker dominated government because it left them alone.

The Pennsylvania pattern of church and state did not foster secularization among the sects. Rather, the increase of freedom allowed the sects to create enclaves which fostered a particularly intense and very long lasting fusion of religion and daily life. Unlike the German sects, the members of the Society of Friends were regularly exposed to pressures which would modify their ideas of religion. Many Quakers, especially those who lived in or near Philadelphia, participated in politics and engaged in artisan and mercantile activities. Yet unlike New England where trading patterns undermined the Puritan state, the impact of the meeting upon those most active in the general society remained strong. Quakers involved in the political and mercantile world were among the leaders of the revival of discipline in the 1750s, the anti-slavery crusade, and the withdrawal from politics at the time of the Revolution.

Pennsylvania may have been close to heaven for the sects; was it close to hell for the churches? Clearly, state churches of Europe had to make major modifications in Pennsylvania.[11] The sectarian nature of the state and the lack of official governmental support and respect forced the churches into making adjustments throughout the eighteenth century. The process of creating new institutional forms remained protracted because of the nature of the colonial clergy.

Every denomination dependent upon foreign clergy had difficulty in Pennsylvania. Immigrant pastors required considerable seasoning in which they learned to forget European patterns of deference.[12] Whether the denomination was Old Light Presbyterian, Lutheran, Reformed, or Church of England, the calibre of missionary pastors did not inspire confidence by the laity. In a country where "hireling ministers" appeared one word, a significant percentage of ordained clergy succumbed to drunkenness, immorality, depression, and fraud.[13] They were unable to establish harmonious relations with fellow clergymen and/or their congregations. The first generation of Quaker settlers was extraordinarily quarrelsome. Unfortunately for the institutionalized church, every generation of ministers of Anglican, Lutheran, and Reformed churches until the Revolution behaved like new settlers.[14]

The ministry's problems often originated in Europe. Pennsylvania Presbyterians had to reconcile theological and organization differences among clergy and settlers who came from Scotland, Ireland, England, and New England. Animosities among Reformed or Lutheran pietists and the orthodox and their united opposition to the Moravians were magnified in Pennsylvania.

The European-trained clergy had to determine how far educational standards previously deemed essential could be relaxed in the colonies. They had to survive the climate and rigors of constant travel. They learned how to improvise without governmental support a coetus, ministerium, or presbytery capable of ordaining pastors, settling disputes in churches, and disciplining recalcitrant clergy. Preachers had to accept a church's contract which instead of indefinite tenure allowed the congregation to dismiss a minister with a few month's notice. The clergy also had to endure an uncertain livelihood, since salaries resulted from gifts and not taxes.[15]

The shortage of well-qualified clergy meant that imposters were frequent. Any German with a modicum of education thought he could pass himself off on a rural congregation as a clergyman. Methodists did not pioneer the circuit rider in Pennsylvania; virtually all churches functioned this way. If many ministers so irritated their congregations that they had to change parishes every few years,[16] others were successful in building churches and winning the affection and respect of the people.

The sects began with numerous advantages over the churches. They did not pay their clergy, their meeting houses were cheap to build and maintain, their communitarian nature and time of arrival and work ethic brought prosperity. The German congregations, on the other hand, were largely composed of poor, often indentured servants, who had not come to Pennsylvania for religious reasons.[17] Yet, paradoxically, the freedom which Pennsylvania allowed permitted a positive relationship to develop between the clergy and laity.

The German laity did not wish to be dominated by a church/state alliance as they had been at home. When the Moravians attempted to win over other Germans to their distinctive forms of piety between 1740 and 1746, the people also resisted being anything but full-fledged Lutherans or Reformed. When excommunication occasioned no civil liability, the laity within the churches cooperated with ministers in scrutinizing individuals for moral offenses before allowing participation in sacramental communion. The laity insisted upon deposing elders who brought discredit upon the church by scandalous or immoral behavior. They were willing to contribute labor and to subscribe money to build churches and support the clergy. But if the minister attempted to enforce legally the contract or subscription, the congregation would withdraw and go elsewhere.

Organized institutional religion in Europe was ruled by the clergy. Pennsylvania's settlers did not wish to be ruled by anyone, least of all by a clergyman whom they paid. When the minister was moral and astute, his church flourished. But a cleric who falsely accused a member of immorality could find himself in civil court.[18] The preacher who attempted to allocate pews without the vestry needed more seasoning. When the minister was absent, church members lapsed into sectarianism.[19] In their reports to European church authorities, the missionaries continually lamented the hostile atmosphere of Pennsylvania where the sects were waiting to ensnare dissatisfied parishioners.

The most successful church in colonial Pennsylvania was the Presbyterian. It succeeded partially because of its contacts with New England and mostly because of the nature of migration.[20] But the Presbyterian Church succeeded in spite of several self-inflicted wounds which could have brought suicide. In the early years of the colony, the Presbyterians were a negligible factor. Lord Cornbury's persecution of Francis Makemie in New York and New Jersey made the few Presbyterians support the Friends in preference to the Church of England.[21] When the Presbyterians could have become a powerful factor in the colony in the 1740s, the Great Awakening disrupted the denomination. From 1740 until 1760 the only model the Presbyterians provided was in hatred of each other. The main reason the Presbyterians could become an effective political and religious opposition after 1755 was that Old and New Lights found it more productive to oppose first the Quakers and then the British rather than each other.[22] The animosity between Old and New Lights persisted until the Revolution and emerged again in the nineteenth century.

Neither the Presbyterians' theology nor practice of piety appealed to other denominations. The German churches had no revival of classic Calvinism or predestination. When Whitefield spoke in the Lutheran Church in Philadelphia, Muhlenberg noted that the congregation was largely English.[23] What the Presbyterians offered to their denomination was an educated, moral, and cheap ministry. It was a native-born ministry, requiring no seasoning.[24] The Germans and the Anglicans learned from the Presbyterians the necessity of creating educational institutions like Princeton to supply a learned ministry. The Anglicans never overcame the liability of requiring a prospective minister to journey to England to be ordained by a bishop.

The crucial factor in the growth of the institutional church in Pennsylvania was the commitment of lay men and women. When the clergy arrived in the colony, they did so in response to the laity's requests and served churches founded by the devout. This pattern of church expansion following the people's request for ministerial services continued. In 1748 there were 86 Reformed and Lutheran congregations in Pennsylvania; in 1776, 249. The number of pastors had increased by two per year and the number of churches by eight. The Presbyterians showed similar growth, having 15 or 16 congregations in 1730 and 112 in 1776. Even they had twice as many churches as preachers. Immigration allowed the church people to become numerically dominant over the sectarians. By the decade of the Revolution both sects and churches had a strong position in Pennsylvania society.

The state and the law did not hold Pennsylvania's churches together. Ethnicity, shared piety, theological agreement, and habit replaced external force. The power of the clergy declined while the rights and privileges of the laity increased. The power of the church became less formal, but that does not mean it was less pervasive. A voluntary organization resting upon the consent of the members need not be weak. Eventually, the influence of religion was dispersed from the clergy and the institutional church to the laity. The result was a different kind of power, but it can be termed secularization only if a purely institutional definition is employed.

An alternative indication of secularization would be an increase in the number of those people who after immigration had little formal involvement with the church—a phenomenon known as slippage. Such people did not present their children for baptism, never partook of communion, were not confirmed in membership, and did not attend services. There is at present no way of establishing how numerous the unchurched were. There are no membership statistics for Lutherans, Reformed, Quakers, Mennonites; and only scattered figures for other groups.[26] When in 1759 William Smith calculated "the state of Religious Persuasions" "from ample materials in my hands," he included everybody in Pennsylvania in a religious community.[27] Most descriptions of religion in the colony came from people who wanted something; immigrants enticing countrymen to come over, visitors telling prospective settlers to stay home; clergy and laity beseeching European authorities to provide financial support, build churches, and send over additional ministers. Those who wrote about religion tended to be clergymen and they did not agree on what constituted vital Christianity or irreligion, and bandied terms with slight regard to precision or consistency. A heathen could be an Indian, a black, a Muslim, a Quaker, a freethinker, an atheist, and could be interchanged with the terms unconverted or pagan.[28] The ministers' accounts prove there was slippage, but do not indicate either numbers or motivation.

Motivation is the key because some Pennsylvanians ignored the institutionalized church for religious reasons. A pious immigrant could refuse to go to church because he disliked professional clergy. Pennsylvania's tradition of anticlericalism began with the Quakers and continued throughout the eighteenth century. Christopher Saur used his German-language newspaper to belittle clerical infighting and pretensions. In 1754 the trustees of the Charity School project debated appointing a Lutheran and Reformed pastor for each local school board. Conrad Weiser, whose son-in-law was Henry Melchior Muhlenberg, scotched that proposal by declaring that the prejudice of the people against the clergy was so great, and increasing, that formally involving ministers might hinder the schools.[29]

A Lutheran immigrant who wished to become naturalized had to prove that he was a Protestant. (Only 4272 did so before the Revolution; far more joined churches, showing that for most persons politics was less important than religion.)[30] He might journey from the backcountry to Philadelphia and present himself to Muhlenberg and the elders to become eligible for the sacrament. Since he had been baptised in Germany, he was eligible. After partaking of the sacrament, he asked for a certificate to prove he was a Protestant which would be presented to the magistrate. Even if he never attended services again, the man was counted as a part of the Lutheran Church. What if he never again contributed money? After all, in Germany he had never voluntarily given money. What if he failed to have his children baptised? In Germany, he would certainly have done so; though he might have waited until they became sick and he worried over their future status. In Pennsylvania he was free from clerical supervision. After all, that was one reason why Pennsylvania appealed to him. His neighbors might be Baptists, Amish, Mennonites, or Quakers and they certainly appeared as pious as the Lutherans. None of these people baptised children.[31] Besides, in Pennsylvania the minister was always after money to build a church, pay the schoolmaster, or support himself. Even if our Lutheran father had taken his family to church with some regularity, his vital records might be lost. Few colonial immigrant churches had stability of leadership, and the clergy had other tasks besides keeping vital records. In a folk culture a scrap of paper recording baptism was not as significant as community recognition that the family was Lutheran.

An immigrant to Pennsylvania faced a bewildering variety of claims about church polity. Quakers had no sacraments; Mennonites, Dunkers, and Baptists opposed infant baptism and allowed only adult members to take communion. Old Light Presbyterians and conservative Lutherans and Reformed required a person's assent to a creed plus leading a moral life as test for membership. New Light Baptists and Presbyterians accepted as members those who could testify to their conversion. Pietist Lutherans attempted to have a service of preparation as well as personal examination by the pastors and elders the day before the administration of the Lord's Supper. There were disagreements within as well as between different denominations on liturgy, predestination, and on the necessity for a deeply introspective piety.

What must have seemed most unusual to an immigrant was that

religion was now a matter of choice. Life seemed simpler in Europe where most English were part of the Church of England, the Dutch of the Reformed, etc. Those who took the initiative became something different—a dissenter.

In the confusion of claims in Pennsylvania, ethnicity triumphed in church organization but theology prevailed in inter-denominational harmony. A shared "Germanness" brought close cooperation between Lutheran and Reformed which resulted in the creation of Union congregation and many mixed marriages. Ethnicity kept apart Swedish and German Lutherans and also prevented the German Reformed, Dutch Reformed, and Presbyterians from joining. Organizational separateness did not hinder cooperation among Calvinist clergy, and ministers even moved from one denomination to a similar one.

Eventually two ways of dealing with religious diversity emerged. Pietists insisted that a personal conversion and inward piety were the desiderata no matter what the outward denomination.[32] Others came to believe that all churches advocated pretty much the same ideas and that moral living was the essence. Neither alternative was secular. Holding the first brought involvement in a local congregation; espousing the second did not.

A fourth approach to secularization examines ideas. The colonists become secular under this model if they thought about the daily processes of life in a mechanistic or scientific manner. They could also become secular by ignoring the subject of religion altogether. Christianity, like other world religions, aimed at providing a framework by which people could impose sense or order upon a chaotic existence. For the laity, the issues involving the institutional life of the church were less significant than daily existence. Sickness and health, life and death, agricultural plenty or famine, war and peace, shipwreck or safe arrival, prosperity and poverty were the substance of popular piety. Farming and sailing determined the economic substance of Pennsylvania and both of these activities were at the mercy of the weather. And the weather and nature were under the control of God. Providential history, God's operating either directly or through secondary causes, provided the intellectual framework for German peasant as well as member of the academy.

Christianity dominated intellectual life because there were few other options available. Schoolbooks, sermons, almanacs, newspapers and tracts allowed for little diversity of opinion. During the Revolution the Schwenkfelders declined to serve in the American armies, but offered to pray for their success. Since God determined the future, praying was as important as serving.[33] In colonial Pennsylvania the Schwenkfelders' position was more understandable than the secular option that God has nothing to do with success or failure in battle. The issue for other Pennsylvanians was not the value of prayer but whether prayer also required enlisting. After all, God helps those who also help themselves.

Historians have to be careful to avoid making a theological distinction into a definition of secularism. One gets the impression that scholars can be far more "orthodox" or supernaturally oriented than some eighteenth-century Christians. For these historians, authentic Christianity becomes emotional as well as intellectual, involves the entire person in an existential dilemma, and radically opposes the prevalent culture.[34] This interpretation of religion fits many of those converted in the revival and the pietists. Famous middle colony exemplars were Gilbert Tennent and Henry Melchior Muhlenberg. No one would classify such men as secular.

A second form of eighteenth-century religion stressed reason, order, and the immanence of God in creation. A Philadelphia exemplar of such latitudinarian religion was William Smith, provost of the College of Pennsylvania. Smith taught rhetoric and made his orations examples of correct literary discourse. (He was willing to sacrifice Anglican apostolic succession in order to gain a union with the Lutherans.) He was a political opportunist, a not too honest pamphleteer, and a manipulator of church politics. He attended the theatre and celebrated Britain's imperial destiny. The temptation would be to consider Smith secular, but he was not. He remained an Anglican priest who faithfully used the prayer book, educated ministers, and worked for the advancement of his church.

The absence of an intellectual framework as compelling as Christianity did not mean that there were no skeptics in Pennsylvania. A few denied life after death, the existence of miracles, the efficacy of prayer, and the divinity of Christ. The numbers of scoffers cannot be accurately ascertained, for they left no written records of their beliefs and their existence must be inferred from hostile accounts. The skepticism may have been of the cracker barrel variety, a discussion position one espoused when slightly drunk or in the presence of a supercilious clergyman.

Who might be likely to engage in irreligious discourse? Anyone with no stake in the colony who was willing to defy or scandalize public opinion; most likely, those on the margins of society. Members of the British army, sailors, travelers—groups of males not dependent upon the good will or respect of others—had great freedom of speech.[35] There was a law against blasphemy, but anyone could with impunity attack the claims of any religious group. Rhys Isaac argues that, after 1760, the rise of the

117

Baptists in Virginia allowed people to defy the cultural norms of the planter aristocracy.[36] In Pennsylvania there was no such clear way to upset the authorities. The proprietors were supported by the Anglicans and other church people, including Old and New Light Presbyterians, the assembly by the Quakers and the sectarians. In the absence of a religious opportunity for rejection of dominant norms, an irreligious utterance served as a functional equivalent.

In the eighteenth century it still took courage to defy Christianity; perhaps that was why the legends of Faust and Don Giovanni occasioned such creativity. In Pennsylvania people still believed that wrong ideas could not be divorced from their consequences. The result of questioning God's truth was likely to be a horrible end, if not immediately, eventually. And who would trust a scoffer, for those willing to belittle the Bible would cheat a person. For all their vaunted freedoms, the settlers in Pennsylvania remained dependent upon others for jobs, loans, customers, friendship, and markets. For those within the society, open defiance of Christianity offered neither temporal nor spiritual advantages, since skepticism was able to provide neither the answers nor the assurance furnished by religion, and might bring social ostracism.

The Old and New Testament have a kind of built-in secularism, for both the ancient Hebrews and early Christians opposed nature cults and posited God as involved in but existing apart from the world. The result was that parts of life were visualized apart from organized religion. The issue in eighteenth-century Pennsylvania is whether secularization increased by people neglecting to ask religious questions and creating godless areas of activities. The most likely candidate for such compartmentalization is economics. Eighteenth-century tracts describing land banks, balance of trade, markets, and paper money operate within a world controlled by natural processes. Such an attitude need not be secular, since God is the author and disposer of the natural order. Still, the merchant who ignored ethical responsiblity because of impersonal law was clearly pushing religion to the periphery.

Unfortunately, there seems to be at present no adequate method of establishing whether a denial of the role of Christianity in business took place, or, if it did occur, whether this was something new. Economists have long assumed that persons in all centuries attempt to maximize profits, often within institutional restraints. Even in the supposedly religious fourteenth century, land in London cost more than comparable acreage in Cornwall; scarcity of spices meant that their price was high. Devout merchants did not repeal the laws of supply and demand. Religious leaders have perennially complained about the worship of money

118

and excoriated the hard-heartedness of the rich, assuming that business people pay some attention. The correlation between commercial activities and Puritans in seventeenth-century England is well established, but this does not mean the Puritan merchant was less devout and more secular than an Elizabethan Anglican or Catholic farmer. Accounting books, whether kept in Medici Florence or eighteenth-century Philadelphia, do not often contain the theological meaning of the numbers to those who wrote them down.

A Chester County farmer whose diary contains records of the weather and business accounts cannot be assumed to be irreligious just because God is not named. Neither can he be assumed to have allowed religion to influence his business because he appeared at meeting or in church on Sunday. Letters from eighteenth-century merchants move easily from personal news, to calculations, to piety, to complaints of ill treatment. If disasters occurred, businessmen could use such events to wean themselves from over-reliance upon worldly goods, find a deserved rebuke from the Almighty, or blame their troubles upon bad luck or impersonal fate. Prosperity and profits and a good harvest could, and frequently were, ascribed to God, personal acumen, or both.

In eighteenth-century Pennsylvania, outsiders judged all religious groups because of the presumed hypocrisy of members' business ethics. Only the Friends disowned for failure in business, and even they distinguished between defrauding creditors due to overtrading or injudicious behavior and bankruptcy caused by external circumstances. The most common criticism of the Quakers, reiterated with far too little skepticism by historians, was that the sect had surrendered piety for prosperity.[37] Richard Bushman argues that concern over involvement with land speculation and business practices was a destabilizing force in eastern Connecticut which helps to explain the attraction of the Great Awakening.[38] Yet he does not discuss changes in economic behavior, if any, occasioned by the religious revivals. The Bible contains sufficient strictures against wealth to justify any condemnation of those who prospered, but there are numerous passages equating the blessing of God with peace and prosperity. Either the attainment of riches or the renunciation of them fit into the religious culture of colonial Pennsylvania.

The churches, both clergy and laity, continued to insist on their responsibility for discussing the ethics of economics. People did not view commercial agriculture and trade as inherently immoral or amoral, and the colonists did not assume that buying a yard of cloth, taking grain to be ground and selling a loaf of bread were religious acts. Working hard in one's calling was a religious duty. They defined being cheated or overcharged by the merchant, the miller, or the baker as not just economic misfortunes but moral and religious offenses. In short, the settlers' attitudes to economics were not consistent, and inconsistency continued throughout the colonial period.

The colonists did not define either science or economics as operating outside the province of God; these subjects became intelligible because the operations of God in them were understandable. By the end of the eighteenth century a few churchmen would find the enlightenment emphasis upon reason a threat to Christianity, but that debate did not begin in Pennsylvania until Thomas Paine and others openly attacked organized religion during and after the Revolution. Until that time, the distinction between latitudinarianism and deism was fuzzy. The Library Company attracted the most sophisticated portion of Pennsylvania society, but its shelves had no deists' books before the Revolution.[39] The few free thinkers like Andrew Hamilton and Benjamin Franklin were likely to be members or contributors to Christ Church. Both men ended by being buried in a churchyard. In Pennsylvania being a free thinker meant having some skepticism about the literal acceptance of parts of the Old or New Testament and/or rejecting Calvinism and miracles or the supernatural.

The serious competition to Christianity came from what the enlightenment called superstition and we term folklore.[40] The interpretation of dreams, omens, magic, and witchcraft, all mentioned in the Bible, had for so long been blended with Christianity that it was difficult to distinguish them. The church's attack upon folklore was timorous and uncertain, because neither clergy nor laity had a theological system which established a clear distinction between a legitimate and a superstitious act. Jacob Taylor included in his 1745 Almanack a long attack upon astrology and his rival John Jerman's use of it. Yet Taylor in his Ephemeris for 1726 declared that the stars controlled health and each of the twelve constellations governed one part of a man's body. John Jerman included signs of the zodiac in his almanacs and used astrological lore.[41] Reverend Andreas Hesselius, a Swedish Lutheran, in 1717 listed stillbirths, astral phenomena, and an evil ship captain carried off by the devil.[42] The Presbyterian Synod of Philadelphia in 1728 testified against "judicial astrology" while clearing an accused minister from the charge of practicing it. A practice that might be illegitimate if the devil were invoked, became acceptable if accompanied by prayer to Jesus.[43]

Basil Willey, in describing the English intellectuals of the mid-seventeenth century, found a series of thinkers poised between what he defined as a basically scholastic and a modern way of thought. In medieval patterns of thought, the "why" is the crucial issue; in modern, the "how" questions predominate.[44] With a few exceptions, colonial Pennsylvanians were still preoccupied with the "why." Only a small minority, of whom Franklin is the most famous example, asked both questions. Virtually no one assumed that only the "how" was important.

Franklin is a fascinating example of the limitations of our knowledge of secularization. He was raised a Puritan, but detested Presbyterians. He composed a simplified church liturgy, prayers, and extracts from scripture, but he also wrote a treatise which undermined conventional notions of pleasure and pain, good and evil.[45] He advocated frequent attendance at church for himself and his family and conducted family worship at home. While repeatedly endorsing public prayers, he detested public hypocrisy. Alfred Aldridge argues that Franklin believed in worship of God and providence, but there is no certainty that he related the two beliefs.[46] Was he secular in that, in spite of appearances in church on Sunday, he shunted religious questions to an obscure corner of his mind and never thought much about them? Although scholars have discovered and written more about him than any other colonial Pennsylvanian, we do not know whether Franklin prayed in private. Was his call for prayer at the Constitutional Convention a political ploy, an instinctive reaction, a sign of deep-seated belief? Perhaps he did not know.

The variety of meanings in the commonly used term secularization shows that definition and precision are crucial, yet almost impossible to achieve. Even though working definitions allow a focused investigation, the application of secularization theory remains a problematic enterprise not only because of ambiguities in the concept but also the nature of the issues. There is no reliable method by which historians can assess the depth of an individual's — let alone a society's — religious beliefs and commitments and see how the passage of time changes them.

Still, the historian can use secularization theory to elucidate different facets of a people's religion. He must remember that there is a profound difference between the institutional church and the cultural role of Christianity, even though the two phenomena are often linked. This essay has examined colonial Pennsylvania to answer the following questions:

1. Did religion lose its public functions?
2. Did the power of the institutional church decline?
3. Was a non-Christian world view an intellectual alternative?

In Pennsylvania the separation of the institutional church from the state did not lead to or facilitate divorcing government from Christian concerns. The religious-political battles between Quakers and Anglicans and later between the sects and the churches were over what kind of religious framework would dominate the government. Religious toleration and peace became the central core of the sectarian platform. The alternative after 1720 was not for a state supported church, but for a military establishment and a traditional kind of alliance (as in Virginia and New England) between magistrates and clergy. All religious bodies saw civil government as ordained by God to reform immoral conditions. They also agreed on the religious origins of government. To legislators and people the destiny of the colony lay in the hands of God.

The Pennsylvania Assembly's refusal to become involved in purely ecclesiastical affairs allowed the sects more autonomy and more control over members than in Europe. The churches—Anglican, Lutheran, Reformed, Presbyterian—accustomed to state sponsorship had to adjust to new relationships among the clergy, laity, and general populace. For virtually all the churches a satisfactory pattern of institutional organization had been established well before the Revolution. After 1750 outward signs—increasing numbers of members, more congregations and better edifices, functioning synods—showed that lay initiative and clerical guidance had rebuilt the institutional church. The churches had less legal power than in Europe, but the informal ties between religious groups and the laity who dominated the general society remained very powerful.

The history of colonial Pennsylvania lends little support to the common assumption that her people had or were creating a secular culture in the eighteenth century. In 1690 and in 1760 Christianity provided a "sacred canopy" in which to assess the meaning and significance of basic processes of human life. Christianity had tradition, prestige, a heritage encompassing reason and enthusiasm, and institutions capable of inspiring a few men and women to acts of self-sacrifice. Even to the apathetic, religion provided consolation in times of crisis. The social cost of open defiance of Christian norms of belief and conduct remained a potent force for uniformity. The main alternative belief systems—magic, astrology, spiritualism—were more opposed to a mechanistic, scientific, and rationalistic world view than was Christianity. Protestantism seemed "modern" as compared with hexes and witchcraft, because the doctrine of secondary causes allowed the natural order to operate without divorcing it from God's providence. In a culture characterized by widespread illiteracy and social and political change, Christianity provided a worldview capable of allowing peasants and intellectuals to make sense out of the chaos and order of existence.

122

NOTES

1. Richard Fenn, *Toward a Theory of Secularization*, Society for the Study of Religion, Monograph Series, No. 1 (Connecticut, 1978), 24-40.

2. The varieties of definitions are clearly described in Larry Shiner, "Secularization: Its Meaning and Effects," reprinted in *Religious Influence in Contemporary Society*, Joseph E. Faulkner, ed., (Columbus, Ohio, 1972), 469-485.

3. Peter Berger, *The Social Reality of Religion* (London, 1967), 111-113, 124.

4. Joseph Levering, *A History of Bethlehem, Pennsylvania 1741-1892* (Bethlehem, Pa., 1903), 147, 210-212; Brother Lamech, *Chronicon Ephratense*, tr. J. Max Hark (Lancaster, Pa., 1889), 45, 58, 83, 87, 140, 216, 239.

5. The church/sect classification works better in Europe than in Pennsylvania where Friends combined attributes of both kinds. The classic attempt to apply Weber and Troeltsch's typology to America is H. Richard Niebuhr, *Social Sources of Denominationalism* (1929). For Niebuhr the church was an inclusive institution with ascribed membership and a sacerdotal leadership. Sects, formed by the disinherited, were exclusive, more individualistic, with a strong ethical emphasis, and requiring a definite commitment. Recent commentators have found many variations in sects and have modified Niebuhr's definition to allow changes over time. Bryan Wilson defines sects as characterized by voluntary self-selected membership, exclusivity, homogeneity, self-consciousness and conscientiousness. Sectarian membership need not come from the poor; Niebuhr's emphasis on the disinherited confuses the issue somewhat, although it is a fact that the sects have appealed more to the disinherited than the churches.

In the colonial period Presbyterians, Anglicans, Lutherans, and Reformed saw themselves as churches. By the 1760s the Baptists were tending to ally themselves with the churches, partially because their clergy were college educated. Pennsylvanians described the Quakers, Amish, Moravians, and Brethren as sects. The Quaker experiment in Pennsylvania involved a sect's taking control of a government while attempting to stand against certain emphases in Anglo-American culture. H. Richard Niebuhr, *The Social Sources of Denominationalism* (New York, reprinted, 1957), 17-21; Bryan Wilson, *Religious Sects* (London, 1970), 22-35; Bryan R. Wilson, ed., *Patterns of Sectarianism* (London, 1967). For a discussion of the sectarian political aims in Pennsylvania, see J. W. Frost, "Religious Liberty in Early Pennsylvania," *Pennsylvania Magazine of History and Biography*, CV (October, 1982), 427, 437-445.

6. *Votes of Assembly, Pennsylvania Archives*, III, 2535-2538, 2541-2545, 2555-2557.

7. *The Works of William Smith* (Philadelphia, 1803), Sermon IV, Sermon V, Sermon VIII, 109, 123; Gilbert Tennent, *The Late Association for Defense, Encourag'd* (Philadelphia, 1747). Presbyterians, Baptists, Reformed, and Lutherans had days for fasting in which the difference between their view of the wars and the sectarians became clear.

8. The amount of competition among denominations at the local level in Penn-

sylvania varied greatly. In Chester County as late as 1775, thirteen localities had only a Quaker meeting, four only a Presbyterian church. When there was competition, there were just two congregations — normally Quaker versus Anglican or Quaker versus Baptist. There was one Chester County town which contained both Presbyterian churches and Quaker meetings. In Bucks County there were ten single congregation localities, five with two, and six with three or more. Except for urban centers like Philadelphia and Germantown, there was more denominational rivalry on the frontiers. Berks had five single congregation communities but eleven with three denominations. Lancaster had sixteen localities with three denominations, but only eight with one church. Lester Cappon, ed., *Atlas of Early American History 1760–1790* (Princeton, New Jersey, 1976), 38.

9. Jack Marietta, *Reformation of American Quakerism* (Pennsylvania, 1984), xiii.

10. C. Henry Smith, *Mennonite Immigration to Pennsylvania*, Pennsylvania German Society Publication (Pennsylvania, 1929); Richard MacMaster, Samuel R. Horst, and Richard Ulle, eds., *Conscience in Crisis* (Pennsylvania, 1979); Howard Kriebel, *Schwenkfelders in Pennsylvania* in Pennsylvania-German Society *Proceedings* XIII (1904); Donald Durnbaugh, ed., *The Brethren in Colonial America* (Illinois, 1967); Jacob Sessler, *Communal Pietism Among Early American Moravians* (New York, 1933).

11. Among the histories which pay particular attention to the churches are Martin Lodge, "The Great Awakening in the Middle Colonies," Ph.D. diss., University of California, 1964; John Frantz, "The Awakening of Religion Among the German Settlers in the Middle Colonies," *William and Mary Quarterly* (April, 1976); Jon Butler, *Power, Authority and the Origins of American Denominational Order: The English Churches in the Delaware Valley 1680–1730. Transactions of the American Philosophical Society* (Feb. 1978), vol. 68, Part 2; Guy Klett, *Presbyterians in Colonial Pennsylvania* (Philadelphia, 1937); Leonard J. Trinterud, *Forming of an American Tradition* (Philadelphia, 1949).

12. Henry Melchior Muhlenberg, *Journals*, II, 295. The popular belief was that it required seven years. Charles H. Glatfelter, *Pastors and People: German Lutheran and Reformed Churches in the Pennsylvania Field, 1717–1793. Publications of the Pennsylvania German Society*, XXI (Pennsylvania, 1980), Vol. I contains a biographical sketch of all known German pastors.

13. Trinterud found the failure of the Old Light Presbyterian clergy exemplified by their moral failings. He calculated that eight of twelve Old Light ministers had blemishes on their record. Among the Anglicans, Phillips was accused of seducing the wives of two vestrymen and the daughter of another man. The rivalries between Jenney, Peters, Smith, Sturgeon, Cumings, and Macclenachan kept the political rivalry constantly alive. Even when there were only a few clergymen of each denomination, they quarreled. Boehm vs. Reiff, Leutbecker vs. Stoever vs. Muhlenberg. There were constant difficulties with Lutheran ministers who were depressive, drunk, immoral, or in contention with their congregations. Among the Reformed, Berger, Zufall, and Lange drank too much; Bartholomaues and Wittner were melancholy if not depressive. My favorite character is Domine Stapel. In need of a wife, Stapel drew up lottery tickets with

124

the names of 15 or 16 women. "He passes his time partly in drinking, partly in thinking of the other sex, and partly in practicing medicine." Trinterud, *Forming an American Tradition*, 135–136, 142; R. L. Winter, *John Caspar Stoever*, 92–93; W. J. Hinke, ed., *Life and Letters of Rev. John Philip Boehm* (Philadelphia, 1916), 266; *Minutes of the Coetus of Reformed German Congregations of Pennsylvania* (Philadelphia, 1903), 179–180, 205, 246, 252, 285; Deborah Matthias Gough, "Pluralism, Politics and Power Struggles: The Church of England in Colonial Philadelphia," Ph.D. diss., University of Pennsylvania, 1978.

14. The results of irregularities were described by an Anglican priest: "One irregular Clergyman . . . will pull down more in six months than a diligent Missionary can build up in almost as many years, for such is the uncharitable temper of the new sect of enthusiasts, that from the bad life of one they conclude the character of the whole body of our clergy." William Stevens Perry, ed., *Papers Relating to the History of the Church in Pennsylvania* (n.p., 1871), 245.

15. Glatfelter, *Pastors and People: The History*, II, contains a complete account of the adjustments of Lutherans and Reformed. He shows that many "irregular" ministers served congregations very successfully.

16. The Lutherans of Reading "are just now a suing & execrating one another on the occasion of electing a Minister & this satisfaction they frequently indulge themselves being fonder of new Clergy than new cloths which they are parsimonious enough to wear threadbare & when they are ripe for a change of Pastors they make them do so too, & so starve them out of place with cold or hunger. Their subscriptions are scanty at best & these they continue to withhold annually at pleasure; for in their language they Hire a Minister generally for no longer than a year which renders his office as contemptible as poor." Alexander Murray, 1772, in Perry, *Papers*, 458–459.

17. Glatfelter, *Pastors and People*, II, 157.

18. Israel Acrelius, *History of New Sweden; Or The Settlements on the River Delaware*, tr. William M. Reynolds (Philadelphia, 1874), 238.

19. Acrelius, *History*, 305; Perry, *Papers*, 101, 161, 192; *Hallische Nachrichten* (Reading, 1882) I, 268; H. Harbaugh, *Life and Labors of Rev. Michael Schlatter* (Philadelphia, 1857), 202.

20. The Presbyterians "gain no accessions except from the Importations of their own Society from the North of Ireland." Perry, *Papers*, 367.

21. Boyd S. Schlenther, *The Life and Writings of Francis Makamie* (Philadelphia, 1971), 21–25, 189–244.

22. A striking feature of Synod and Presbytery minutes is the decline in conflict within churches after the 1760s. The main exception is Philadelphia where conflict persisted in the Second Presbyterian (New Light) and Pine Street churches.

23. Muhlenberg, *Journals*, II, 181, 433, 441.

24. In 1775 the New Light Philadelphia Presbytery announced that there were no vacancies and recommended that candidates go elsewhere. First Philadelphia Presbytery, Minutes, April 5, 1775, 189; Glatfelter, *Pastors and People*, II, 213, 235.

25. Glatfelter, *Pastors and People*, II, 145–146. Patricia V. Bonomi and Peter

Eisenstadt have demonstrated that the assumption that eighteenth-century Americans were unchurched needs revision. Their calculations, more successful for New England and the South than Pennsylvania, show that a significant percentage of the population was involved in the institutional church. Laura Becker linked between 87 and 93% of the population in Reading to a specific denomination. Stephanie Wolf found a much greater degree of non-involvement in Germantown. Patricia U. Bonomi and Peter R. Eisenstadt, "Church Adherence in the Eighteenth-Century British American Colonies," *William and Mary Quarterly*, Third Series, XXIX (April, 1982), 245–286; Laura Becker, "The American Revolution as a Community Experience: A Case Study of Reading, Pennsylvania," Ph.D. diss., University of Pennsylvania, 1978, 232–244; Stephanie Wolf, *Urban Village* (Princeton, 1976), 203–206, 240–242.

26. Baptists included figures for those who were members and attenders. Muhlenberg estimated the ratio of attenders to members at six to one and complained that settlers would go to hear any visiting preacher. A. D. Gillette, ed., *Minutes of Philadelphia Baptist Association* (Philadelphia, 1851).

27. Horace W. Smith, *Life and Correspondence of Rev. William Smith, D.D.* (reprinted, 1972), I, 220.

28. *Hallische Nachrichten*, II, 40–41; Perry, *Papers*, 178, 220, 222, 261, 329. Thomas Barton to the Society, July, 1761, "What number of infidels may lurk under the Mask of Religion is difficult to know. But I am not acquainted with any in this Mission who oppenly avow themselves to be such, or at least, whose guarded outside does not give the same pretence to a different character."

29. Glatfelter, *Pastors and People*, II, 321.

30. Ibid., 332.

31. In 1768 the New Light First Presbytery of Philadelphia debated whether a child of unbaptised parents could be baptised. After a year's deliberation, the Presbytery could not decide and left the decision to individual congregations. First Presbytery of Philadelphia, Minutes, 111, 119, Ms. at Presbyterian Historical Society. Hugh Neill at Oxford complained in 1761 of the people attending services who were not baptised, because of the general prejudice against baptism of infants. In Reading, Alexander Murray found people unbaptised because they lived among Friends, were indolent or neglectful, or they demanded "perfection" in "point either of Morals or knowledge in some abstruse party tenet." Perry, *Papers*, 337, 345.

32. Dietmar Rothermund, *Layman's Progress: Religious and Political Experience in Colonial Pennsylvania, 1740–1770* (Philadelphia, 1962) contains an overall interpretation of the evolution of religion in Pennsylvania. His discussion of secularization (pp. 57–68) differs from the interpretation offered here.

33. "Draft of Letter of Reverend Christopher Schultz to Sebastian Levan, Member of Assembly, Dated, Hereford, Aug. 12, 1777," in Kreibel, *Schwenkfelders*, 213.

34. Perry Miller, *Jonathan Edwards* (New York, 1949) and Alan Heimert, *Religion and the American Mind* (Cambridge, Mass., 1966) exemplify this neo-

orthodox or existentialist tendency. Edwards and the New Lights become, at least implicitly, heroes whose ideas and action create an American culture. Neither Miller nor Heimert ever claimed that the Old Lights and rationalists were not religious.

35. Marcus Rediker, "Under the Banner of King Death: The Social World of Anglo-American Pirates, 1716-1726," *William and Mary Quarterly*, Third Series, XXXVIII (April, 1981), 221-222.

36. Rhys Isaac, "Evangelical revolt: The Nature of the Baptists' Challenge to the Traditional Order in Virginia, 1765-1775," *William and Mary Quarterly*, Third Series, XXXI (1974), 345-368.

37. Richard Bauman, *For the Reputation of Truth: Politics Religion and Conflict Among the Pennsylvania Quakers* (Baltimore, 1971), 38-40; Frederick Tolles, *Meeting House and Counting House* (Chapel Hill, N.C., 1948), 123-125; Marietta, *Reformation*, 98-105.

38. Richard Bushman, *From Puritan to Yankee* (Cambridge, Mass., 1971), 107-143.

39. Gough, "Pluralism, Power," 144-147.

40. Keith Thomas, after listing an impressive number of causes for the decline of magic in late seventeenth-century England—the intellectual revolution, rise of science, ideology of self-help, more control over environment, economic transformation—is extremely cautious about drawing too firm a conclusion. He recognizes that the sources and people he has cited may not be representative and that students of folklore in the nineteenth century found many examples of omens, divination, etc., and that popular religion and spiritualism contained much that could be defined as magic. Jon Butler, whose discussion of magic and religion in colonial America breaks new ground, concludes that Thomas is possibly wrong in dating the decline of magic in England in the seventeenth century, and certainly wrong for America. Butler draws many examples of astrology, etc., from eighteenth-century Pennsylvania, but never discusses the Pennsylvania Germans at length. Butler's conclusion is that magic declined in mid-eighteenth-century America, perhaps due to the rise of evangelical religion. Keith Thomas, *Religion and the Decline of Magic* (New York, 1971), particularly 665-667; Jon Butler, "Magic, Astrology, and the Early American Religious Heritage, 1680-1760," *American Historical Review*, 84 (April, 1979), 317-345.

41. Jacob Taylor, *A Compleat Ephermeris for 1726* (Philadelphia, 1725) and *Pensilvania 1746, An Almanack* (Philadelphia, 1745); Thomas Godfrey, *Pennsylvania Almanack for 1734* (Philadelphia, 1733); John Jerman, *An Almanack for the Year 1723* (Philadelphia, 1722).

42. Acrelius, *History of New Sweden*, 279-282. Acrelius's history was published in 1759.

43. *Records of the Presbyterian Church in the United States of America Embracing the Minutes of the General Presbytery and General Synod* (Philadelphia, 1904), 91.

44. Basil Willey, *The Seventeenth-Century Background* (London, 1934), 3-4,

14-15. Willey believed the ambiguity changed in England after 1660, at least for the intellectuals. He did not specifically discuss secularization or the extent to which men like Newton reflected popular taste. In Pennsylvania the existence of sects, German speaking immigrants, and the high degree of illiteracy made the culture more conservative.

45. Benjamin Franklin, "A Dissertation on Liberty and Necessity, Pleasure, and Pain," often reprinted.

46. Alfred Owen Aldridge, *Benjamin Franklin and Nature's God* (Durham, N.C., 1967), 39–40, 175–178, 256–259.

The Women's Aid Society:
A Historical Document

At Fortress Monroe in Virginia on 24 May 1861 General Benjamin Franklin Butler refused to hand over three fugitive slaves which a Virginia militia officer demanded be returned under the Fugitive Slave Law. General Butler argued that the slaves had been used to build fortifications in support of the rebellion, and that he was therefore confiscating them as contraband of war.[1] With this action, Butler supplied a name for the slaves who fled behind the lines of the Northern troops. Although Butler was not certain that he had acted properly, Congress seemed to follow his lead. On 6 August 1861 it passed the first of a series of confiscation acts, providing a policy which in effect freed the slaves in Confederate areas controlled by the Union army. Lincoln's Emancipation Proclamation of September 1862 was directly in concert with these Congressional acts.[2]

As the number of blacks escaping to behind Northern lines swelled, the army officers realized that they had a major refugee problem. Organization of offical "contraband camps" began in the West when General Grant appointed John Eaton, Chaplain of the Twenty-seventh Ohio Infantry Volunteers to be in charge of the black refugees. A parallel process of organization began in the East under General Butler, who appointed Private Edward L. Pierce to organize the refugees into work groups. Pierce appealed to friends in Boston to provide aid for these refugees, and their response soon took the shape of the New England Freedmen's Aid Society. Northerners began to form similar aid societies in many cities, and the masses of freed blacks were cared for during the entire Civil War largely through the efforts of these groups.[3]

The Women's Aid Society, a group of Philadelphia Friends, organized one such relief effort on 12 March 1862, largely to provide clothing for the freedmen.[4] This group of women preceded the formation of the "Friends' Association of Philadelphia, and its Vicinity, for the Relief of Colored Freedmen" (hereafter referred to as the Friends' Freedmen's Association) by more than a year and one half.[5] The formation of the men's society was indicative of the increased interest in, and organization on behalf of, the freedmen. At this time the Women's Aid Society expanded its functions and organized auxiliary groups in the outlying regions of Philadelphia.

Beginning in December of 1863, the Women's Aid Society had lithographed a series of eight circulars which it sent to its auxiliary groups to provide them with some information about the circumstances of the freedmen they were helping, and to "enhance their interest" in the work they were doing. These circulars commonly contained extracts from letters received from the contraband camps to which the Women's Aid Society regularly sent supplies.

Transcribed below is the first of these circulars,[6] which is notable for several reasons. In addition to two letters, the circular printed an address given by an Ohio Quaker who had just visited several contraband camps on the Mississippi River. Many of the persons mentioned in the letters had important roles in the government's organized efforts to manage the freedman, and the address cited a public review of black students attended by Ulysses S. Grant. More importantly, the circular provided evidence of the attitudes towards the freed slaves of those northerners working with and for them. Both the Women's Aid Society's choice of material to send to its auxiliary groups and the attitudes expressed and implied in the speech and letters are significant. The women expressed joy in the blacks' religious faith, and surprise and pleasure at the blacks' ability to learn. A statement by Louis Gerteis seems applicable to the document: "Like most missionaries, they found the blacks appealingly quaint and picturesque, as well as apallingly degraded and ignorant."[7]

Finally, the document suggests what information the aid societies were receiving about the condition of the contraband camps. Although the accounts of illness and scarcity of clothing were accurate and gloomy, the accounts regarding the labor and education processes were too rosy. Although the structures of the labor systems were accurately described, the operation of these systems was less successful than is implied. The general opinion was that the blacks learned quickly, but there were also less jubilant evaluations of the blacks' intelligence: "Higher than I had expected—keen and bright when they wish to understand;—stupid and idiotic when they do not," and "Better than many suppose. Good as any could expect under the circumstances."[8]

At a meeting of the Women's Aid Society held 12th mo 12th 1863, it was mentioned that many friends, in country places, who are now working assiduously in behalf of the "Freedmen," are too remotely situated to attend our meetings, and are, in consequence, comparatively unacquainted with many of the stirring facts to which we have access; and that a knowledge of some of these, would greatly enhance their interest, and might be a benefit to the cause. Upon this suggestion the following report has been drawn up, and is offered to the Auxiliary Societies in country places. E. C. Collins. Secretary.[9]

Philadelphia 12th mo: 12th. 1863.

Feeling it really due to some of our friends in the country, who are diligently aiding in the great work of providing relief for the poor, suffering "Freedman," that they should share a portion of the interesting items of information continually flowing in to stimulate our own— energies, we propose to transmit to you an occasional report of the proceedings of our meetings, with such extracts from our correspondence as may convey the clearest idea of the condition of these suffering people, and of the appropriation made of the labor so generously added to our efforts.

At our mtg this afternoon, we had the company of Levi Coffin,[10] a friend who is Agent for the Freedman's Relief Association of Cincinnati, and has devoted his time and energies to this work for a year past. He gave us a deeply interesting account of his visits to the "contraband" camps on the Mississippi; in all of which together, there are at least 50.000[11] of these claimants upon our sympathy. This number only embraces women, children, and infirm or aged men—the able bodied men being all employed by Government.

He had seen as many as 800 come in at once, almost in a state of nudity—and everywhere the cry was going up for more clothing—both wearing apparel and bedding. He spoke with peculiar interest of the progress of education amongst them;—of the general eagerness of both young and old, to acquire knowledge,—and of their extraordinary aptness—not so much from any superiority of intellect, but because it is a boon for which they have waited and *prayed*, and which they now seize upon with avidity, as coming from their Heavenly Father's hand. One school, on President's Island,[12] was mentioned, as especially interesting. Lucinda Humphreys, of Chicago, had opened it, by special permission from General Grant,[13] and had proven her qualification for the service by the remarkable influence she had exerted over both children and adults, and by their rapid improvement under her instruction.

She had recently made a public examination of the pupils which was attended by General Grant, and a number of other Officers and soldiers,—several of whom made addresses. Amongst the scholars there was one old colored man, 95 years of age, — upon whose hoary head the blessing of liberty had just descended; — he had been *praying all his life* that he might be enabled to read the Bible before he died — and now that long desired privilege was nearly won; — he seemed to learn almost intuitively, and already, after so few lessons, could read in easy sentences.

This old man also made a speech, before the assembled company; — it was simple but full of feeling; raising both his hands and looking upward, he said, "Dis is de Lord's work. — dis is de window of Heaven opened to the colored people." And so they all seem to regard it — this opportunity so long delayed — as the window of [*sic*] opened to let in light upon their poor benighted minds. L[evi] C[offin] spoke especially of their devotion and trustfulness — invariably referring all blessings to Divine Providence. He said it was most comforting and satisfactory to find them, as a people, looking to the Savior, and exercising a simple faith in Him.

Everywhere you will hear the same thing — "We have been praying and praying, these many years. — and now the Lord has heard our cries and *has come down* to deliver us."

One old woman, just arrived, was asked her age; she replied, "Dey use tell me I was 21, and made me do a Gal's work, but I guess if dey'd said *75*, dey'd a come nearer to it." Then she proceeded to narrate the story of the grievous wrongs she had endured all her life long. Her large family of children and grandchildren had gradually been apportioned out to the different branches of her Master's family, until almost all had been removed from her; "but," said she, "I had been praying to de Lord always, dat He would look down on our troubles, and set us free — and I never lost faith dat He *would* do it. You see," said she, placing her hand on her whitened hair, "I was growing old, but I never lost faith dat de Lord would deliver us, and dat I should see it. One day I was out milkin' de cows — stoopin' down and prayin' dat de Lord would send de Yankees, when I heard a great noise and looked up, and, "Bress de Lord, dere was de Yankees' faces right over de fence — right on Massa's place; so I put down my bucket and ran to 'em — and dey said dey come to take we all — so git ready"! [*sic*]

Here she described quite amusingly the overwhelming joy of her heart, which was ready to leap from its sable bounds into the quick possession of promised liberty. A squad of Union Cavalry had made a raid into that section, and passing over the adjacent farms, had gathered up all the negroes on their way, and amongst the motley group on which the old woman's eye now rested, were the happy faces of her collected descendents, children and grandchildren, eager to carry her with them in their onward march to freedom. She was no longer a slave, and her voice could mingle in the glad refrain—*"Bress God, we's free!"*

Their patient submission to all the trials dispensed, is very instructive; an instance was given of one poor woman, whose husband and 2 oldest children had been sold away from her and carried, she knew not whither; with the two youngest she had contrived to escape and come within our lines, when the elder of these was taken sick and died; just before LC.'s visit the other also died, and was buried; quite a concourse of negroes gathered at the grave, and the attending Missionary said, that after the regular funeral services had been performed, the poor, stricken mother stepped forward and added these words; "This was my last child—I know not if I have any other living; I have prayed to the Lord that its life might be spared—but I always prayed *in submission*; now He has taken it away—my heart is pierced, but my happiness is not gone. I have trusted in the Lord my Savior and He will help me." "Which of us," said the Missionary, "could have said more than this?"

In speaking of the capabilities of the people for supporting themselves, he mentioned that many of the evacuated farms are rented out to them by Government, thro' Commissioners;[14] in most cases, however, they are leased to whites, who have to employ the Freedman to cultivate them; these pay to Government a certain percentage on every bale of cotton and every bushel of grain raised, and are bound to pay a stipulated price for labor.[15] The whole proceeds pass through the hands of the Commissioners, in order to secure the dues of both Government and the negroes. Often the farms are leased directly to the Freedman;—and one instance was mentioned, of a place of 600 acres near Corinth, which had been leased to 28 colored men, who, with their families, made a little community of 230 persons, on the farm where they had formerly been worked as slaves.[16] Everything was in good order; altho it was the 6th mo: they were planting corn, with confidence that it would have time to mature; the cotton was nicely up, and the cotton gins all in working order. When asked if they were able to support + take care of themselves, without a *driver* to follow them, they replied, "oh, yes, Massa—we used to take care of ourselves and Massa too;—surely we can take care of ourselves without him, now!" [space] Having been always accustomed to the kind of labor required for the culture of those lands (of which there are 60.000 acres confiscated in the Department[17] of the Tennessee) they are much more capable of preparing it for a good yield and bringing in the handsome profits, than the whites would be; and now, occupying both the old negro huts, and Massa's spacious domain, *these* families are well provided for. But it is for the *un*provided—the new-comers, that appeals are so earnestly going out to the benevolent, who are sharing largely of the bounties of Providence. L Coffin said it was his conviction that the half had never been told of the miseries and sufferings of these poor creatures; and that, having witnessed *so much*, he could not be silent, but felt an increased desire to encourage others to renewed exertion, and to do his own part more earnestly than ever. — The association with which he is connected in Cincinnati, have contributed largely to the relief of the Freedmen, yet all their efforts are "but a drop in the bucket"; they have sent out and are supporting 28 Teachers and 3 Physicians — and have done a great deal toward supplying the large demand for books. He assured us that the work was assuming greater proportions and that we need not be afraid of doing too much. The need is immense.

After this Friend had withdrawn, we entered upon the general business of the association, which was not of striking interest, except to those daily connected with it. There were one or two letters, however, which were so full of interest to *all*, that we copy portions of them for your benefit also.

A large amount of clothing had been forwarded to New Berne, NC. in response to a pressing demand from that place; and to the Friend who wrote, announcing that it had been sent, the following reply was written.[18]

New Berne. NC. Dec. 7th. 1863.

"My dear Sir,

My husband, Chaplain Horace James,[19] is absent on Roanoke Island, where he is making arrangements for the comfort of 15.000 of the Freedmen under his care.[20] In his absence I will reply to your favor of the 20th Nov. which has just reached me. We are truly rejoiced that the Women's Aid Society have sent us this box,[21] as we have *nothing* on hand to-day. The Schooner has not yet arrived in port, but I will see to it that the box is obtained as soon as she comes. x x x In reply to your question about the wants of the Freedmen, I hardly know where to begin — for so large a portion of them want *everything*. x x x There are 17.000 blacks in the Department of N Carolina who come under Mr James' care; of these we have 9000 in and around New Berne. The others are scattered at Elizabeth City, Plymouth, Roanoke, Beaufort, Washington, Hatteras Inlet, +c +c.[22] A portion of these are self-sustaining; *multitudes* more *would* be, if they could get any work. Many of the men are in the army — *wages unpaid*; by careful computation Govt owes these blacks $60.000.

Our *greatest* need now, is occasioned by the presence of the Small-pox in New Berne.[23] It is yet on the increase. I quote from an official communication of the medical director of this district to Chaplain James. "Every particle of the bedding and clothing of these patients is destroyed as a sanitary measure, and they are true objects of charity. During the next month, we shall discharge in this way, (naked) at least 100 patients, and we can only look to *you* for clothing." We are doing everything we can for these people, but the supplies are *far, far* short of the demand. This very day I have been obliged to say to the Surgeon, who sent for clothing for 12 women to be discharged, that they must wait; — but I was happy to add that a box was on the way from Philadelphia and when it came I hoped to supply him. I have personally known many families of escaped slaves, who by patient careful industry, had got up a house, and made themselves comfortable for this cool, damp winter, — thus stripped of everything; and they leave the Hospital to find their houses torn down and burned — themselved enfeebled by loathsome disease. Can you wonder they are well-nigh discouraged? And yet *no one* is willing to say he would rather be a slave. "Bless de Lord, we's free, Missus! we 'spect to suffer a heap, — but our chil'n 'll be better off!"

The people, when discharged from the Hospital, come directly to this office, + while we welcome them and give them sympathy, we *cannot* give them clothes — for we have them not. But it is really needful for their health that they have 2 suits of under-clothing. x x Your hearts will tell you there *must* be a great deal of suffering; but can you not help us to relieve a portion of it? I attend personally to work of issuing supplies, and will pledge myself that all shall be faithfully done. The *schools* are in a fine state. Mͬ James has 28 Teachers at work, and the children are fast becoming unfit for slaves.

With great respect, yours'
Helen James."

The following Extracts are from the pen of one who has been earnestly engaged in promoting the welfare of the Freedmen, for more than a year past.[24] Her letter is dated from Norfolk, Va. and addressed to a friend of the cause, in this city.[25]

"It is all work here — and to take time for writing seems like robbing the negro. At this moment, while I write at Dͬ Brown's[26] desk, women and children are stepping from a steamboat upon the Dͬ's wharf, directly under my window, who are just born into freedom! They are representatives of 400 set free at once, by *colored* soldiers. They say hundreds more would come from their neighborhood if they were not locked up and carefully watched. They tell terrible stories of torture in days past;

tho' they say "slashing is pretty much done with, since the Union came here." They were hung to trees by their feet; beaten with planks in which holes had been made; stripped & cow-hided; and maltreated in many ways.

From whatever quarter the runaways come, they bear a universal testimony to the shameless untruth of their masters. ["]They told us the Union was poor, and wanted to sell us, to raise mone to carry on the war." "That we should be sold to Cuba"—"or have our eyes put out,—that the northern people have horns, and have come down here to destroy we colored people." The refugees are sent transiently to "Hall's Jail"; and many of them remember well when they wore chains within those walls. Sarah and I spend a great deal of time within the high walls of the Jail yard. We form classes for the refugees, as soon as they enter, and they learn with amazing rapidity. How eager they all are! Their faces kindle with transfiguring joy at every new word; for they find their way into words almost as soon as they look at the Alphabet. Almost daily, modest, pretty, neatly dressed women come to the yard to look for lost members of their family. "I have had seven head of children stole from me, and I look at every new face, perchance I may find them." Some of the visiters can hardly keep their hands from us—"Oh, I love you so! I don't like you, I loves you. What you are doing for these people, perhaps some good white ladies are doing for my children.["] Some of the mature almost worship their books. One old woman, slow to learn, said, "Oh, if I could have had this chance ten years ago! But I'll do the best I can—and I prays the Lord night + day, to give me knowledge and understanding." Yesterday I showed a woman, whom I have taught to write, the various ways of making the same Capital letters. When I asked her which she preferred, she replied, "Oh I loves them *all*; they are beautiful to me![")
_____ _____ The poetry of thought, feeling, and language, which characterize semi-barbarous people, is sometimes touchingly + beautifully demonstrated by the simple among the negroes. Those of reverent, religious nature, are sensitive, appreciative + grateful; prizing their opportunities, and seeing the Heavenly Father's hand in all things. "Oh, I want to learn, every chance I can get, for I so love to read. Every once in awhile I come across the name of God, and the love of it, it is so sweet, makes me want to read + read." — To a number of old men, good readers, I have given coarse printed Testaments—and each recipient has rejoiced with exceeding joy. Our life on Craney Island was savage + unsocial, compared with our present civilized city life— tho' our days there were the happiest we have passed in Virginia. Eight-

een hundred negroes were with us *out at sea*! And we were perpetually stimulated by the consciousness of their unlimited needs. When, in the Spring, hundreds of them were removed to the Government farms,[27] Dr Brown wished us to come into the neighborhood of Norfolk, that we might have the Scattered people under our charge. So we find our way out to the farms, learn the wants of the negroes, — help them with hints — listen to their wants, teach them, clothe them and do whatever we can for them. But comfort is some thing new for us — tho' we have been marvellously helped all the time. x x x x x Please tell MC + SW.C.[28] I wish they had been able to look into the Jail yard, the day after they were there — to see the boys, seated on the floor — on boxes — on benches, and all about — mending their ragged jackets + pantaloons! It was a very picturesque and moving sight. We have no pantaloons on hand, and so they were obliged to mend their clothes without removing them. Having made themselves whole, they illuminated their countenances with becoming pride in their patches.

Every day brings something new. x x x x x

Thine &c Lucy Chase.["]

NOTES

1. Louis Gerteis, *From Contraband to Freedman*, (Westport, 1973), p. 13.

2. J. G. Randall and David Donald, *The Civil War and Reconstruction*, 2nd. ed., (Boston, 1961), pp. 372–73.

3. Bell Irvin Wiley, *Southern Negroes 1861-1865*, (New Haven, 1938), p. 176; Henry L. Swint, ed., *Dear Ones at Home*, (Nashville, 1966), pp. 1–2.

4. Women's Aid Society 1862-64, Roll 1B, microfilm of MS, Friends' Freedmen's Association, Haverford College, 12 March 1862 minutes.

5. Executive Board Minutes, 1863-1880, Roll 1AE, microfilm of MS, Friends' Freedmen's Association, 7 November 1863 minutes.

6. Folder 950, Quaker Collection, Haverford College.

7. Gerteis, *From Contraband to Freedman*, p. 28.

8. John Eaton, *Grant, Lincoln, and the Freedmen*, (New York, 1907), p. 65.

9. Elizabeth Cope Collins joined the Women's Aid Society on 26 March 1862, and served as its secretary for over two years. Her obituary in the *Friends' Review* noted her "active interest in benevolent enterprise" and her "winning gentleness of manner." Women's Aid Society, 1862-64; *Friends' Review*, 34 (1881), 408.

10. Levi Coffin was a Quaker who became prominent in the Underground Railroad. He moved to Indiana in 1826 and to Cincinnati, Ohio, in 1847. In Ohio

he continued the anti-slavery activities which earned him the title, "President of the Underground Railroad." He helped to found the Western Freedmen's Aid Commission during the Civil War, and travelled to England in 1864 to raise money on its behalf. He published his well-known autobiography, *The Reminiscences of Levi Coffin*, before his death on September 16, 1877. See, Charles Ludwig, *Levi Coffin*, (Scottdale, 1975).

11. By 5 July 1864, there were 113,650 freedmen under John Eaton: 41,150 in the military; 62,300 were self-supporting on plantations, in cities, and in other occupations; 10,200 were on assistance from the government. See, Eaton, *Grant, Lincoln and Freedmen*, pp. 133–34.

12. This camp was one of the three near Memphis, Tennessee, the other two being Camp Holly Spring ("Camp Fiske") and Camp Shiloh. President's Island was the largest of these camps, containing 1,540 blacks as of 18 November 1863. These camps were just south of Memphis. In James E. Yeatman's 17 December 1863 report, the man in charge of the island was Mr. A. J. Thompson, who was aided by a Chaplain Kingsbury of Illinois. There were also several teachers and a missionary whom the Presbytery of the United Presbyterians of Mansfield, Ohio, had sent. See, James E. Yeatmen, "A Report on the Condition of the Freedmen of Mississippi," (St. Louis, n.p., 1864), pp. 2–4.

13. Lucinda Humphreys is a relatively obscure figure, and there is no record in Grant's papers of any letter granting her permission to open a school. One reference which seems to be to this woman is on page 164 of L. P. Brockett and Mary C. Vaughn, *Heroines of the Rebellion*, (Philadelphia, 1888). A "Miss Humphrey" is mentioned in connection with Mrs. Elizabeth Porter of Chicago, who served as a nurse at the Battle of Shiloh and became interested in the black refugees while her husband was stationed at Memphis in the summer of 1862. I suspect that the author both dropped an "s" from Lucinda Humphreys's name and confused "Shiloh" (Pittsburgh Landing) with Camp Shiloh; however, Levi Coffin may have confused a few details himself. There is no mention of Lucinda Humphreys in Yeatman's rather thorough report, but there is mention of Mrs. Porter on page 2 as one "of the first teachers."

14. In an order of 5 April 1863, General Thomas appointed a commission of three men—George B. Field, Captain A. E. Shickle, and Reverend Mr. D. S. Livermore, to "superintend the leasing of plantations." See Eaton, *Grant, Lincoln and Freedmen*, p. 59.

15. At the time of Levi Coffin's visit, the tariffs were two dollars per bale of cotton and five cents per bushel on corn and potatoes. Wages were, by Eaton's evaluation, low: seven dollars per month for able-bodied men over fifteen; five dollars per month for women; half rates for those between twelve and fifteen; no children under twelve could be employed. These rates were raised after Yeatman's report of 17 December 1863, which criticized the system. Eaton believed that there were problems of administration under both systems. See Eaton, *Grant, Lincoln and Freedmen*, pp. 59–60, 145–47.

16. Eaton, writing to Levi Coffin in 1864, estimated that of 100,000 acres under cultivation, "about 7000 acres are leased and cultivated by blacks. Some Ne-

groes are managing as high as 300 or 400 acres." Eaton, *Grant, Lincoln and Freedmen*, pp. 133-134.

17. The "department" was the basic territorial division during the Civil War. The army division operating within a department usually took the name of that department. Mark Boatner III, *The Civil War Dictionary*, (New York, 1959), pp. 234-35.

18. This letter was most likely addressed to J. Wistar Evans, a Quaker active in the Friends' Association of Philadelphia and its Vicinity for the Relief of Colored Freedmen. The Women's Aid Society enlisted the help of men to forward the boxes they prepared, and J. Wistar Evans is one of two who volunteered their services as early as 26 November 1862. He is listed as one of five members of the Purchasing and Forwarding Committee of the Friends' Freedmen's Association; this committee, formed on 11 November 1863, was responsible for helping the Women's Aid Society and acting as a liaison between the Women's Aid Society and the Association. Evans had been actively involved in assisting the Society in forwarding supplies for over a year at the time of this letter. Women's Aid Society, 1862-64; Executive Board Minutes, 1863-1880; *Statistics of the Operations of the Executive Board of the Friends' Association of Philadelphia and its Vicinity for the Relief of Colored Freedmen*, proc. of a public meeting of Friends, 19 January 1864, (Philadelphia, 1864), pp. 31-33.

19. Horace James, 1818-1875, originally was a Congregational Minister in Worcester, Mass. He was the Chaplain of the Massachusetts Twenty-fifth Regiment, and became the Superintendent of the freedmen for all of North Carolina under General Butler on 5 December 1863. He had arrived in New Bern in May 1863, and had begun work among the escaped blacks. He had gained an offical capacity for aiding the freedmen on 10 September 1863 by orders of Major General Pleck. After the war, he became Superintendent for the New Bern district of the Freedmen's Bureau, but was discredited by the murder on 1 March 1866 of one of his workers whom he had placed under armed guard because he had been caught stealing. After a trial, he returned to Boston and the ministry. See, Gerteis, *From Contraband to Freedman*, pp. 31-37; Horace James, *Annual Report of the Superintendent of Negro Affairs in North Carolina*, (Boston, n.d.), p. 24; Fred Ainsworth and Joseph Kirkley, eds., *The War of the Rebellion: A Compilation of the Official Records of the Union and Confederate Armies*, (Washington, 1899), pp. 1139-44.

20. Roanoke Island was one of James's major projects. It had dwellings on one side of the island and twelve acre plots for the freedmen to work. It only housed a little over 3,000 freedmen in 1865, although it seems from Mrs. James's letter that he had grand designs for it. See, Gerteis, *From Contraband to Freedmen*, p. 41; James, *Report of the Superintendent*, p. 3.

21. The box contained, "One counterpane, 1 shawl, 26 skirts, one pair shoes, 11 chemises, red flannel garments for children 20, Men's shirts 9—Women's dresses 59—3 pairs infants' shoes, 2 hats, 3 blankets, 7 children's dresses—Total 143." Women's Aid Society, 1862-64, 28 November 1863.

22. The figure reported by James for 1864 was 17,419 for North Carolina,

8,591 for New Bern, 860 for Plymouth, 2,426 for Beaufort, 2,741 for Washington, and 89 for Hatteras Inlet. The loss of Plymouth to Confederate forces in January 1864 led to the evacuation of Washington, which was midway between Plymouth and New Bern. This evacuation swelled the numbers of freedmen in New Bern, Beaufort, and Roanoke to 10,782, 3,245, and 3,091 respectively by January 1865. James, *Report of the Superintendent*, p. 3.

23. Smallpox was not a major problem during the Civil War compared to other diseases for which the causes and cures were unknown. Vaccines did exist, although they were not always reliable. Smallpox cases in the army occurred throughout the war. In North Carolina, during the winter of 1863-64, almost fifty per week died in February from smallpox—the victims being mostly blacks. A concomitant outbreak of yellow fever affected the whites more than the blacks. See, Paul Steiner, *Disease in the Civil War*, (Springfield, 1968), pp. 4-5, 15; James, *Report of the Superintendent*, pp. 16-17.

24. Lucy Chase, the author of the letter, and her sister Sarah were the daughters of Anthony Chase, a businessman in Worcester, Massachusetts, and the sisters of Thomas Chase, President of Haverford College from 1875-1886. Lucy was 41 and Sarah, 27, when they received appointments as teachers from the Secretary of the Boston Education Commission in December 1862. They began work in January 1863 on Craney Island, near Norfolk, Virginia, where in June 1862 Major General John A. Dix had ordered the freedmen to be collected for the winter of 1862-63. 30 September 1863 was the last day the sisters and the freedmen were on the island; after this date the sisters moved to Norfolk and the freedmen, to outlying areas. Lucy continued to teach in various southern locations, including Richmond, Virginia, and Lake City, Florida, until 1869, when she returned to Worcester, where she died in 1909. Swint, *Dear Ones at Home*, pp. 1-9, 88; Gerteis, *From Contraband to Freedmen*, pp. 21-26.

25. This particular letter was probably addressed to Elizabeth Collins, as the Secretary of the Society.

26. Orlando Brown was originally the surgeon for the Eighteenth Massachusetts Infantry and then the Twenty-ninth Massachusetts Infantry before being placed in charge of the freedmen on Craney Island. He was officially appointed Superintendent of the freedmen below the James River in Virginia by General Butler on 5 December 1863. After the war, in March 1865, General O. O. Howard appointed him Assistant Commissioner of the Freedmen's Bureau for the state of Virginia. Swint, *Dear Ones at Home*, pp. 19-20n; Gerteis, *From Contraband to Freedmen*, p. 29.

27. In April 1862, Secretary of War Stanton directed Brigadier General Rufus Saxton to take charge of the abandoned plantations in Virginia. Saxton appointed superintendents to care for each plantation: these plantations were then cultivated by the freedmen who were paid wages for their labor. Problems with obtaining money from the Treasury Department resulted in very low wages for the period February 1862 to January 1863. This failure led to the general adoption of the incentive system initiated by Edward Phillbrick, one of the plantation superintendents. The system provided each family with a garden plot and ex-

pected them to provide for themselves. See Wiley, *Southern Negroes*, pp. 178–80, 198–99; Gerteis, *From Contraband to Freedmen*, pp. 53–54.

28. These initials refer to Marmaduke Cope and his wife, Sarah Wistar Cope. They travelled to Hampton, Norfolk, and Yorktown Virginia between 7 and 17 November 1863, and Marmaduke published a report of his visit at the request of the Friends' Freedmen's Association. Marmaduke, born on 3 July 1804 to Israel and Margaret Cope of Philadelphia, earned a sufficient amount in the silk and dry goods business with his cousin Caleb to retire at age twenty-eight (after six years in business) and to devote his time to charitable organizations. Besides his activities in the Friends' Freedmen's Association, he also was one of those who organized the Institute for Colored Youth in Philadelphia in 1847. He remained a trustee of this school until his death in 1897. See, "Brief Account of M. C. Cope," *The Friend, Philadelphia*, 71 (1897): 139; Marmaduke Cope, *Report on a Visit to Hampton, Norfolk, & Yorktown*, (Philadelphia, 1863).

PART THREE

Modern
Quakers

The Road to Manchester, 1895[1]

During the early years of the nineteenth century there was growing tension in the sessions of London Yearly Meeting between the Friends who stood by the conservative quietism of the eighteenth century—however arid and somnolent its reality in silent local meetings—and the growing number of weighty Friends whose religious experience expressed itself in vigorous evangelical terms, attaching more importance to the authority of the literal interpretation of the Bible than to the power of the Inward Light in the searching soul.[2] The tension came to a head in the stormy Yearly Meeting of 1836; the Epistle of that year declared: "whatsoever man says or does, which is contrary to the Scriptures, though under the immediate profession of the Spirit, must be reckoned and accounted mere delusion."[3] And this provided the Quaker base from which evangelical Friends dominated the sessions of London Yearly Meeting for most of the rest of the nineteenth century.

The evangelical members of the Society of Friends in Great Britain rescued it from the spiritual inertia which threatened its very existence in the first half of the century. Their passion to share the experience of personal salvation restored the validity of going to meeting expecting vocal prayer and ministry; and their conviction that the Society had experience to share with their fellow-citizens turned Friends to look outwards to the religious needs of others, particularly among the poor. By the late 1880s the membership in London Yearly Meeting had risen from a mid-century low of under 15,000 to over 17,000. There were about 25,000 members of adult First Day Schools associated with local meetings and another 15,000 children.[4] Leadership in the schools was provided by about 1500 young men, mostly Friends.

It was evangelical enterprise which, in the late 1840s, had seized on the early adult schools of Joseph Sturge and others in Birmingham, developing the idea from literacy classes with some biblical instruction for the unlettered poor into lively biblical centred teaching fellowships which came gradually to have an elasticity of doctrinal inclination. For the experience of teaching thoughtful weekly wage earners often led the young Quaker leaders to provocative religious reflection of their own. Many of them found the preparation and discussion more satisfying than either the conventional evangelical ministry in some meetings or the dreary silence in others.

The very success of the First Day Schools affected the society in two contradictory ways. It united Friends in asking themselves why so comparatively few of the First Day students joined the society; it divided Friends about where to search for the way forward.

It was in these circumstances that, towards the end of the century, the evangelical dominance in the Yearly Meeting evaporated, abruptly but peacefully. The occasion was a great Quaker conference held in Manchester over three days in November 1895. The conference was called by Yearly Meeting at the instance of a strong newly-appointed, evangelically inclined Yearly Meeting Home Mission Committee.[5] The conference never had an informative title but was summoned in wide general terms to consider how Quaker witness should be presented to the outside world. The conference was the decisive point at which the society turned away from its evangelical years to find a new way forward in the direction of a liberal Christian faith with an associated radical social concern. What has been a puzzle for many years is how a predominently evangelical committee came to organise a conference that precipitated the eclipse of evangelical influence. Recently the minutes of the committee have become available in the archives of Friends House in London.[6] They open the way to interpret this significant episode in Quaker history and elucidate the part played by a number of Friends still remembered in London Yearly Meeting but who have left lamentably little personal record of their Quaker diplomacy.

In the early 1880s the evangelicals, looking beyond the adult First Day Schools, began to discern what they thought to be lessons to be learnt from the pastoral experience in some of the American yearly meetings. They had no stated intention in London of abandoning the practice of unprogrammed meetings based on silence, but they believed that the provision of a parallel "mission" type of exercise with vigorous evangelical teaching, preaching, prayer, hymns, and temperance advocacy could provide a bridge from First Day associateship to full membership. In 1882, at the height of evangelical ascendency, yet in face of some critical doubts, a Home Mission Committee was set up, formally by Yearly Meeting appointment, but in effect by virtual self-appointment.[7] It received authority to raise privately subscribed funds to support moderately remunerated volunteers who satisfied the committee that they had a personal religious concern for residential extension service, either in urban slum areas or in rural and middle-class areas where "mission" could go hand in hand with the revival of moribund meetings.

By 1892 there were about forty-two of these residential "workers,"[8] on some of whose evangelical preaching activities there was an increasingly critical focus from those who can be usefully identified as a new "emancipatory" strain. Their concern was to emancipate the society from what had, to a large extent, become thought-starved evangelical declamation, without turning Friends back towards the anti-thought bonds of conservative quietism. The emancipators were convinced that the way forward lay in finding ways of bringing the quality of thinking to the service of shared Christian experience in awakened meetings for worship.

In the 1880s there had been three signposts pointing in the emancipatory direction. In 1884 a hundred page paperback entitled *A Reasonable Faith*, written by "Three Friends," was published anonymously.[9] It was a direct, lucid, readable presentation of contemporary liberal Christianity, firmly but courteously critical of evangelical theology. Friends ill at ease with the general tenor of the current ministry in meeting were offered a different approach to biblical understanding and inspiration. Once the book was in circulation, its authors, William Pollard, Francis Frith and W. E. Turner, identified themselves. They were not professional scholars, but thought deeply and wrote well. The book stirred the emotions of the society noticeably, yet without evoking any sense of crisis. In 1886 this line of Christian exposition was taken further in a more scholarly way by Edward Worsdell in *The Gospel of Divine Help*.[10] It created less stir than *A Reasonable Faith* but strengthened the foundations from which the emancipators were able to push forward.

Then in 1888 a difficult and divided Yearly Meeting declined to accept the Richmond Declaration of 1887.[11] Some Friends formulated theological criticisms, but the weight of the objections lay in fear that the declaration was akin to a creed. This was probably the one point at which, had the sense of the meeting been different, there might have been a crisis, precipitated by resignations or even a separation initiated by the emancipators. As it was, the evangelicals remained remarkably unperturbed, perhaps because of the hold which Joseph Bevan Braithwaite, Sr., had on the society at large. For thirty years, after the death of J. J. Gurney, he had been the leading evangelical Friend, drafter not only of the London Epistle year after year,[12] but also of the Richmond Declaration itself,[13] a constant traveller in the ministry, a revered patriarch with warm-hearted and perceptive pastoral gifts and some standing as a biblical textual scholar. Braithwaite took the Yearly Meeting's decision with pained but quiet generosity as the sense of the meeting.[14] Yet in view of his personal status the non-acceptance was all the more significant.

The emancipators emerged from Yearly Meeting with raised hopes of change. Two younger men in particular had made their mark, Edward Grubb (b. 1854)[15] and John William Graham (b. 1859). Grubb was one of the first Friends to gain a post-graduate degree of the University of London; he was a teacher of religious studies in schools, but had also become active in trade union life since he perceived that philanthropy was no adequate answer to the scale on which social problems were emerging. Graham was a Cambridge mathematician, an able controversialist, shortly to join the faculty of Manchester University. Yet while the idea of emancipation was in the air there was not yet any coherent thought about how to sharpen the focus or share the vision; nor had glowing imaginative leadership emerged.

In the early 1890s tension grew sharply between the evangelical conviction that extension lay in the development of remunerated residential "mission work" and the emancipatory conviction that the key to new life lay in the liberal religious education of members of the society itself. So the prospective triennial review of the membership of the Home Mission Committee at Yearly Meeting in 1892 aroused tremendous interest.[16] In two long, crowded sessions the critics did most of the talking, ostensibly on the dangers, even the iniquities, of what they dubbed "the one man system," but with an undercurrent of theological criticism. The upshot of the exercise was the summoning by Yearly Meeting of a representative conference in the fall of 1892. Over two days, three hundred Friends wrestled with the question whether "mission" work in the hands of paid Friends was or was not a threat to "the distinguishing views of the Society." There was no clear answer. But the general principle that Friends should be looking outwards was warmly embraced and two administrative steps were recommended to the next Yearly Meeting which would give room for local and individual initiative along other lines than residential "mission." The first change was that, while a Home Mission Committee should be continued, its membership should be entirely through nominations from the seventeen quarterly meetings, with no additional members appointed directly by Yearly Meeting in order to provide a stable evangelical core. The second was that no paid "worker" should be stationed without the approval of the local monthly or quarterly meeting, and that the status of any "worker" so stationed should not be any different from that of any local Friend.[17]

The proposals were accepted by Yearly Meeting in 1893[18]; the lack of a stabilising core was resisted by the "old guard" but the clerk ruled that

148

there was no good reason why in a single session Friends should overturn the sense of a well-attended representative conference held over two days. So the responsibility for initiative shifted after sixty years from a Yearly Meeting hierarchy to Friends in the country.

Meanwhile, the emancipatory concern was given time to mature. This was helped by changed ownership of one of the two current Quaker periodicals. The *British Friend* had been founded in 1843 as the monthly journal of the conservative quietist strain. For nearly fifty years it had carried on its front cover a verse from Jeremiah to differentiate itself from the evangelically orientated *Friend*, founded in the same year: "Stand ye in the ways, and see, and ask for the old paths, which is the good way and walk therein." In 1891 the *British Friend* passed into the hands of the emancipators, with W. E. Turner as editor. The verse from Jeremiah was abandoned in favour of giving the paper a vigorous liberal temper,[19] still differentiating it from the *Friend*, though both were less aggressive than when founded fifty years earlier. The *British Friend* now gave Turner, Grubb, Graham and others a channel for the systematic presentation of ideas about how Quaker extension could profit from liberal biblical, scientific and social criticism and thought.

Moreover, three other Friends were now becoming influential. Fyfe Stewart (b. 1835) and William Charles Braithwaite (b. 1862),[20] one of the sons of Joseph Bevan Braithwaite, Sr., had become members of the first Home Mission Committee with ideas of their own for broadening the meaning of "extension," without necessarily abandoning residential "mission." Then at Yearly Meeting, 1893, John Wilhelm Rowntree (b. 1869)[21] entered actively into the situation. At the end of 1892 he had written a rousing article in the *Friend*, calling young Friends to recognise that the responsibility for the future was theirs.[22] Six months later at Yearly Meeting he made a brief but penetrating declaration that the ministry that members of his generation heard in meeting was incomprehensibly doctrinal and that it was difficult to say so to their "revered elders." What was needed was "plain, uncontroversial sermons upon the practicalities of life" in language that was understood.[23] There was nothing of substance in this that had not been said before over the previous twenty years by the authors of *A Reasonable Faith* and more recently by Grubb and Graham. What made this different was that it came from a twenty-four year old, testifying with the passionate Christian commitment of a recent release from agnosticism. It was presented with the acumen of the able business executive that he was, and with the charisma of his engaging enthusiasm for amateur dramatics. He laid hold of Yearly Meeting. Whether the weighty evangelical hierarchy relished his reflections or not, here was the warmth and flame that was at the heart of their own ministry at its best. And it brought a glow and the prospect of leadership to the emerging insights of the emancipators.

Between the Yearly Meetings of 1893 and 1894, while the Quarterly Meetings were working on their nominations to the new Home Mission Committee, the emancipators wrote busily and addressed meetings throughout the country. An anonymous editor published a small pamphlet entitled "Is there not a cause. . . ?"[24] It was a collection of extracts from articles in American Quaker publications by British Friends describing in glowing terms what they believed energetic pastoral developments could do for London Yearly Meeting. If, in context, the extracts were fair, the pamphlet presented an alarming picture of the hopes of some of the London evangelicals.

When at Yearly Meeting in 1894 the nominations were received for the new Home Service Committee it was found that twenty-nine of the eighty-four members had been members of the former committee and many of the new faces were known to belong to "mission" sympathisers.[25] On the other hand, though the numerical representation of the emancipators was small, it included Turner and Graham from Lancashire, while Stewart and W. C. Braithwaite had the confidence of both wings. Neither Grubb nor J. W. Rowntree was appointed from Yorkshire. Grubb's trade union activity may have placed him under some cloud and J. W. Rowntree was, perhaps, something of an *enfant terrible.* In any event there were two other Rowntrees among the Yorkshire six.

Turner was disappointed. He had been the first of the emancipators to spell out in Yearly Meeting that what Friends needed was systematic spiritual education for themselves as well as offering instruction to others. Writing in the *British Friend* immediately after the names of the new committee were known, he reflected sadly:

> It is fairly clear that the majority of Friends sent up are wishful to make no sudden break in the old regime. We had hoped for a more robust and sensitive Quakerism. . . . patience. . . . avoid partisanship. . . . enter into sympathy with those efforts towards which we are bound to withhold complete approval.

And he finished with regret that there were so few younger members.[26]

The new committee arranged to meet over two days at three-monthly intervals. When this group met for the first working session in October 1894, Turner's disappointment was justified, for it turned down decisively a proposal from two Lancashire members (of whom Graham was almost certainly one) to abandon the ten-year-old practice of helping Friends financially to reside in named centres for the furtherance of "mission" work. The proposal was not accepted because:

no course which would in any way interfere with entire freedom of service in any of those whom the Lord has called into his harvest field can be satisfactory.[27]

What is astonishing is that within thirteen months of this emphatic endorsement of the evangelical "mission" inheritance, the same committee organised the Manchester Conference which opened up the way in a markedly different direction.

Alas, there is a deplorable lack of primary material in the form of letters, notes, memoranda, or diaries by the major participants to explain the extraordinary speed with which the new route was cut. The only clues lie between the lines of the minutes of the Home Mission Committee and its Executive, which have recently become available, and in the reports — or lack of them — in the Quaker journals.

In a brief report of the October decision to continue the "mission" work, the evangelically oriented *Friend* referred to the "free criticism indulged in. . . ."[28] That there would be tension is not surprising in the historical context, but that it was so sharp must have worried the new committee's officers, Charles Brady, the Clerk, W. C. Braithwaite, the Assistant Clerk, and Fyfe Stewart, the Acting Honorary Secretary. These men had held the same offices in the latter years of the old Committee, and loyal as they were to the "mission" work at its best, they yet knew its limitations in practice and recognised that the emancipators had a burning concern that would certainly not be allowed to rest quiescent. What happened next after this October meeting strongly suggests that the officers saw that if the future of the committee was not to be burdened by the sharpness of the division at its first meeting, then the next meeting in February must be an occasion for unity. As indeed it was.

The first twenty-four minutes of the February meeting deal with the affairs of the "mission stations." Minute twenty-five relates to the final session on the second afternoon:

> We have had laid before us in an interesting way the comparative ignorance and misconception which exists around us as to the Society of Friends and the importance of concerted action in the endeavour to dissipate the views to some extent current. . . . all legitimate means for making known our distinguishing views and bringing ourselves as a Christian Church into contact with the people, embracing in this thought not only the poorer classes of the community but also the more cultured and educated portion of society. The needs of the thoughtful and educated young people of our own Society have been adverted to. . . .
>
> It has been suggested that the whole subject is one that the ensuing Yearly Meeting might properly be invited to entertain. . . . If the outcome . . . should

be the appointment of a special conference . . . the Home Mission Committee might be a convenient body to arrange it.[29]

The tone of this minute, coming at the end of a long second day, surely indicates that the Committee had been presented with a carefully prepared proposal drawing together themes of the various interests within the society which had been discussed in the crowded tension of recent Yearly Meetings. "Ignorance and misconception" refers to a current public view that Friends had no use for the Bible and that their views were entirely negative; "distinguishing views" refers to the conviction of many Friends that the "mission" work was obscuring the distinctive form of Quaker worship; "contact with the people" probably refers to a recent public meeting in York attended by over a thousand people and addressed among others by Grubb, Joshua Rowntree, and two other Yorkshire Friends asking whether the churches were in touch with the people; the "poorer classes" acknowledges the urban "mission" and adult school service; the "more cultured portion of society" refers to the concern of Caroline Stephen, author of *Quaker Strongholds*,[30] and a member of a distinguished Cambridge family (she was the aunt of Virginia Woolf), that the sophisticated agnostics should not be neglected; the "young people of our own Society" is a clear recognition of the dramatic impact of young John Wilhelm Rowntree and his associates. The minute was a skilled piece of diplomacy, pulling themes together into a proposal that would give the satisfaction to Yearly Meeting of seeing that a committee which had been born in tension was working well together.

Almost certainly W. C. Braithwaite was the Friend who laid before the committee in "an interesting way" this proposal for an inclusive conference. At the age of twenty-five he had become Clerk of Westminster and Longford Monthly Meeting with twelve hundred members, and over the next eight years he had shown himself to be an effective administrator and conciliator. He had the advantage of being the son of J. B. Braithwaite, yet was his own man and was trusted right across the spectrum. He was the Assistant Clerk of the Home Mission Committee which gave him the status to lay a major matter before the meeting at its fifth session and be taken seriously.

But nobody makes a proposal for a difficult conference without doing preliminary groundwork. The main committee had appointed a well-balanced Executive Committee.[31] It met three times after the October meeting and before the February meeting of the main committee. Its minutes give no hint of the birth of the conference idea. The only possible inference is that the officers had talked together about how to move forward out of the October tension and had decided to act informally.

152

They probably drew Turner into their deliberations. It was he who, at Yearly Meeting, 1892,[32] had proposed the conference that eased the tension by opening the way for the new-style Home Mission Committee. He was a member of the Executive and the oldest of the emancipators. He would already have been talking with his Lancashire neighbour, Graham (who was not a member of the Executive), about the latter's frustration at the October rejection of his proposal. Grubb and J. W. Rowntree were not on the Home Mission Committee, but the campaigning experience of the one and the youthful drive of the other could not possibly have been overlooked as factors threatening to heighten tension. From what happened at the February meeting and over the next eight months of conference preparation, it seems highly probable that Brady, Braithwaite, and Stewart agreed that the best way to keep the temperature low was for Braithwaite to propose an inclusive conference but without making any arrangements for the elaboration or refinement of the proposal before the minute went to Yearly Meeting in May. This would leave room for the emancipators to take a quiet planning initiative.

This supposition is supported by the fact that again in its three meetings between February and Yearly Meeting the Executive gave no thought to the matter. Discussion at Yearly Meeting was friendly in general. The minute approved the holding of a conference open to all Friends, to be held at Manchester in November, "on the subjects of their [i.e. the committee's] minute."[33]

The committee met in strength immediately on the rise of Yearly Meeting to consider how to pick up the task. But what were "the subjects of their minute"? The relevant committee minute reads:

> Various suggestions have been made as to the subjects to be brought before the Conference of which notes have been taken for the guidance of the Executive. ~~The following are some of them~~ (sic) The Executive is left at entire liberty to deal with the various subjects as they think fit.

Why the deletion and why was the Executive given such complete freedom of action?[34]

All Friends know the patience required of a committee while the Clerk drafts a detailed minute. In this instance the committee was meeting in hurried, unplanned session at the end of two weeks of Yearly Meeting when members may well have been anxious to get home. The all-inclusive vagueness of the February minute left plenty of room for prolix elaboration and there can be little doubt that as the Clerk struggled with a new minute somebody came to the rescue with a suggestion that the sense of the meeting should be embodied in conventional Quaker terms. Somebody may have added that decisions were urgent since six months' preparation was short enough and that in any event the next ordinary meeting of the full Home Mission Committee would be over two days at the beginning of July in five weeks time.

The Executive met the next day under the new chairmanship of Joshua Rowntree. It quickly settled the conference time-table; there would be three sessions daily, each to receive three or four papers, about thirty in all. Then, late in the meeting, but seemingly without any consideration of conference substance it appointed a conference sub-committee of Joshua Rowntree as Chairman, W. C. Braithwaite, his elder brother J. B. Braithwaite, Jr., Turner, Fyfe Stewart, and the new full-time Secretary, Ellwood Brockbank. None of the evangelical members of the Executive Committee was on the conference sub-committee.[35]

The sub-committee was given no more than a week to report back to the Executive which then minuted:

> A list of proposed chairmen and speakers has been considered. The [sub] committee is authorised to communicate with the Friends whose names have been brought forward and to proceed with the. . . . arrangements.[36]

Thus within ten days of the Yearly Meeting decision to hold the conference the programme had been mapped out in some detail by an emancipatory sub-committee, but without the inclusion of any names in writing.

In the interval Joshua Rowntree had become the key Friend in what was happening.[37] He was a most reassuring person, a fifty-one year old lawyer, who had been both Mayor of his home town, Scarborough, and subsequently its Member of Parliament for six years; a courageous supporter of Home Rule for Ireland when it was unpopular; and the first candidate to hold meetings for women though it was thirty years before they had the vote. His gift for personal relationships was quite outstanding. He was an active and faithful Friend who had taken very little vocal part in the extension controversy. The course of events makes it clear that he had been well-informed about the emancipatory planning, the more naturally since both Grubb and Graham had been recent Scarborough residents and J. W. Rowntree was a neighbouring young cousin in a close-knit Yorkshire family that enjoyed united and critical interest in every aspect of Quaker life. The main committee had appointed him chairman of its Executive immediately after Yearly Meeting and the Executive had appointed him chairman of the conference sub-committee when it met on the following day.

154

No minutes of this sub-committee have yet been found. So we know nothing of its considerations in the next four weeks before it reported again to the Executive on 3 July, which simply minuted: "A suggested programme has been read and considered."[38] The main committee met on the following two days. Its relevant minute reads:

> Joshua Rowntree has laid before us. . . . some general particulars as to the plans they [the Executive] propose. We feel deeply the importance of the intended meetings and approve of the suggestions made so far as they have been indicated to us. Some further hints have fallen from Friends as to other points of interest of which notes are to be taken by the Secretary for the guidance of the sub-committee.[39]

There is a hint of dissatisfaction with the meagreness of the information supplied, but acquiescence wins. Maybe three or four evangelical members of the committee had already been included in the programme and found their hands tied. Maybe, since four-fifths of the committee's time was spent on mission stations, the evangelicals were satisfied with the security of their own line of concern. Either way, the committee's "hints" do not seem to have been effective.

A few days later a substantial article, which must already have been in print, appeared in the *Friends Quarterly Examiner*. It was by W. C. Braithwaite on "The Aims of the Society of Friends."[40] Faith, he wrote, needed to go out to meet the issues of the day which he defined as the altered intellectual atmosphere, the rising pressure of fundamental social relationships, and the craving after reality in religious life. As affecting the society this meant that Friends must open their minds to scientific thought and that "the same fearless and open mind should be shown towards the higher criticism of the Bible." Friends had played a notable part in specific social problems such as opium, slavery, and temperance, but itemised philanthropy was not adequate "to fundamental principles which should control the relationships of men to one another in social life," as Woolman had pointed out in his essays on poverty. Friends must discard the formalism of the evangelical salvationist ministry in meeting and educate themselves for a ministry that would relate Christian experience to the whole of daily life. He finished by saying that the article "has more bearing on our future work than as existing aims accepted by the Church now," and that he does not know how to map out the road ahead.

Braithwaite's points were identifiably at the heart of the conference when the time came; yet only a few days earlier the main committee had minuted that it had not been told much about the agenda. Moreover in the August issue of the *British Friend* the titles of the sessions were printed exactly as they finally appeared. Equally surprising, though in another direction, is an article in the evangelically oriented *Friend* of 16 August.[41] It refers to Braithwaite's article in the *Quarterly Examiner* as of the first importance and gave a whole column to a summary—but with no reference either to the particular point about the need of the society to open itself up to scientific thought and higher biblical criticism or to the general point about the forthcoming conference. Who knew what, and in what direction Friends were having their thoughts directed, is thoroughly confusing.

The Executive minutes of August carry the matter no further and in September merely report that an outline of the proposed meetings has been read and considered, the details being left in the hands of the sub-committee for completion. In October, the Executive minutes make no reference at all to the conference. When the main committee met the following day it was presented for the first time with written material—a large elaborately printed "Provisional Programme" with the titles of the papers and a full list of chairmen and speakers. The minute reads:

> At this and our previous sitting we have engaged in considering the arrange-ments proposed by the Executive for the forthcoming Conference in Man-chester [a copy was attached]. After protracted and careful discussion they are with slight modification adopted. . . . The Executive is requested to endeavour to add another name to the list of those who are responsible for the introduc-tion of the subject "The Attitude of the Society towards Modern Thought".[42]

The headings of the sessions under which about thirty papers were scheduled were; Early Quakerism—its Spirit and its Power; Has Quakerism a message to the World to-day?; The Relations between Adult Schools and Mission Meetings and the Organisation of the Society of Friends; the Attitude of the Society of Friends towards Social Ques-tions; the Attitude of the Society of Friends towards Modern Thought; the More Effectual Presentation of Spiritual Truth; and finally, the Vitalizing of our Meetings for Worship.

Obviously it had been a difficult meeting. Here, six weeks before the occasion, was the first time the Home Mission Committee had seen a list of either subjects or speakers. There may well have been unease that only five of the names were those of Friends belonging identifiably to the evangelical main stream while at least fourteen names were of identifi-able emancipators. The latter included every one of the conference sub-committee as well as J. W. Graham, Edward Grubb and J. W. Rown-tree. Certainly there was alarm about two of the headings. For at the opening meeting of the conference itself, Theodore Nield, a member of the main committee but on this occasion welcoming the conference to Manchester as a local Friend, referred to the fear of some that "we are going to discuss social questions" and went on to justify their inclusion.[43] The much greater tension arose around "Modern Thought" for it was here that the only effective intervention was made by the main committee. The term "Modern Thought" was bound to raise hackles since it was a code word used to avoid, but to link, Darwinian Evolution and Higher Biblical Criticism. The three speakers on the provisional programme were Rendel Harris (b. 1852),[44] who had held a chair at Johns Hopkins University and was now reader in Palaeography at Cambridge; Silvanus Thompson (b. 1851),[45] Fellow of the Royal Society, and a distinguished theoretical and experimental physicist and electrical engineer; and J. W. Graham. It would have been difficult for any branch of the Christian Church to field a better team to present the liberating quality of "Modern Thought" to a lay audience. It is surprising that the Executive had not earlier insisted on the inclusion of an evangelical contributor. Maybe the sub-committee had convinced the Executive that it would be impossible to find an evangelical scholar of equivalent standing and unfair to invite a weak one. The one evangelical Friend who was a recognised Biblical scholar was Joseph Bevan Braithwaite, Sr. Maybe one of his sons had talked with him and found that, at the age of seventy-six, the old man had declined. For when, at about this time, a younger member of the family had asked him whether his outlook had been in any way affected by modern scholarship, his reply had been: "My dear, my mind was made up on these matters sixty years ago."[46] However that may be, the committee pressed its point and the upshot was Braithwaite's inclusion as one of the four contributors on "The Attitude of the Society of Friends to Modern Thought."

The obscurity of how the conference was planned, and how the minds of Friends were prepared for it, remains. In the event, the Manchester Conference captured the steady attention of a thousand Friends in residence, with thirteen hundred present for what proved to be the critical "Modern Thought" session.[47]

The first of these papers was by J. B. Braithwaite who sustained his conviction that the Scriptures alone were the ultimate test of Truth and that the archeologists were doing much to support this by authenticating the basic historicity of the Bible. He was followed by Rendel Harris of whom it was said that his lifelong love affair with Jesus Christ gave him an engaging freedom to reflect on the Scriptures.

"The doctrine of evolution. . . . is certainly not going to be restricted to protoplasm and zoology; it is just as applicable to the Scriptures, to Churches, to Sacraments, and will tell us just as romantic tales in interpreting the growth of these as it does in the lowest forms of animal life .... the question is our own attitude to our own thoughts, not whether we are afraid of thought, but whether we are afraid of thinking." Silvanus Thompson spoke of his thorough enjoyment in being a scientist, a Christian, and a Friend: "We have no right to neglect our intellects any more than we have to neglect our bodies." J. W. Graham dwelt on the limitations of words in the spiritual life: "The whole vocabulary of religion. . . . is earthborn metaphor. . . . All words used for the unseen are borrowed from things seen, so that words hinder thought in this supreme department."

The conference agenda allowed for papers to be followed by discussion from the floor. In this instance feelings for and against "Modern Thought" made themselves so immediately evident that peace of a sort was only kept by closing the session without discussion. The evangelicals were hurt that there was no room for the free expression of their emotions. Their response took another form later on.

The emancipatory impact of the session, and indeed of the conference as a whole, is captured by a reflective article in the *British Friend*:

> To many . . . it was as though their private and perhaps most hidden convictions were being fearlessly proclaimed from the house-tops and they felt it to be a new liberation of the soul.[48]

The divergence between the evangelical and emancipatory outlooks was steep but not divisive. Both were looking for ways of sharing their Christian Quaker experience with the outside world. What helped to sustain the unity of the society over the next ten years was that evangelicals and the emancipators were able to keep out of one another's way.

The first meeting of the Home Mission Committee following the conference was in February 1896. Minute four tidies up administrative details; it goes on to define, retrospectively, the objects of the Conference as: "the removal of misconceptions and strengthening the attachment of Young Friends. . . ." It concludes with satisfaction that "both these objects were promoted to a somewhat unusual degree. . . . We believe these questions and other important matters which arose . . . are of vital moment to the well-being of our Society and should continue to press upon the minds of Friends with the thought that further thought and action may result."[49]

And with that anodyne sentiment the Manchester Conference disappears for good from the minutes of the Yearly Meeting Home Mission

Committee, presumably because it was too divided to be able to initiate any action itself in the new direction. On a diminishing scale its "mission" work continued well into the twentieth century.

Yearly Meeting itself, in May 1896, received a remarkably uninformative report from the Conference Chairman. The two sessions on Social Questions received ten lines, Modern Thought even less: "several papers from various standpoints. No opportunity offered, however, for their discussion."[50] The weight of the evangelical hierarchy could still paralyse Yearly Meeting.

Yet further thought and action did, indeed, flow from the conference — but not through the official channels of the society. The follow-up to Manchester was pure private enterprise led by John Wilhelm Rowntree with a lively group of associates, particularly Edward Grubb, W. C. Braithwaite, Rendel Harris, J. W. Graham, Edward Worsdell, George Cadbury, and Rufus M. Jones. They instituted a great series of summer schools; they launched systematic adult religious education for Friends through the foundation of Woodbrooke and in other ways; they re-established the sustained publication of Quaker thought and experience through the series of "Present Day Papers" and the Swarthmore lectures; they initiated the writing of the great series of Quaker historical studies by W. C. Braithwaite and Rufus M. Jones.[51]

It was the amalgam of widely shared, sinewy study, teaching, learning and publication which provided the membership of London Yearly Meeting with the mental muscle to respond positively to the destructive pressures of the first World War and to look forward through its gloomy aftermath.[52] But toughness of mind would have been barren without the inspired sense of religious commitment which John Wilhelm Rowntree laid before the Manchester Conference in the words of prayer with which he concluded his own contribution:

> Then, O Christ, convince us by Thy Spirit, thrill us with Thy Divine Passion, drown our selfishness in Thy invading love, lay on us the burden of the world's suffering, drive us forth with the apostolic fervour of the early Church! So only can our message be delivered; — "Speak to the Children of Israel, that they go forward."[53]

John Wilhelm Rowntree died in New York in 1905 at the age of thirty-seven. After his death the seeds fertilised at Manchester were nurtured to maturity by his friends and by the resources of the Charitable Trust[54] founded by his father, Joseph Rowntree,[55] himself the author of one of the seminal papers at the Manchester Conference.[56]

But that's another story.

NOTES

1. The title refers to a conference which was held that year. See *Proceedings of the Conference of Members of the Society of Friends, held, by direction of the Yearly Meeting, in Manchester from eleventh to fifteenth of Eleventh Month, 1895* (London, 1896). Hereafter abbreviated as *PMC*.

2. Roger Wilson, "Friends in the Nineteenth Century," *Friends Quarterly*, October, 1984, pp. 353-363.

3. *Epistles from the Yearly Meeting of Friends*, London, II, 1858, p. 272.

4. *PMC*, p. 111.

5. The names of members and their quarterly meetings are included in London Yearly Meeting Minutes, 1894, pp. 33-34. Hereafter abbreviated as *LYM*.

6. London Yearly Meeting Home Mission Committee Minutes and its Executive Committee Minutes, 1882-1896, Friends House Library, London. Hereafter abbreviated as *HMC* and *HMCE*, respectively.

7. *LYM*, 1882, pp. 21-33. *Friend*, 6th mo., 8, 1882, pp. 137-147. *British Friend*, 6th mo., 1882, pp. 138, 146, and 7th mo., pp. 175-179. Throughout their nineteenth century existence these two journals had different editorial policies; therefore I often cite them both. However, they seem to have shared reports of spoken contributions in yearly meeting.

8. *LYM*, 1892, p. 26. The number had risen from twenty-six in 1891.

9. *A Reasonable Faith: short religious essays for the times, By three 'Friends'*, (London, 1884); see also "A Reasonable Faith," *Friends Quarterly*, October, 1894.

10. Edward Worsdell, *The Gospel of divine Help*, (London, 1896); see also *Friends Quarterly*, October, 1984.

11. *LYM*, 1888, pp. 27-48; *Friend*, 6th mo., 8, 1882, pp. 158-164; *British Friend*, 6th mo., 1882, pp. 153-157.

12. Joseph Bevan Braithwaite, Diary (MS), 1893, p. 93, Friends House Library, London.

13. Allen Jay, *Autobiography*, pp. 361-362, (London, 1910); see also J. B. Braithwaite, "Notes on the Richmond Conference," *Friends Quarterly Examiner*, 4th mo., 1888, pp. 272-288.

14. J. B. Braithwaite Diary, 6th mo., 21, 1888, pp. 286-289.

15. J. Dudley, *Life of Edward Grubb*, (London, 1946).

16. *Friend*, 27 May 1892, pp. 353-357, and 10 June, p. 389; *British Friend*, 6th mo., 1892, pp. 127-132, and 7th mo., pp. 5, 146-147.

17. *Friend*, 28 October 1892, pp. 711-712, 721-722; November, pp. 744-754; *British Friend*, 11th mo., 1892, pp. 260-268, 12th mo., pp. 284-286.

18. *LYM*, 1893, pp. 32-34; *Friend*, 2 June 1893, pp. 356-359. *British Friend*; 6th mo., 1893, pp. 168-171.

19. *British Friend*, 1st mo., 1893, p. 1. The new motto was from 1 Corinthians: "For the Kingdom of God is not in word but in power," reaching back to the Yearly Meeting Epistle of 1827, when the orthodox Quietist strain was struggling to define itself in face of the growing vitality of the evangelicals.

20. Thomas and Emmott, *William Charles Braithwaite*, (London, 1931).

21. John Wilhelm Rowntree, *Essays and Addresses*, ed., Joshua Rowntree (London, 1905), "Introductory Biographical Sketch," pp. ix–xlvii.

22. *Friend*, 16 December 1892, p. 828.

23. *Friend*, 2 June 1893, p. 350; *British Friend*, 6th mo., 1893, pp. 148–149.

24. "Is There not a Cause? The Society of Friends and the Late Home Mission Committee," anon., (London, 1893), Friends House Library, London.

25. *LYM*, 1894, pp. 33–34.

26. *British Friend*, 6th mo., 1894, p. 168.

27. *HMC*, October 1894, minute 3, p. 30.

28. *Friend*, 12 October 1894, pp. 654–656.

29. *HMC*, February 1895, pp. 75–79.

30. Caroline Stephen, *Quaker Strongholds*, (London, 1890).

31. *HMC*, October 1894, p. 10.

32. *Friend*, 27 May 1892, p. 353; *British Friend*, 6th mo., 1892, p. 127.

33. *LYM*, 1895, p. 54.

34. *HMC*, 30 May 1895, minute 5, pp. 110–111.

35. *HMCE*, 31 May 1895, p. 135.

36. *HMCE*, 7 June 1895, p. 144.

37. S. E. Robson, *Joshua Rowntree*, (London, 1916).

38. *HMCE*, 3 July 1895, p. 152.

39. *HMC*, 4–5 July 1895, minute 7, p. 126, and minute 15, p. 134.

40. *Friends Quarterly Examiner*, 7th mo., 1895, pp. 321–341.

41. *Friend*, 16 August 1895, pp. 539–540.

42. *HMC*, 3 October 1895, minute 10, p. 144.

43. *PMC*, p. 14.

44. I. Pickard, *Memories of J. Rendel Harris*, (Woodbrooke, 1978); also H. G. Wood, *Woodbrooke, 1903–1953*, Ch. II, "The First Director of Studies," (London, 1953).

45. J. S. Thompson, *Silvanus Thompson, Life and Letters*, (London, 1920).

46. *Joseph Bevan Braithwaite*, by His Children, (London, 1909), p. 88.

47. *PMC*, pp. 203–247.

48. *British Friend*, 11th mo., 1895, p. 299.

49. *HMC*, February 1896, minute 4, pp. 170–171.

50. *LYM*, 1896, pp. 21–24.

51. Roger Wilson, "We Shall Never Thrive upon Ignorance," in *A Quaker Miscellany for Edward Milligan*, ed., Blamires (Manchester, 1985).

52. Thomas C. Kennedy, "The Quaker Renaissance and the Origins of the British Peace Movement, 1895–1920," *Albion*, 16, 3 (1984): 243–272.

53. *PMC*, p. 93.

54. Roger Wilson, "Of Changing Faces and Strengthening Hands," *Report of the Joseph Rowntree Charitable Trust*, 1982–4, York, pp. 36–37.

55. Ann Vernon, *A Quaker Business Man,* (York, 1981).

56. *PMC*, pp. 266–272.

Additional Sources

In addition to references identified in footnotes, the following sources have been of general use:

The Friend, published in London monthly from 1843 till 1892, and subsequently weekly. It changed the identification of months from ordinal number (1st Month) to secular designation (January) at the same time.

The British Friend, published in Glasgow monthly from 1843, and later on from London, Birkenhead, and back to London.

Rufus M. Jones, *The Later Periods of Quakerism*, Vol. 1, Chapter ix.

Richenda Scott, "Authority or Experience," *Friends Historical Society Journal*, (London, 1960).

Richenda Scott, "Tradition and Experience," Swarthmore Lecture, London, 1964.

E. B. Bronner, *The Other Branch*, Friends Historical Society (London, 1975).

The Friends and
Academic Freedom:
Some Experiences and
Thoughts of
Henry J. Cadbury

Throughout his long life, Henry Joel Cadbury, New Testament scholar and leading American Quaker, insisted that belief could follow action as well as action, belief. The religious impulse which in some persons led to a mystical opening, and in others, a theological insight, in still others might take the form of principled action. The action in turn could deepen spiritual sensitivity and lead to a more profound commitment to a Christian ethic. It was a way of restating the early Quaker message that if one took a step in the light, more light would follow.

This proposition is well illustrated in Henry Cadbury's own experiences with academic freedom. An interest which stemmed originally from a liberal Christian perspective became one of the abiding concerns of his life after he himself had known various curtailments of that freedom. The original basis of these experiences was his commitment to the Quaker peace testimony in time of war, but his concern broadened through the years to embrace many other aspects of academic freedom, in particular, and civil liberties in general. His knowledge of Quaker history led him to be a frequent resource to civil libertarian lawyers on such matters as the right of Jehovah's Witnesses to refuse to salute the flag, the right of young non-registrants for the draft, of tax refusers, to have their day in court, and the right of persons accused of subversion to take the Fifth Amendment. He was often an expert witness in such cases, sometimes at great personal expense. He might well have pursued these interests if he himself had not been involved, but the compassion he felt for victims of infringements of liberty clearly stemmed from his own experiences as victim.

163

Active with the Young Friends movement before the outbreak of World War I, Henry Cadbury was one of the organizers of the Friends National Peace Committee in 1915, a group which wrote to all monthly meetings, urging them to remain true to the Quaker peace testimony, and began to make plans for conscientious objectors in the event of the American entry into the war. He also gave a series of public lectures on the psychology of peace and war, wrote articles on the Christian view of war, and addressed a series of letters to the public press urging President Wilson to try mediation, and defending the pacifist position. As chairman of the Friends National Peace Committee he was the convenor of a meeting 30 April 1917 of all branches of the Religious Society of Friends to form a new group, the American Friends Service Committee, to provide "a service of love in wartime," as a witness for peace and an outlet for young conscientious objectors. Thereafter Henry Cadbury was deeply involved in the Committee, serving as a volunteer executive secretary in August of 1917, and working especially hard to counsel individual conscientious objectors on their options in what became a confused situation because of the government's unwillingness to provide any clear-cut alternatives to military service. He was soon commuting between the Service Committee's new office at 20 South 12th Street, Philadelphia, the War Department in Washington D.C., and the Haverford College campus, where he lived and taught.

Henry Cadbury had been a student at Haverford from 1899 to 1903 under President Isaac Sharpless. When he first became interested in entering the field of biblical literature, he had consulted Sharpless, who had encouraged him to continue his Harvard studies in this area. In 1910, when Cadbury was still working on his Ph.D., Sharpless invited him to join the Haverford faculty as Instructor in Greek. Sharpless's faith in the young scholar was rewarded; Cadbury's brilliant Ph.D. dissertation at Harvard, "The Making of Luke/Acts," won him recognition in the world of New Testament scholarship, and in 1916 he became secretary of the Society of Biblical Literature, the youngest man to hold that post. In 1914 Cadbury received his degree; in 1915 Sharpless offered him the post of Assistant Professor in Biblical Literature for a term of three years, and in 1917 promoted him to a five year term as Associate Professor in the same field. According to rules of tenure developed by Sharpless in 1915, no assistant or associate professor was to be discharged except after a conference between a faculty and Board Committee, and an opportunity to state his case.

In 1917, Isaac Sharpless resigned and William Wistar Comfort, a Haverford graduate of 1894, and the head of the modern language department at Cornell, came to Haverford as the new president. He walked into a unique situation; the AFSC was using the Haverford campus to train men for overseas duties and two of his professors, Rufus Jones and Henry Cadbury, were constantly away from the college, working for AFSC in Philadelphia and in Washington, D.C. Rufus Jones was a highly respected figure throughout Quakerdom, and kept a low profile in the press, but Henry Cadbury did not. In April just after the American entry into the war, he had written a rather argumentative letter to the *Philadelphia Public Ledger*, in response to an editorial which suggested that pacifists were treasonable. Clearly, he was beginning to see himself as something of a public spokesperson for the pacifist view, and the local papers so perceived him.

In mid-September of 1917, just a few weeks after classes began at Haverford under the Sharpless administration, Cadbury was the subject of an attack in *The Press*. Under the headline "Quakers Prepare for Acts Which May Violate Law," *The Press* revealed that a letter and questionnaire mailed in a plain brown wrapper, had fallen into their hands. The letter, written by Cadbury, stated that AFSC believed there could be no division of military service between combatant and non-combatant, and asked each individual to make his decision at the "high tribunal of his own conscience," then let the committee know if he had decided to go voluntarily to a mobilization camp or not. "On several occasions statements have been made by Dr. Henry Joel Cadbury, chairman of the Philadelphia Young Friends Committee which has shown the willingness of Friends to ignore the law if it does not coincide with their own ideas of what should be done," the newspaper reported accusingly.[1]

It was a time of passionate patriotism, and not all Friends were loyal to the peace testimony. Just after the United States entry into the war, some 120 members of Hicksite meetings signed a public letter announcing their view that in this particular crisis all Christians should support the national cause. No such public expression came from the Orthodox Friends, but many were wavering. Alumni and students at Haverford were divided, and the college administration undoubtedly felt the brunt of criticism whenever the Quaker position against war hit the public press.

Henry Cadbury could not accept the idea of a division of opinion among Quakers over pacifism, and he could not keep quiet about his sentiments. In early 1918 he wrote an article for the *Friends Intelligencer*, asking "Are We Honest?" and pointing out that though Friends bodies had unanimously approved the peace testimony, individual Friends felt free to disregard it, and some representative members of the Society had actually encouraged participation in the military.

> To a certain extent any representative of the Society who by word or example commends as justifiable for Friends any form of participation in war, either voluntary or compulsory, makes if not himself, at least others guilty of perjury.[2]

There was a note of frustration and of sharpness in the piece. Henry Cadbury lived by his own high standards, and as a young man he expected the same of his colleagues, especially those who were members of the Society of Friends. While many of his fellow teachers have spoken of his popularity, others who felt the sting of his disapproval were not so sure that he was universally liked at this juncture in his career.

The war hysteria was clearly threatening academic freedom. Scott Nearing had been dismissed by the University of Pennsylvania in 1915; Emily Greene Balch would soon suffer the same fate at Wellesley. In an article published in the March issue of the *Haverfordian*, "Freedom of Thought and the Colleges," Henry Cadbury argued that such freedom was not so much a right as a duty, for students as well as for faculty. New ideas had to be explored with a certain detachment if solutions to world problems were to be obtained. And how were minds to remain free if hysteria against all things German prevailed?

> Even before the war we had begun to hear a good deal about academic freedom. It was then something so largely "academic" as to seem a very minor issue. It was something quite commendable, to be sure, the right of scholars to seek the truth fearlessly without restraint of loss of station. It was a protest against the arbitrary treatment of professors according to the economic interests of trustees or the political prejudices of state legislatures. The war has made this need more apparent by certain flagrant cases of patriotic academic execution. But after all, this kind of liberty is not the great need. It is a question of rights: I would plead for academic freedom as a duty, and a duty for students more than for faculties. . . . Most Americans were shocked at the Manifesto of the ninety-three German intellectuals justifying the war. It appears to have been prepared and signed by imperial request. But how much more shocked we should be if such general agreement were due not to special pressure but to the more imperious force of a perverted public opinion. The latter is apparently our greatest danger here.[3]

As the months passed, Henry Cadbury became more and more upset to see the anti-German passions in which the nation was indulging sweep aside all logic. Even the Society of Biblical Literature capitulated; one scholar suggested that Biblical scholarship in this country break its dependence on the German scholars. "We can no longer go to school to a nation against which we feel a moral aversion."[4]

The American Friends Service Committee experienced a growing complex of problems at this time. Vincent Nicholson, the young executive secretary, was drafted, and though Rufus Jones attempted to use his influence, he failed to obtain an exemption for him. The Committee needed to find a successor immediately. In early July, Rufus Jones wrote to President William Comfort, asking if Henry Cadbury could be spared for the next academic year to take Vincent Nicholson's place. Comfort wrote back tersely that Haverford could not release Cadbury unless he would continue to teach twelve hours of elementary Greek while heading up the A.F.S.C., "but I suppose he could not do so." The A.F.S.C. should look in other directions, Comfort urged. The tone of the letter suggests frustration with Cadbury's preoccupation with the Committee, and perhaps also with his habit of making his unpopular view public.[5]

In the fall of 1918, Henry Cadbury read the newspapers with growing despair. The hatred expressed against Germany seemed to be cresting to unbelievable heights as the allied armies advanced toward the Rhine and Germany made peace overtures. All his sense of outrage at the abandonment of Christian toleration or even human decency toward the enemy, he poured out in a letter to the *Philadelphia Public Ledger*, written on college stationery:

Haverford College, October 7, 1918
To the Editor of the Public Ledger
Sir:

As a Christian and patriotic American may I raise one cry of protest in your column against the orgy of hate in which the American press and public indulges on the receipt of peace overtures from the enemy. Whatever the immediate result of the present German request for an armistice, the spirit of implacable hatred and revenge exhibited by many persons in this country indicates that it is our nation which is the greatest obstacle to a clean peace and the least worthy of it. Never in the period of his greatest arrogances and successes did the German Kaiser and Junkers utter more heathen and bloodthirsty sentiments than appear throughout our newspapers today. Intoxicated with the first taste of blood and flushed with victory, the American public hastens to condemn in advance the soberly phrased pleas of a conciliatory foe. While the English press wisely refrains from comment until an official answer can be given, Americans with insatiable lust for vengeance cry More! More! Every concession on the part of the enemy is counted as a mark of weakness and is made an excuse for more humiliating and unreasonable demands. While the war-weary people of Europe long for peace, we conceited newcomers into the fight prefer to sacrifice their youth and ours by the millions in order that we may dictate a peace to suit our insane hysteria. Surely it behooves us at this hour, when not retaliation for the past but the assurance of a safer and saner international fellowship is the world's need, distinguishing justice and mercy from blind revenge, to keep ourselves in the mood of moderation and fair play. A peace on other terms or in any other spirit will be no peace at all, but the curse of the future. Signed: Henry J. Cadbury.[6]

Of all the letters Henry Cadbury had written to the press during the war years, this one, published on 12 October, was the most angry, and it produced an immediate, angry response. Many letters were written to the *Ledger* denouncing Cadbury as neither a Christian nor a patriot, and reiterating the charges of German outrages. Similar letters poured into Haverford from angry alumni. By using college stationery, was Henry Cadbury implying that his views were those of the college? Many of the non-pacifist alumni had been disturbed the past summer when Haverford had refused the War Department's invitation to establish an army training group on campus. Now they demanded that Cadbury be dismissed immediately in order to make it clear that Haverford did not share his unpatriotic views. A group of twenty alumni met with former President Isaac Sharpless to press for his dismissal. Henry Cadbury also received anonymous threats to lynch him, and to burn his house down.

Both Henry Cadbury and his wife, Lydia Brown Cadbury, were stunned by this response. Cadbury immediately went to see President Comfort to explain that his letter had not been intended as an attack on anyone, but only a call to Christian principles. The interview was apparently not a great success, and afterwards Cadbury put down some of his thoughts in writing:

> The letter was intended to bespeak the same Christian freedom from hate and revenge which President Wilson and Secretary Lansing so finely expressed in their recent speeches. It was not intended to express an opinion on the relative guilt of the belligerents, on peace terms, or on any other matter of national policy. Owing however to the present tense state of public feeling and the vigor of the language in which my views were expressed it has caused more comment than I anticipated. I freely confess this error in judgment, and so far as the results affect myself I shall bear the personal disadvantage as deserved. I can make this confession the more readily as I know thee will construe it as no surrender of cherished Quaker principles but as the confession of one whose judgment is fallible and whose zeal is not always wise.
>
> Equally surprised am I at the way some persons have associated the position of an individual on matters of national morality with the institution in which he teaches Greek. For this I have the deepest regret.[7]

Regret, unfortunately, turned out to be not enough. More criticism poured into the college. It became apparent that the only way Cadbury could defuse the issue for the administration was to resign. Rufus and Elizabeth Jones came next door to confer with the Cadburys. No one knows what went on in this interview, but it seems apparent that Rufus Jones had no alternative course to offer. In the course of the interview, Henry Cadbury wept, according to family recollection. The realization that he would actually have to resign from the college where he had been a student for four years and a teacher for eight, was to be remembered as the most painful of his life.

On 21 October he submitted his resignation, and on 24 October he wrote a letter to the faculty saying that his attitude was one of "confessed indiscretion and sincere penitence."[8]

A special meeting of the Board of Managers had been called on 22 October to consider the situation. President Comfort defended Cadbury's scholarship and integrity, but said that "certain personal characteristics and combative tendencies lessened his usefulness." Former President Sharpless spoke to the same effect. Board members agreed on "their unanimous emphatic disapproval of the letter," which they described as "this indiscretion on his part, following, as it did, numerous similar but less serious ones." They were, however, divided about equally between those who thought Henry Cadbury's resignation should be accepted immediately and those who feared that such action would be a blow to academic freedom. A subcommittee was appointed to consider the case and make a public statement. As a result, an article appeared in the *Philadelphia Evening Bulletin*, which reported that Henry J. Cadbury, "who bewails the fact that America is not ready yet to shake hands with the Huns . . . will have to give up his college position," and that no one on the Haverford Board disagreed.

> 'There was absolutely no division on the question of the impropriety of Mr. Cadbury's public statement,' said Asa S. Wing, president of the Haverford College Board . . . 'There was a division, however, on the question of academic freedom and the dignity of taking too precipitous action on the matter.'[9]

At a second special meeting of the Board held 1 November, the committee recommended that Cadbury be given a leave of absence for the rest of the academic year, and his resignation reconsidered no later than March. The Board accepted this recommendation, along with the statement:

> The precious privilege of free judgment and utterance where the conscience is truly concerned, Haverford College respects and maintains. But the habit of

169

temperate judgment and consideration for the feelings of others with whom one has associated oneself should always characterize the utterances of a scholar, especially upon matters touching the public conscience. We hold that Professor Cadbury in his letter to the Public Ledger of October 12 reflected upon the integrity of the present spirit and aims of a vast majority of our fellow citizens, and used intemperate and unjustified language, which Haverford College repudiates.[10]

Apparently neither the faculty nor the students raised any protest to this decision. They knew that Cadbury was being given leave with pay and the opportunity of being reinstated in March. Technically, one could not say that he had been dismissed, and the question of tenure was therefore not involved. Many stressed his insensitivity in appearing to speak "for the whole." Since he had annoyed at least some of his colleagues with his strong pacifist stand, the general view seems to have been that he had created the situation. By apparently accepting the Board's decision, and keeping a low profile, he helped to confirm this view.

Yet Cadbury did not want to back down abjectly from a principle which he still believed to be right. Among his papers there has survived an interesting exchange of letters with Clarence Pickett, a Friend from Kansas whom Cadbury had first met at the Winona Lake Peace Conferences. Pickett was now a Quaker pastor in the town of Oskaloosa, Iowa. His pacifism here was so unpopular that his house had been painted with yellow stripes and members of his own Meeting had offered to buy a war bond for him to prove his loyalty. Hearing of Cadbury's troubles, Pickett wrote to express sympathy. Cadbury's response reveals that he was not yet settled in mind about the Haverford experience:

> Dear Clarence,
>
> Your letter of sympathy was needed and appreciated and I hear you are having troubles of your own. Well, let's "stick it". Of course I don't wish to defend myself. I was said to be intemperate and indiscreet. But as thee says we mostly err on the other side. I am impressed with how different the penalties are for missing the golden mean on its two sides. Over-caution rarely gets what thee and I get. I am most concern (sic) to convert it all into good—with thy assistance and friendship.[11]

Meanwhile, the Selective Service agents had reported Henry Cadbury to the United States District Attorney, Francis Fisher Kane, as a traitor, and Cadbury was asked to appear at Kane's office to defend himself. Fortunately Kane's view of the Espionage Act was a liberal one, and it may be also that he felt that Haverford's professor had suffered enough.

Throughout the rest of his life, Henry Cadbury reflected on his suspension from Haverford as a turning point in his life. Had it not occurred he might have gone on quietly teaching at Haverford, and never been known outside Quaker circles. But in a much deeper sense it changed him and shaped his emerging view of himself and of the role of religion in his life. He had never known that he would feel so deeply about pacifism, and that he would become — though inadvertently — known as one of the martyrs to academic freedom. The depth of the conviction that led him to take an unpopular stand seemed to well up from the bottom of his being, beyond his conscious choice. The experience of bearing the brunt of so much public anger, and trying not to be angry himself, in turn deepened his sense of conviction and of leading. Taking action, taking a stand, then could be seen as itself a road to spiritual growth. He had helped young men, with an incoherent feeling that they could not kill, find service with the AFSC, and through that service articulate an increasingly clear sense of what religious pacifism might mean. He would see himself thereafter as a traveler on that same road. The experience was a turning point also in his developing interest in the history of the Society of Friends. The delicate balance between the individual's freedom to seek and articulate the Truth — which left unchecked would lead to anarchy — and the group discipline of corporate decision making — which could and often did lead to inertia and conformity — became a theme of his. He himself represented the two tendencies — what one might call the yin and yang of Quakerism. He had grown up in the heart of the Society, eager to please and to conform, but harboring a questioning mind and a seeking heart. By vigorously advocating the peace testimony — just what a young Quaker should do — he had somehow overstepped the invisible line between appropriate and inappropriate behavior. To his intense surprise he found himself in the ranks of the small number of men and women whose prophetic voices had moved the Society forward in such testimonies as the abolition of slavery and the equal treatment of women, but who had suffered at the hands of the Society as a result. Henry Cadbury never saw himself as a radical, but he became interested in the lives of the Quaker radicals of the past, and supportive of those of his day, and he nudged the Society forward on many issues. At the same time, his interest in arriving at a true sense of the meeting grew, after the Haverford incident, until it became one of his characteristics. Never again did he risk the accusation of speaking for the group, unless he knew that the group supported him.

Having been suspended by Haverford, Cadbury was free to work for the A.F.S.C. By this time, however, the top positions for which he had been sought were filled. There was a need however for someone with Cadbury's gift with words to convert the unfolding story of Quaker service abroad into articles for religious publications. Cadbury became a volunteer public relations man. Later during 1920, he spent a summer touring the child feeding projects in Europe, and writing about them for the American press.

News that Henry Cadbury might be available for a new teaching post had meanwhile spread through the academic community during the early months of 1919. In February, Rufus Jones had an inquiry about Cadbury's teaching ability, along with the question of whether or not his pacifism was of the "offensive" sort. In mid-March, just before the deadline for Haverford's decision to act upon his earlier resignation, Henry Cadbury received an offer from Andover Theological Seminary in Cambridge to become assistant professor of New Testament for the academic year 1919–1920.

To be in Cambridge, where he could work with his former teachers on New Testament research, and have available one of the finest libraries in the country was an exciting prospect. It meant that the obscure Quaker scholar was gaining national recognition. Harvard University, with which the Andover Seminary was affiliated, had no pacifist background. Indeed some of its theologians had been active in war work. Yet the value placed on academic freedom and scholarship seemed absolute.

Henry Cadbury was, moreover, quite sure from the attitude of the president of Haverford and some members of the board that the passage of time had not diminished the anger felt against him for his fiery letter to the *Ledger* and that they were "against my retention, even for the remainder of my unexpired term of service," and intended therefore to accept his earlier letter of resignation.[12]

To forestall this, he wrote to inform the Board of Managers that he had accepted the Andover position and that they were free to consider this as a new letter of resignation, "unless you believe it to the advantage of the college to act upon my earlier offer to resign upon the basis suggested when that offer was made."

Although he may still have regretted the language he had used in the *Ledger*, Henry Cadbury by this time felt sure that Haverford was going to be embarrassed by the charge that it had violated academic freedom in placing him on leave the fall before, and he wanted to give the Board of Managers an opportunity to refuse to accept the original resignation and thus clear Haverford's good name.

> I have no personal desire to prevent such a decision, nor to take the matter out of your hands, but rather to offer you the opportunity to avert the unjust criticism which might have been brought upon the college by a disposition that you could have made of my case as postponed from your meeting in the

Eleventh Month. Of course I have no desire willfully to cut myself off from service to the college and to the ideals of a liberal religious education which your Board has cherished for Haverford and for the Society of Friends.[13]

President Comfort, however, chose to interpret the fact that Cadbury had accepted Andover's one-year offer as grounds for severing his connections with Haverford, and the college moved to accept his standing resignation. The case, as Cadbury predicted, became a famous one, and was included in a study of examples of wartime hysteria, *Preachers Present Arms.*[14]

A former student of Henry Cadbury's, William Henry Chamberlain, wrote about the incident in his *Confessions of an Individualist*, published in 1940:

The letter would have been generally recognized as elementary commonsense ten years, or even one year later. But the mood in America at the time was suggestive of a Soviet purge or a Nazi pogrom. . . . A chorus of vituperation was raised against Henry Cadbury, and Haverford, to its shame, bowed to the mob sentiment and let him go. This would certainly have seemed to be an issue on which a Friends college should have stood by a pacifist professor, even at the cost of a little, temporary unpopularity. Fortunately, Dr. Cadbury's subsequent academic advancement was not adversely affected by this incident.[15]

Haverford never formally apologized for its action, and at the time of preparation of *Preachers Present Arms*, in 1932, the Haverford administration would make no statement on the case. In 1933, however, at the time of the college's centennial, the Board awarded their now famous son an honorary degree. In the 1950s, when President Gilbert White invited Henry Cadbury, upon his retirement from Harvard, to return to Haverford to teach Quaker history, he did so with some sense of righting an earlier wrong.

In Cambridge, Henry Cadbury settled into his one year assignment at the Andover Theological Seminary with ease. Andover, founded in 1808 as the first school for the training of professional clergy in New England, had moved to Cambridge and became affiliated with the Harvard Divinity School in 1908. The two schools did not merge; Andover, founded by a strict Calvinist, was legally bound to the Andover Creed, a conservative statement under which each professor was supposed to promise that he would "maintain and inculcate the Christian faith . . . in opposition not only to Atheists and Infidels, but to Jews, Papists, Mohametans, Arians, Pelagians, Antinomians, Arminians, Socinians, Sabellians, Unitarians, and Universalists." Few modern theologians were willing to subscribe publicly to this creed, and by 1908 it was in abeyance, though still in place, preventing merger. But Harvard and Andover combined their libraries, and in 1911, when the new Andover Hall was built on Francis Avenue, there was a library wing with ample stacks for 200,000 books as well as a large reading room. Later in his career Henry Cadbury became the director of this library.

The one year assignment stretched to seven years, while Henry Cadbury, at the peak of his creativity, made important contributions to the methodology of New Testament study. He might have become a full professor had he been willing to forsake his Quaker principles against "the hireling ministry," and become an ordained minister. The dean of the school wrote to Rufus Jones in private to inquire whether Cadbury might in fact accept ordination without violating Quaker principles. Needless to say, this was not possible. However, he continued on a year to year basis, his growing popularity and scholarly reputation making his retention seem assured.

In 1922, a more complete merger of Andover and Harvard was arranged somewhat hastily. The Visitors of the Andover Theological Seminary, a somewhat pro forma body, felt that they had never been properly informed of, or approved, this merger and took the matter to court. In September, 1925, the Supreme Judicial Court of Massachusetts ruled that the merger was illegal, and that every Andover professor must subscribe to the Andover Creed. When this ruling became final in January of 1926, the whole faculty resigned. Most of the professors were subsequently hired by Harvard, but Cadbury as the most junior member of the faculty, and the only one not an ordained minister, was let go. Thus at age forty-two, and the father of three children, Cadbury lost his position a second time because of his beliefs.

This time there were many offers, including a tempting one from Yale, which wanted to prepare Cadbury to become head of the Divinity School. But the emphasis would be on the training of "hireling ministers," and Cadbury continued to feel that this was not possible from the point of view of his Quaker beliefs. In the end he went to Bryn Mawr as Professor of Biblical Literature. Back in his home community, he was able to play a significant role in Quaker affairs, including the founding of Pendle Hill, and serving as Board chairman of the A.F.S.C. It was, as he would have said, a congenial situation, and he remained there for nine years (including a one-year sabbatical at Woodbrooke in England and The American School of Oriental Research in Jerusalem) before accepting an urgent invitation to return to Harvard as the Hollis Professor of Divinity.

This should have been the happy ending to the saga, but for a time it appeared likely that Henry Cadbury might once more have to leave his position in the interests of academic freedom. In June of 1935 the State of Massachusetts had passed a law requiring all teachers to sign an oath of allegiance to the Constitution of the United States and of the Commonwealth of Massachusetts, and Harvard professors were not exempt. Henry Cadbury found that he had until November 30, 1935, to sign the oath, or lose his position.

As a Friend, Henry Cadbury was opposed to oaths. That could be easily remedied; he could instead file an affirmation. But more seriously, he was conscientiously opposed to the very concept of the loyalty oath and its threat to academic freedom. And as a pacifist he was aware that the pledge to support the constitution implied the use of force. Yet most of his learned colleagues urged him to sign. The contributions he was making to the field of New Testament scholarship and to the education of future scholars and preachers, they told him, were far more important than his uneasiness at taking such an oath. To sort out all the arguments that were advanced, Henry Cadbury wrote a play script, in the form of a dialogue between the harassed professor and all his volunteer advisers.

Several others at Harvard were in the same quandary. Dr. Kirtley F. Mather, a geologist, was refusing to sign on the grounds of civil liberties. Eventually he signed with qualifications and was able to continue to teach. Professor Earl Winslow at Tufts, a Friend, also refused to sign, and ultimately lost his position. So did another Tufts professor. A larger group, consisting of seven teachers at Andover-Newton Theological Seminary, and Dr. Seal Thompson, Professor of Biblical Literature at Wellesley College, and a good friend of the Cadburys, urged Cadbury to unite with them in joint action, demanding the right of signing with stated reservations. For the sake of this group, Cadbury undertook correspondence with the American Civil Liberties Union and a Boston law firm on possible courses of action.

After the painful sense of isolation he had experienced when suspended from Haverford, he felt the need of consulting widely before making a decision which might change the course of his life. Lydia Cadbury of course was supportive, but she had hated the episode at Haverford, and the thought of being again uprooted was disturbing. Cadbury wrote to Harold Evans, a Philadelphia lawyer, to Otto Reinemann, a Quaker scholar with German background, and to Joshua Cope, a Quaker ornithologist teaching at Cornell, to get their views. Evans felt he had taken a similar oath as a lawyer without much trouble, Reinemann did not see the parallel with the German oath, and Cope confessed he had not given the matter much thought.[16]

175

Hearing of his quandary, Friends in Philadelphia were fully sympathetic. The Board of Directors of Pendle Hill had offered Cadbury the job of director for that year. The position remained unfilled, and several board members wrote to assure Cadbury that if he felt he had to leave his Harvard position they would welcome him with open arms. So would Bryn Mawr. Clarence Pickett thought the AFSC ought to get behind a drive against such laws. The Yearly Meeting Peace Committee wrote that they were "shocked."

After much agony of spirit, Cadbury decided to unite with the Andover group in a joint protest, and to try to find a way to make the affirmation without violating his conscience. He first attempted to rewrite the wording on the blank. The state sent this back to him as unacceptable. He made a second effort to state his objection to the oath on a sheet of paper attached to the blank. This too officials returned.

A few days after the deadline, President James B. Conant called him in. Conant himself had objected to the oath but had signed it, stating that "it was unthinkable that Harvard should disobey the law," and on that same basis he had urged the Harvard faculty to sign. Cadbury approached the interview expecting the worst. Instead, Dr. Conant indicated that Harvard would refuse to accept a resignation, and asked if Cadbury would be willing for the University to use his case as the basis for testing the constitutionality of the oath. If they decided to do so, they would carry the case as far as the Supreme Court. They did not believe that they would win, but they thought they might at least gain time for a new legislature to come into being, and perhaps be able to keep Cadbury on the faculty for another two years while the case progressed through the courts. Cadbury wrote his brother Ben Cadbury to describe the interview: "This is the first sign of spunk in the University since the law was passed and I am cheered. But of course nothing is settled, still less public."[17]

Immediately after the interview with Conant, Henry Cadbury went to Yale to deliver some lectures. On his return he heard from his colleagues at Andover-Newton that they had decided to try once more to file with reservations. Seal Thompson was doing the same. Henry Cadbury decided to go along with this last ditch effort for the sake of the others. On 26 December he addressed a letter to Dr. James B. Conant and James G. Reardon, Commissioner of Education, outlining his objections to the oath.

> Any political control or dictation in education can easily become for a conscientious teacher a form of political interference with the free exercise of religion, and this is especially true of teachers who like myself are teachers of

religion or for those who teach in private or parochial schools. I may best illustrate the ground of my difficulties by referring to three traditional principles of the Religious Society of Friends (commonly called Quakers) a Society to which I have belonged since birth and whose religious sentiments I share.

(a) Honesty of speech is a proverbial Quaker tradition. This honesty applies to all utterances and not only oaths, to which Friends have long objected as profaning the Divine name and for which they have been allowed to substitute, as in the present instance, a solemn affirmation. A law requiring wholesale swearing or affirming, in a promise not explicit in wording, performed under coercion, either with mental reservations or without due consideration of authorized interpretation, they regard as tending to dishonesty in itself and as detrimental to the general standard of truth speaking in the community.

(b) The maximum of religious liberty has been a fundamental aim of Friends. To win it and to maintain it they have suffered abundantly, sometimes even unto death. Frequently they have suffered under laws which though ostensibly intended for political purposes were abused for religious persecution. Whenever in a position or in influence to do so they have advocated and established not for themselves only but for all forms of religion in fullest toleration.

(c) The Society of Friends has maintained that in every case of apparent conflict of loyalties, God is to be obeyed rather than man, and that the conscientious individual in such cases is justified in yielding neither to pressure nor to punishment nor to pleas of human sovereignty, law, necessity or defense. This principle is historically illustrated in practice in Friends' disobedience to the fugitive slave law and in nearly three centuries of continuous refusal to pay tithes or to assist directly or indirectly wars waged for or against the powers that be.

He stated that he was signing the attached affirmation conditionally and that if at any time he felt the law was jeopardizing freedom of thought and expression for himself or for others "I shall be at liberty to revoke the accompanying affirmation and the solemn promise therein contained." This letter must be kept on file both at the University and at the office of the Commissioner of Education, he stipulated.[18]

On 2 January 1936, came the prompt reply. The Commissioner was accepting his affirmation and, although it could not be a matter of public record, was going to file the accompanying letter. The same decision had been made for Cadbury's partners in conscience. For the moment the crisis had passed.

In February, Henry Cadbury was asked to give a lecture to the students and faculty of the Divinity School on the topic, "My Personal Religion." He spoke of his maturing concept of a religion of conscientious action, and illustrated what he had to say with the ordeal he had just been through:

When a man deals religiously with issues that others settle in other ways, in fact takes seriously the religious implications of behavior. . . . tries to practice fully the standards conventional religion officially endorses, and to make his whole life consistent if not conscious, he is in my opinion practicing religion as much as the one who skillfully builds the dialectic structure of a well rounded theology or as the man who through public and private devotion lives in that mystical drama of a religious imagination. . . .

. . . . If you could have lived with me through the strain of many weeks this autumn and early winter when I was dealing largely in the secret of my own conscience with the question of my relation to the teacher's oath, you might have seen what I mean by a living religion. I refer not to questions of my personal welfare, they never bothered me at all. But if real moral questions are at stake (even in a very slight degree) and if loyalties are genuinely in conflict, and if moral questions are only too easily confused with merely political or strategic considerations, a course of right action in personal behavior taxes much more than you might suppose the genuinely religious elements that a man can bring to such a problem. . . .[19]

At the Friends General Conference held at Cape May, N.J. the following summer he lectured on "The Quaker Concern for Academic Freedom." He mentioned William Penn's efforts to intercede with James II against filling the chair of Magdalen College, Oxford, with "a rogue and papist" in 1687, and the experience of Friends who suffered during the Revolutionary War for their refusal to take a loyalty oath. Academic freedom was necessary for the sake of the honest pursuit of the truth, he said. "Nor can the truth set us free, unless men are freed to seek the truth." But he spoke primarily of the special obligation of Friends to be vigilant:

Furthermore, as Friends we are interested in social change by the slow and peaceful method of education. The method and issues touch our special concerns: religious freedom from the state, the rights of conscience, militarism in education, pseudo-patriotism, the suppression of economic discussion and reconstruction, and sincerity in the taking of an oath.

What part can we play in the securing of academic freedom? We can know and interpret the signs of the times and help liberal public opinion by pointing out the futility of the measures used; prevent the passage of gag laws and secure by court decision or legislative repeal their nullification; join others in organizations working for this end; and we can bring the Society of Friends and the example of its institutions into line, and if necessary, take personal and institutional risks in defiance of such control.[20]

This was a much stronger statement in defense of academic freedom than his earlier article in the *Haverfordian*, written before his own first hand experience with its denial. True to his own admonition, Henry Cadbury kept close track of the passage of loyalty oaths by the various states, and the attempts to have them ruled unconstitutional. He also kept files on those individuals who refused to sign, most of them not subversives at all but Quakers like himself. During the McCarthy period, he became deeply involved in fighting the climate of fear and active in support of the cases of several public school teachers who refused to sign loyalty oaths. With several other Harvard professors, he signed a public advertisement in 1953 decrying the police state methods of the various government investigating committees, and declared that they would not testify if called upon to do so. A Massachusetts legislator, Thomas Dorgan, who called himself the father of the teacher's oath, wrote to the *Harvard Crimson* to say he felt that these same professors were bound by the oath they took to testify if called upon. Henry Cadbury drafted a spirited letter in response, saying that the promise he had made to support the Constitution would be violated if he testified before one of the investigating committees, which he believed themselves violated several Constitutional safeguards.

> If under these conditions I participate as a "witness" in a process which I thus regard I commit an offense — I violate the very oath which Mr. Dorgan and his associates once required me to take. To avoid this present crime and self incrimination I do well not to try to clear myself, as I could do, of charges of communism, violence or conspiracy, but to stick conscientiously to my former promise whatever the consequences.[21]

He continued to dig up examples from Quaker history of Friends who suffered because of their refusal to sign an oath. In 1955 he published an article, "Friends and the Law," in the *Friends Intelligencer* summarizing the experience of Friends in dealing with loyalty oaths as well as the right to refuse to incriminate oneself.[22]

This article caused a few critics to ask why Henry Cadbury had in fact signed the loyalty oath at Harvard, even with his stipulations. No one put the question directly to Cadbury, so we do not know what his answer might have been. It is clear from what he wrote at the time, and subsequently, that he felt he had battled with his conscience and come up with what seemed a right leading at the time. Characteristically, he might have said that the right answer for him might well be the wrong answer for another, and that the right answer at one point of time might not hold for today.[23]

Although he sought examples from the Quaker past on various issues facing modern Friends, he always made it clear that he himself did not believe that such examples sanctified present action. Friends' testimonies evolved as way opened, he believed. He was therefore delighted when he detected a new testimony in the making.

Such was the case with the developing sensitivity over the loyalty oath. In 1967 he wrote in his column, "Letters from the Past," in the *Friends Journal*, of his pleasure in the recent Massachusetts Supreme Court decision ruling the teachers' oath law invalid, and in the part Friends had played nationally in ending the era of the oath. Characteristically, he made no mention of his own role:

> To suppose the era is already near its end may be too optimistic. There has been some change of climate since the McCarthy era, but anti-communism is still a widespread preoccupation, as the war in Vietnam shows. The U.S. Supreme Court decisions have not been unanimous, and the lower courts may not act uniformly on the issue. Meanwhile, the role of Friends continues to be an interesting phenomenon not identical with early Friends' scruples against swearing; a sensitiveness — if not with uniformity or psychological clarity — to the implications of the objectionable legislation, and a tendency to act accordingly and not merely to voice dissent.[24]

For those who exhibited that sensitivity, and suffered as a result, Cadbury's support was never abstract. For the draft refuser, the tax refuser, the oath refuser, he was always cheerfully available, willing to travel, to testify, to produce nuggets of relevant Quaker history, to add a voice of calm reason to the situation. His encouragement to these risk-takers, coupled with his own experiences with academic freedom, helped the Society as it groped its way toward a new concern, and thereby wrote of a new chapter in Quaker history.

NOTES

1. *The Press*, 18 September 1917.
2. *Friends Intelligencer*, 3 August 1918.
3. *The Haverfordian*, March 1918.
4. Earnest W. Saunders, *Searching the Scriptures*, (Chico, Pa. 1982) p. 31.
5. William W. Comfort to Rufus M. Jones, 12 July 1918, Rufus M. Jones Papers, Quaker Collection, Haverford College Library.
6. *Philadelphia Public Ledger*, 12 October 1918.
7. Henry Cadbury to William Wistar Comfort, 16 October 1918, Henry J. Cadbury Papers, Quaker Collection, Haverford College Library.
8. Henry J. Cadbury to the faculty, 24 October 1918. Cadbury Papers.
9. *Philadelphia Evening Bulletin*, 23 October 1918.

10. Minutes, Haverford College Board of Managers, 1 November 1918, Quaker Collection.

11. Henry Cadbury to Clarence Pickett, 9 November 1918, Archives of the American Friends Service Committee, Philadelphia.

12. 1903 Haverford Class Letter of November, 1919, A.F.S.C. Archives.

13. Minutes, Haverford College Board of Managers, Quaker Collection, 21 March 1919.

14. Ray H. Abrams, *Preachers Present Arms*, (Scottsdale, Pa., 1933) pp. 230–231.

15. William Henry Chamberlain, *Confessions of an Individualist*, (NY, 1940) pp. 34–35.

16. Letters in the Papers of Henry J. Cadbury, Peace Collection, Friends Historical Library, Swarthmore.

17. Henry Cadbury to Benjamin Cadbury, 5 December 1935, Uncatalogued Cadbury Family Papers, Quaker Collection, Haverford College Library.

18. The Teachers' Oath and Religious Reservations, Henry J. Cadbury, mimeographed statement marked (not for publication at present), Henry Joel Cadbury Papers, Peace Collection, Friends Historical Library.

19. "My Personal Religion," Harvard Divinity School lecture, February 1936, Henry J. Cadbury Papers, Quaker Collection, Haverford College Library.

20. *Friends Intelligencer*, 1 August 1936.

21. Draft of a letter to the *Harvard Crimson* May 1953, Cadbury Papers, Swarthmore. This letter was apparently never published.

22. "Friends and the Law," *Friends Intelligencer*, June, 1955, vol. 112, No 23, pp. 320–323.

23. C. Marshall Taylor Papers, Friends Historical Library, Swarthmore. Restricted; used with permission of the Director.

24. "Helping an Era to End," in Henry J. Cadbury, *Friendly Heritage: Letters from the Quaker Past*, (Norwalk, Conn., 1972) pp. 312–314.

Thomas Kelly Encounters Nazi Germany: His Letter from Strasbourg, 1938

Thomas Kelly, a devout Friend and a philosophy professor at Haverford College, left for Germany in late June 1938 as an emissary of the American Friends Service Committee to offer spiritual support and to find out the condition of Friends under Hitler. He was also invited to give the annual Richard Cary Lecture at the German Yearly Meeting in August. He spent most of his time making visits with German Friends, and with other dissidents and Jews who had established close contacts with the Friends.

A letter to his family from Strasbourg, 16 August 1938, is of great significance for an understanding of Thomas Kelly's life.[1] It contains the fullest account he ever provided of the discovery which had begun in November or December 1937 and continued through the next summer of what he called "the experiences of Presence" or as "an increased sense of *being laid hold on* by . . . a gentle loving, but awful Power," resulting in a "new sense of unreserved dedication of oneself to a life of child-like dedication to God." Kelly insisted on the lack of connection between the experiences of that summer in Germany and these mystical openings. The new sense of dedication

> comes not out of the feeling one has of having looked into *awful depths* of human woe, overwhelming as that is. What I want to say does not grow out of any specific external influence—it seems to grow out of an *internal influence* which is so overmastering that I can only recognize it as God working within me.

Still, the same passion and understandings underlie both parts of the letter: that dealing with social and political Germany, and that dealing with his inner life and the inner lives of others whom he met.

The letter reveals an important aspect of Thomas Kelly's relationship with his wife during his period of religious upheaval. In the last pages of the letter, addressed solely to his wife, he pleaded with her for under-standing and companionship in his new inner life. As he said at the outset of the letter, he was afraid of seeming a wholly new person, which indeed he felt himself to be. Throughout the letters from earlier in the summer, he wrote, in a tone that seems at times almost pathetic, of how much he missed his family and could not bear the separation. He expressed deep anxiety for all the tasks his wife had to bear alone, and imagined what she and the children were doing at all times of day. His desire for daily companionship faded from his letters as he became more engrossed in the German situation, but reappeared here, as a desire for inner com-panionship, in the Strasbourg letter. There is no record of Lael Kelly's re-sponse to the changes in her husband's life.

The Strasbourg letter shows conditions in Germany during the summer of 1938 and vividly portrays the sufferings and powerlessness of Jews and dissenters in the Nazi regime. We can see how much an American in Germany could discover about Nazi totalitarianism, violence, propa-ganda, policy, and preparation for war, as well as how a well-educated American observer attempted to come to terms with Naziism before the war. Much that Thomas Kelly wrote from Strasbourg is now familiar; the Jew-hatred and the theory of blood purity, the omnipresent eye and cruelty of the Gestapo, the censorship and the propaganda, the emphasis on sport and the Hitler youth, and the economic renewal. Thomas Kelly was, of course, in an especially good position to see the suffering going on in Germany because the Society of Friends had developed extensive contacts with the Jewish community. Jews suffered insult, violence, discrimination, unemployment, and dislocation. Dissenters were being watched and, if they became too active, carted off to concentration camps. Terror had succeeded in paralyzing both Jews and dissidents. The "brave few" Thomas Kelly mentioned were capable only of symbolic resistance, such as refusing to say "Heil Hitler!" Most would not venture even that far, fearing for their own lives and the lives of their children. They were becoming desperate. "Dr. Heschel told of being in Vienna recently. In the apartment house he was in, scarcely a floor had not had its suicide." One could strive to save one's personal honor, like Pastor Mensching, "unswervingly honest" and careful that hate never enter his heart. Or one could try to emigrate. Neither was easy.

In writing back to America, Kelly realized that what he had to say would seem unreal, that it even could seem unreal to himself. "O, its all crazy, I know. The only thing about it is that it is *real*. One pinches oneself and asks, *Is this the world* or am I insane, that such crazy history should be in the making." Thomas Kelly had been traveling among those

184

Germans who had thus far been the main victims of the regime, and he had shocking things to say. He had to explain everything he said and argue against Nazi ideology and practice not only because he himself had to wrestle with the meaning of what he saw, but because the terrors of Naziism were new to much of his audience.

It has sometimes been suggested that the German people themselves did not know the full dimensions of the treatment of the Jews. But at least one foreign visitor had no trouble at all seeing their desperation and suffering. The persecution was public. "The treatment of the Jews is *so* scandalous that the German people as a whole apologize for it and look upon it as an aberration of their government. I have not yet met a single person who defended the present treatment." The German people knew about the treatment of the Jews, at least in 1938, but they could not or did not do anything about it.

In September 1939 more than a year after Thomas Kelly's letter from Strasbourg, there were 30,000 persons in concentration camps inside Germany, with something more than 100,000 in new camps in Austria and Czechoslovakia.[2] Nevertheless, Jews and dissenters continued to *live* in Germany throughout the summer of 1938, and they enjoyed a certain freedom of movement. Germany was still wide open to foreigners. The German Friends could hold their Yearly Meeting and invite Thomas Kelly to speak. He, in turn, could follow the contacts of German Quakers with dissidents and Jews to meet and talk with them. Hertha Israel could go into a restaurant if accompanied by non-Jews and could translate Thomas Kelly's lecture, even though she could not eat in a restaurant alone or have her name acknowledged in the printed translation. Other stories Thomas Kelly wrote down reveal the same ambiguity. A man could be arrested for tearing down anti-Jewish posters and then be freed within the hour by the regular police. A family could think to ask Thomas Kelly for a list of English books its son in concentration camp could try to translate.

Jews may have been desperate and dissidents may have been powerless, but "the restaurants are the same as ever, and life bustles along." To us, Germany in the summer of 1938 is an historical moment which will not stand still, rushing as it did toward world war and the death camps. But Thomas Kelly could insist, "There *is* a bright side," and Albert Martin, who had been in Germany longer than Thomas Kelly, could propose to the London Yearly Meeting that Quakers foster pacifism and internationalism among those Germans opposing Hitler. He believed Hitler was about to fall of his own weight. Admittedly, Martin's proposal did not get much support, both because many Friends backed away from the

Religious Society's being so straightforwardly political and because few could agree with his analysis.[3]

Thomas Kelly saw the angry Nazi militarism as the return of the pre-World War I military clique, given renewed life by the humiliation of Versailles. He agreed with the Germans who analyzed their character defect as a training in authoritarianism and obedience. He discovered the end of unemployment, which Hitler had effected by gearing up for war, on which so much of Germany's faith in Hitler was based. He saw the massive nature of Hitler's military preparations.

Neither European leaders nor Thomas Kelly wanted war. But he distinctly recognized the possibility when he wrote, "If, as is the possible thing, Germany *does* push by force into the East, that is the Balkans, or if the inflammatory situation in Czechoslovakia blazes, then they must have their western borders solid, against England and France. . . . But the nation is already at war. The atmosphere is tense." He saw war as possible, but not inevitable. "I see no real hope, in my *few weeks* experiences, except that the Party purify itself. . . . It may be, if no war breaks out—and Germany knows she can't risk a war inside a year or more—that in ten or twenty years some more reasonable form of totalitarian state may develop out of this, as personalities change through the years." Thomas Kelly wanted to hope for the best. He also seems to have felt he should hope for the best. "This gloomy picture *needs to be corrected* by more association with ardent supporters of the Third Reich. . . . There *is* a bright side . . . I am not sure but what, in the years' perspective, something will grow, of real value. We are all too near it to see it clearly. There are many honest, devoted earnest, thoughtful Germans who have hope that the good will *ultimately* outweigh the evil. I pray it does." The German Quakers, "extremely intolerant of any thought of good coming out of such a regime," could see more clearly than Kelly wished to admit.

Thomas Kelly did not talk directly of political action against Naziism, but he did talk about the positive "translation of *love* into *deed*" in a way that impressed his hearers. On 6 September he wrote a letter to Dr. Heschel expressing his thanks for the spiritual communion they had shared and exhorting him to find some practical way to take the sufferings of his people (the Jews) upon himself.[4] He never wrote down what such a practical way might be.

How Thomas Kelly came to terms with the suffering, oppression and terror of Nazi Germany had to have been shaped by the fact that he was returning to America in less than a month. He was ambivalent about leaving because it meant losing contact with deep, disturbing, compelling reality. In the last analysis, the situation in Nazi Germany was, for Thomas Kelly, an intellectual problem to be resolved in the mind, the wisdom gained to be applied in another, safer world. On 24 August he wrote to his family again, now from Zurich, giving a sort of abstract of the issues he had dealt with in Strasbourg a week earlier. He tried to gain some perspective on the picture he had painted, and to identify the personal significance of that summer's experience.

My dear Precious Ones: —
 . . . I feel now that much that I wrote in Strasbourg was onesided, in that it raved on about the dark side. But that fact itself is significant. — that I, a foreigner, only 2 months in Germany, should be so affected by the pressure of the situation there that it took a while for it to wear off. Now, I feel more balanced about the situation there. and can see many things of promise, in the midst of so much that is dark. But it is a relief to be in a republic again, where one may say what one likes, within the limits of politeness, without the shadow of a Gestapo system. — On the religious side of what I wrote, I feel the same, but believe I thrust out what I had to say so quickly and in short compass as to give no background for it. But, darling, one feels as if one can never live for oneself, in such a tragic world as this. Europe and Asia alike are in such tense states. Only America seems to remain, — a paradise: or is it a fool's paradise? And, on the other side, the wonders of the inner life have *so* amazingly opened up that I am astounded. It is as if one had caught a glimpse of Hell and of Heaven. And one must *be* what is the consequences of such a trust.[5]

The only mystery of provenance concerning the Strasbourg letter is whether or not it actually circulated from Maine to Wilmington to Philadelphia and back to Lael Kelly, as the postscript requests. Those who would have read it in Maine and Ohio are dead. Barbara Cary, to whom the letter was to have been sent in Philadelphia, is presently Barbara Curtis. She explains that most correspondence for the American Friends Service Committee at that time filtered through her hands, but she has no memory of this particular letter.

The Strasbourg letter was printed in part in *Thomas Kelly, A Biography*. Those parts of the letter omitted were large segments of the discussion of conditions in Germany. The *Biography* was concerned with outlining the course of Thomas Kelly's religious life and mystical "openings," so that it was the discussions of suffering of soul, compassion, and his own internal revelations and strivings which constituted the bulk of the letter as it was printed.[6] The long discussion of the treatment of the Jews was excised, as was most of the attempt to describe, explain, and come to terms with Naziism.

187

STRASBOURG, le Tuesday afternoon, Aug. 16, 1938
15, rue de 22-Novembre[7]
My own dear wife and precious precious children:[8] — This is the first time since July 1[9] that I am free to write without reserve. I crossed the border into France[10] in order to spend some time in writing, and I want to unburden my soul as I dare not do in Germany.[11] I must write to you about two things. 1st, the conditions in Germany, and 2nd the spiritual upheaval which such a summer has brought. I wonder if this letter will sound as if it came from another world and from another person than the ones you know. If so, that is correct. — But where shall I begin? First let me say that even in writing to you I shall not give *names* or *places*.[12] Until you have *lived* in this world of despair and fear and abysmal suffering of soul you can never know how serious the consequences of a chance anecdote may be, in the way of life imprisonment, beatings with clubs, family separations, death. This is the first thing you must learn in Germany, if you are with the oppressed and despairing — you must look to see if *anybody* can *possibly* see or hear, through a corridor. It is called *der deutsche Blick*, the German Glance, which is a bit of what is called *Galgenhumor*, or Gallows-humor. Many a time we have sat in the *middle* of a room and whispered. The Martins[13] always removed their telephone from the wall (it plugged in in two places) when they wanted to talk seriously. Now nine tenths of the time *nobody* hears. But there is *always* the *chance* that someone will hear. And that *chance* keeps *thousands* on edge. I called on one man in a certain city, whose leadership in earlier movements was nation-wide. He now runs a little shop as big as a hole in the wall, selling cigarettes to keep alive. We debated about telephoning to him, knowing the danger of phones being watched. Finally someone called him, whose voice he knew, and said he was sending a friend around to see him. And the man, when I arrived, took me upstairs to his apartment and there we talked alone. He told me how he jumped at every phone call, and how he had waited till he knew the voice. — Well, I could go on indefinitely telling of incidents which make people *on edge* all the time. *There is no security*, anywhere, for the great masses of people. And when this goes on and on and on, year in and year out, no wonder the German people are *sick*. I'm amazed they are as well, spiritually, as they are. But I must not plunge into the dark side too soon, as though that were all. On the surface, Germany is *spruced up*, slicked up, freshly painted. Great public works are in progress, some of them much more fantastic than any W.P.A. projects, in their lavishness and thoroughness. Unemployment is entirely gone, etc, etc. And if one looks at such things one feels that this is the bloom-time of Germany. That is what

hasty tourists see. And there are *plenty* of Germans who are convinced that this is great, and that, in spite of the terrible shortness of money, or lowness of pay, they're on the upgrade at last. New super-highways are built, like the one between Worcester and Boston, Hitler is trying to get it so that Germans can run autos like Americans, etc. The *material* side of life is fostered in every possible way, to the cheapening of the *real* German soul, that has been much deeper than such material things. And, in other ways also, Naziism can be looked on as having some good in it. It has emphasized the good of the group, in a way that is at the opposite pole from our American individualism. But that good-of-the-group has gone to such extremes as to destroy *so* much of individuality and initiative and responsibility and ability ever to rectify their own mistakes by self-criticism. The almost fantastic group-consciousness of being das *Deutsche* Volk is unbelievable. Love of land and country can turn into a *narrowing, cramping* — thing. The *Nationalism* of National Socialists is a *wild* and *crazy* frenzy, tinged with a pathetic beauty. On the *socialist* side of the National-Socialist idea there is this sense of the importance of the *whole*. Der Einzelne ist nichts, das Volk ist alles.[14] It has in it a touch of *democracy*. For if *all* are Germans, then their Germanism is a *levelling* medium, and all are one brothers together. This expresses itself in the schooling of children, so that there are few chances for an *aristocratic* education. — One thing that strikes me right away is the *terrible* difference the loss of a free press makes. The tentacles of the government reach out *over all*, All newspapers are the *same* newspaper. And the news is not reported in an *objective* fashion, but always the reader is told, by suggestion how the events are to be interpreted. And it is wild to read the accounts of doings in other countries. All other countries, (except Italy and Japan) are just babies, or awkward callow youths. Only the Germans are sensible. It is Laughable to read. And one wonders how England and France and the U.S.A. ever have managed to wobble into world-powers. And Germany is bent upon becoming a *political* wizard. Hitler, or one of the top men, has said that Germany now has abandoned her old function of producing poets and thinkers, and is now going to excel in politics. But if there is anything that Germany can never excel in, it is *politics*. They lack the subtle touch, and the ability to appreciate other views than their own. One hears it said, and I am beginning to wonder if it is not so, that Germany suffers from an inferiority complex. Sub-consciously she feels her defects, and so *over*-blows her own horn. And one doesn't announce beforehand one's intention to become great in a certain department of human culture. That is a matter which arises as an acknowledgement of an *accomplished* fact. It is as absurd as the recent celebration of *Kunst* or Art, in Munich. The newspapers, that is, the government announced, Now we will think about art. Now we shall do great things in *this* field. But art never can arise by a command from a government.—it grows out of the inner richness of souls who are much alone. Some of the utterances of Hitler on art were recognized everywhere as laughable, sad platitudes, trite sayings. There are many, many, who pay no attention to the newspapers at all. Why *should* they? —I will talk later about the Juden-hass, of Jew-hatred. But in this connection I must speak of the weekly magazine, or journal, *Der Stürmer*, that spews out Jew-hatred in its most tragi-comic form. I have for some time been afraid to try to bring home copies, feeling they would be confiscated at the border as putting Germany in a bad light. But I am told that the party, is *proud* of Der Sturmer. But it is so infantile. It has no really sound arguments. It just pictures the hook-nosed Jew in all forms of vulture activities, week after week after week. —While on the matter of newspapers I must pass over to the intellectual life. There is a serious development of *sport* here, a theory of mind-body as a unity, which is being driven to the limit. When Germans get hold of an idea they *do* have hold of it, and ride it to death. One sees soccer fields, and handball courts. etc. (Tennis is an *aristocratic* game and has none of the wide development we know.) The boys and girls are schooled to train and discipline their *bodies*, to harden them, to have great endurance, never flinching. A mental attitude of hard resolution is cultivated along with the physical side. In Breslau, 3 weeks ago they had a great national sport carnival with 600,000 people there, and all the power of the Reich on display. —what a bitter blow it was when Joe Louis knocked out Max Schmeling in 2 minutes! They had expected to show, through that prize fight, the superiority of *German sport* training,—but this drive on *sport* leaves the student less of a *student*. Parading, marching, hiking, all sorts of things, have reduced the academic level of the school system seriously. Switzerland has compelled all *German* students who come to Switzerland for educations, to start *one year lower down* in the university scale than formerly. Last night I was at supper with a *very* cultured family, in which the daughter reported, laughing, the absurdities of teaching she was having to listen to. From a scientific point of view, I told her, some of the stuff she reported was 1890 stuff. The intellectual level of the schools is *so* seriously crippled. And, add to this the fact that the small school children are taught *systematically* what we would loudly call *propaganda*. Teachers *must* teach what the party tells them, or lose their jobs, And the old time respect for the teacher has disappeared. The pupil is the boss. He listens to what is said in the class room, and reports at home what he is taught.

If the teacher isn't teaching what he is supposed to, or makes any slip, he is thus reported to officials, who chuck him out. One hears varying estimates of how whole-heartedly the students accept what they are taught. Some say they accept it completely. Some say there is much inward criticism among the young people themselves, then you discover how wholly impossible it is to get any estimate of young peoples' opinions. They are in the Hitler Jungend.[15] They are moving about in *troops*. They *don't* and *can't* make Ausflugs[16] privately, as was formerly the case. I was with one girl who had been in prison about 6–8 weeks for going on an unauthorized, non-Hitler Jungend Ausflug.[17] Such representative gatherings as our Student conferences are just out of the question. And the young people are *always in droves*. That is a *serious* damage to the human soul. For a person must have periods *alone*, or with a single companion or two, to roam these magic German forests and learn their message. But one sees, instead, hordes of boys, and troops of girls, with heavy knapsacks, and blanket rolls and cooking equipment, marching, chatting, going somewhere, The superficiality of the restless person, whom we know so well in America, is being systematically produced. The soul of Germany is being hollowed out, from within. It breaks your heart to see it. Yes, they're having a *good time*, and losing their depth. A hardening, paganizing, materialistic world is being *systematically* produced. And the principle of discipline — Germany is really living, as a vast army, on a wartime basis — is taking away every ability to decide for oneself. The *obedience* of the German is as great now as ever. More than that, the whole principle of the totalitarian state, with one-party government and *ruthless* repression of all rival views, leads to a terrible conclusion. For no form or order is permanent, in this world of change. And if an overturn in government *were* to take place, *there is no substitute form*. Loss of the present règime would leave Germany *floundering*. Intolerant of any rival ideas within herself, she can only go on being what she is, in order to defend herself against her enemies. The two bogies are Communism and Democracy. Democracy, it appears to a Nazi, as I understand, is a mid-victorian dream from which a few countries have not yet awaked. They suppose they *tried* Democracy, in the days of the Weimar Constitution and the Republic, what we knew.[18] They never really did, and anyway were so well disciplined in *authoritarianism* that they had a great deal to unlearn if they were ever to make a go of democracy. Comunism is their other great bogey. The standard defence of Naziism is that it saved them from falling into Communism in 1932.[19] I don't know a great deal about this, but I always feel this point is enormously overdriven, and that the danger was not as great as they make out. However, Naziism is here, and I have a hunch it is here for a good long time, — unless a war blows the whole of this witches cauldron to pieces. — One realizes how the entire structure and process of government sucks the money out of the people. People are taxed for everything imaginable. They *must* join organizations, they must belong to the Arbeitsfront[20] (an ominous word itself, — It is the organized labor group, and the word *front* is a *war* word). One *must* give to the Winterhilfs.[21] Then little placards 2-3 inches square are put up at your door bell to show which organizations you have joined. Each city block is watched over and every family is waited on, and pressure put on in case some member has held out. A certain man refused to give to the Winterhilfs (like our community chest), because he was supporting the wife and six children of a man who had been put in Concentration camp because of religious views. This man, for his refusal, lost his job, and is now himself in concentration camp. The ominous uncertainty of what will happen if certain things are done is a terrible strain on the nerves. and most people do what they are pressed to do. *There is no law* by which the Secret Police is governed! They may do as and what they please. And once a judgement is rendered against a man there is *no* appeal, *anywhere*. No review of the case. Many and many are the people in prisons and concentration camps who have had no adequate trial or even the half semblence of a public trial. They are taken, they are gone, — and sometimes the family gets the ashes, I have heard of only one corpse returned to the family, and its condition was such as to show why the man died, — clubbed, beaten, dragged over briers, — all the hellish things of the Middle Ages. Lael, you may see the wife of this man some day in the U.S.A. I heard the other day of a man who had been a friend of a certain Jew. Authorities got after him, his "trial" was really a *prosecution* by the *judges* (!), and he was clapped into concentration camp. There he was so amazingly cheery and loved that serious steps were taken. And he was so mistreated that, over a long period of time, he broke and took his own life. He had managed to write up a little of the last treatment and hide it in his watch, and it got out of the camp. — But I mustn't get started on these things yet. — The government, which gets such sums from the people, by all kinds of sources *never gives an account of what it* does with the money. An enormous amount of the heavy industry of the country is occupied with war materials. It is because such sums are being spent in this way, rather than in the Roosevelt way of W.P.A., that a certain part of the unemployment has been reduced. If the nation were running as a peace nation, I have no idea how much unemployment there would be. One hears rumors of all kinds of secret movements of men. You see the government *owns* the people, and can transport and transplant them at pleasure. *All* right is in the state. It is not a *divided* right, as with us. We, as citizens, have rights, and the state as an entity has rights. Each can sue the other. Not so in a totalitarian state. One hears of large public works that have been left 3/4 finished, the men all carried away to rush the fortifications along the French, Belgian, Dutch and Luxembourg border. If, as is the possible thing, Germany *does* push by force into the East, that is the Balkans, or if the situation in Czechoslovakia blazes, then they must have their western borders solid, against England and France. So it is reported—there is no way of confirming such reports,—that this work is going on at a furious pace. But the nation is already at war. The atmosphere is tense. Yet the restaurants are the same as ever. and life bustles along. It can't be described. It has to be experienced at first hand. — I've given long lectures to you now about political things. The thing that is the burning blazing blot on the present government is the treatment of the *Jew*. One can separate the principle of National Socialism from the principle of blood-purity. Fascism in Italy has existed for more than ten years without a *race theory*. But now, tragically enough, that too is getting going in Italy. Before I talk about the *infamous* treatment of the Jews, let me talk about the theory on which the persecution rests. There is a systematic effort to get all thing that are purely *German* at the center of things. Christianity is *not* German, but an importation, and—to be sure, started by a *Jew*, Jesus. Christianity therefore, must be looked upon as a deteriorating influence. Only that which stems out of German soil and is born of German blood is reliable. This is the *Blut und Boden*[22] conception. *We* have the expression, *Blood speaks*. They take that literally. If one's veins are filled with pure German blood one has in oneself the wine of life, the elixer of divinity. In fact the theory of *Blood* is an inverted form of the theory of the *Inner Light*! — Pure blood in one's veins is a materialistic Inner Light, that will lead the Germans on to greatness, and glory. This blood must be taken literally. The problem of a sound country is not, as they see it, sound economics, or sound ethics, or sound scholarship, but it is a *biological* one. Get one's *body* right and the products of life will flower. (This you see is related to sport also). But mixed marriages between races is a detriment to the country. The worst blood in the world is the Oriental blood (they do some scrambling to get the *Japanese* freed from this stigma) and the Jews are the worst of all. Therefore anyone who is a Jew, or who marries a Jew, or has friendship with a Jew, is in danger of polluting the pure blood of the German people. O, its all crazy, I know. The only thing about it is that it is *real*. One pinches oneself and asks, *Is this the world* or am I insane, that such crazy history should be in the making. So everybodys ancestors are thoroughly searched, and any Jewish blood of 1/8th or more, that is, one great grandparent a full-blooded Jew, classes a person as non-Aryan. Stores have signs up saying, Juden nicht erwünscht, *Jews not wanted here.* I saw recently a sign in Berlin. A store advertized "Aryan since its founding in 1867." In Saxony I found the stores almost universally marked with a single word on the door or window. *Arisch.* (Aryan). Saxony is one of the most *hot* Nazi places. They go to great excesses there. Jews cant go into restaurants and get a meal (our own Negroes have long known this shame. Now the Jews are treated fully as badly. No, *worse* than negroes, for there is an *active persecution* of the Jews. The woman who translated my Cary Lecture was Hertha Israel, a full-blooded Jew, and a peach, about our age—as Jewish in looks as you get, but a fine spirit, and a *very* good member of the Society of Friends. She has all kinds of humiliating experiences. (You noticed I never mentioned her name. Her name cannot appear in the printed lecture, as the translator!)[23] If one of us is along, she can go anywhere, without being stopped, But if she were to go into a restaurant, sit down, and anybody sitting near didn't want to be in the presence of a Jew, he would go to the proprietor, and the proprietor would come and put the Jew out. Jews have great trouble in getting places to live. If they live in an apartment block and anybody says, I don't want to live with Jews, out they go. Elise Behrend doesn't know when she will have to leave her one-room flat.[24] She is a "poison" to the purity of the place. I heard in Frankfurt day before yesterday of a Jewish family that had lived in an apartment 46 years. Now the old lady is 81 years old. Two members of the family are bed-ridden with illness. But they have received 2-weeks notice to move, and the have to go, —with no place to go. It will certainly lead to reestablishment of Ghettos. The Jews in Germany evidently have, in many cases, been rascals, and sharp dealers. But now they have *more* than attoned for any sins, and those that are *wholly innocent* are suffering terribly. They have no employment. The government, which is really a glorified Al Capone regime in many respects, —pure gangsterism—forces them to go out of business and sell their stores at *confiscatory* prices, (and then on the side gets a slice out of the bargain, —I never knew the beat of the way the government gets money.) I heard the other day of a Jew in a certain city who had not paid a fine for a traffic violation in 1923. That, recall, was the time of the inflation. The fine was the equivalent of 2-3 marks, but at that time, 100,000 marks in inflation money. The government has now collected 100,000 marks for a 2-3 mark fine— from a Jew. If a Jew *should* succeed in emmigrating, *90%* of his ~~pro~~[25] money is confiscated. I have heard of cases of their taking their furniture with them, then at the border they were asked to give a statement of the cost at the time of purchase, no matter how old. Then they were *taxed* that amount! In other words, they had to buy their old furniture back at *new* prices, and the gov. got the money. — Jewish children cant *play* with other children. They are shunned. Why? Because the parents of the Aryan children are afraid *they*, the Aryans will be complained against, to the Gestapo, (Secret Police), so they keep their children away. In Berlin they have, in the parks, benches painted red for Aryans and yellow for Jews. An edict has just gone out all over Germany. On Sept, 30. *all* Jewish physicians will cease practising medicine! Humiliation, on every hand, poverty, no hope, no outlet, baffled, despairing. They don't know what is to happen next. I had dinner or Abendbrot last Sunday in Frankfurt with a *peach* of a Jew, a scholar, a Rabbi, an understudy of Martin Buber, one of the world-known Jewish religious thinkers. This man, Dr. Abraham Heschel, is a dear. About our age, clear thinking, modest, an author, with several books to his credit, he gave me two. We had a fine 2½ hours together. Then he and Alfons Paquet[26] and Rudolph Schlesser[27] and I spent the evening together, and we had one of the most searching joint probings of the final ground of *suffering*. Dr. Heschel conducts something like seminars or week end conferences for rabbis, throughout Germany. — I understand that the Jews in Wien are in terrible terror. Almost 10% of Vienna were Jews. They have been quickly dis-placed by non-Jews, under the Hitler regime. All the slow growth of Jew hatred and humiliation that has been developing over 5 years in Germany has been put thru there in a few *months*. Dr. Heschel told of being in Vienna recently. In the apartment house he was in, scarcely a floor had not had its suicide. Every pressure is put upon them to get out of the country. — but there *is no place to go*. The other night in Kassel 8 of us sat around a table and just canvassed the countries of the world, and in all cases the laws prevented immigration except in very restricted form.[28] Australia, — no, except certain farmers, in a trickle, New Zealand? No. Brazil? Farmers only, in small numbers, and under 30. Argentina, the same. The Quota for the USA is 28,000 from Germany in a single year. Applications have come in so fast that the numbers to 1940 are more than covered by applications. Canada, only a few farmers. England is closed. Scandanavia is not open. Russia is open, but *Jews* have been persecuted bitterly in Russia. I heard of a Jewish family the other day that had, in earlier years fled from Russia to Germany to escape Jew-hatred and persecution, then had fled from Germany to Italy, as *this* development of persecution developed. And now that Italy, apparently as a political swap of some kind, is starting on the crazy theory of *race* purity, and *blood*, they are trying to escape from Italy. — At a trial of a Jew recently, for some small offence, the lawyer was a non-Jew. *He* (the lawyer who defended him), was imprisoned afterward on some pretext. Another non-Jew lawyer took up his case, and *he too* is now in prison on some charge! The treatment of the Jew is *so* scandalous that the German people as a whole apologize for it. and look upon it as an aberration of their government. I have not yet met a single person who defends the present treatment. One meets plenty who point out that the Jew in the past had been *over-sharp* in driving bargains, that the Jew was getting into places of economic control throughout the land, etc. But, granting all that, they have no excuse for the *excesses*. In Dresden, in the lovely suburb called *der Weisse Hirsch*,[29] they have signs along the street, showing a hook-nosed Jew being butted by a goat, with the delicate suggestion, *Juden sind hier nicht erwoünscht*. (Jews aren't wanted here). There have been disturbances in many places. S. A. men, (these are the brown shirts. — large numbers of party men in uniform, the party army, the private army of the Fuhrer, are on the streets), S. A. men will break into a Jews store, and smash it up, or paste it with placards of obscene insults. A friend of ours, seeing one of these stores so terribly plastered with signs, in a fit of anger, tore one down. He was arrested, but the regular police, into whose hands he fell, were so decent that he was released in an hour. The same man is also working in a factory — no, I mustn't put that on paper. Do you realize how thorough the espionage system is? A man went to Prague on a business trip. (It is extremely difficult to get permission. — for a German — to get out of Germany, one has to have all kinds of testimonials.). While there he was invited to a tea. At the tea he was introduced to a number of people, one of whom happened to be high up in the Czech government. A week after he returned to Germany and was at his office, he was called on by the Gestapo. They said, You went to Prag. Your application said you were going on business. How does it come that you met Mr. _____? Then they produced a *photograph* of the man, snapped just as he was shaking hands with this Czeck at the tea! The man was dismissed from his job. Of course this espionage system *outside* of Germany cant be perfect. But there are enough cases of such watching that Germans everywhere are jumpy. I heard a similar story of a chance meeting of people in Louxemburg, in a restaurant. The outcome in that case was imprisonment. One grows to understand more why *one must be careful*. I have heard, in Berlin, the actual words reported, of a Haverford student who returned to Haverford and gave a public talk and made remarks of too specific a kind.[30] It isn't that *he* is in danger, or that *I* am in danger. But a specific remark or incident *gets back* here, and the person is identified, and then there is the devil to pay. Now imagine living in this year after year after year. — I was at the home of a family not long ago, that has several children. One of the sons had been so deeply touched by the suffering of families whose fathers had been put in prison that he became too active in relieving distress. He was helped by someone near the Quakers. This near-Quaker connection was taken up as a case of his being in connection with a foreign country, and he has been in prison four years and has two more to serve. The family wanted me to suggest English books he might try to get permission to translate in prison.[31] — One tragic thing about "modern" concentration camps, as I understand it, is that except by special permission, *no writing material* is given. When a man is a student, this is a terrible thing. I called on a man not long ago who was just out of prison five weeks, after being in for two years. He told of his best friend, a university professor, whom he had come to know in prison, who had suffered so terribly because of this privation, of all books and writing matter. The professor, by the way, had published (several years ago), a book which showed by statistical studies that free labor, in the long run, was more efficient than watched, controlled labor. That was a contributory cause, at any rate, to his loss of professorship and his imprisonment. — A man of whom I have heard a great deal, and have been in correspondence with, was head of a small private school here. He followed the practise of reading a small bit out of the Bible each morning to the pupils. One morning, without any thought of the matter, he read a passage in, I believe, the 4th chapter of John, in which, incidentally, this verse occurs, "Salvation is from the Jews." The children reported it at home. The parents reported it to the authorities, and the police came. He is now forbidden to conduct the school. He is permitted to act as its business manager, but not direct its *studies*. He has been put out of all his professional associations, teacher's association etc. He is nearly sixty, and is being forced to *sell his* school. This is quite a crazy world. — It isnt so bad to suffer physical privation as mental frustration and spiritual humiliation. Physically, Germany is getting along, on a *very much* lower scale of living than we are accustomed to. But it is almost impossible to be unswervingly *honest* in Germany. Take the matter of Heil Hitler. *Plenty* of people don't want to do it. But they see their bread and butter may be taken away, if they don't. I know some people who *don't* Heil Hitler, but say *Guten Tag*. But they are brave souls, who take their future in their hands. For you may be complained against, as disloyal, lose your job. etc. Women particularly are meticulous about Heil Hitler. If they should go into a store and fail to do it, they might be reported, and their *husbands* lose their jobs and their children go hungry.

Thus a false front of dishonest conduct is *everywhere* to be met. — along with others who are quite sincere. For their is also a lot of undisillusioned idealism among the Nazis. — No, a foreigner is not expected to Heil Hitler. In fact, it would hardly be the proper thing for him to do. So I say Grüss Gott or Guten Tag. — Then there's the matter of hanging out flags. You're expected to be properly beflagged. Now and then a person feels he is forfeiting his inner decency by succumbing to such discipline, and is bold enough to refuse to hang out a flag. But that is rare. I know one young fellow, a teacher, who has done it. He is now *abgesetzt*, (dismissed) and is without a job now for 1½ years, with wife and two children. But in these days a small matter, like a flag, or a little placard on the door, can become a symbol of great heroism or great weakness, as was the case in the days of Early Christianity, when a pinch of incense on the altar would save a Christian's life from the flames. But most people are *succumbing*, and are doing what they *don't want to do*, and are inwardly uncomfortable about. But the hunger of children is what they fear — losing their jobs. This is a great undermining of character, that is sad to see. The Germans have coined a phrase for this. They say, we have no *civil bravery*, That is, Put a German in uniform and he is *brave*, but put him before the obligations of citizenship as he sees them and he is not brave, but an obedient fellow, sacrificing his conscience. — A real hero is Pastor Mesching, and his wife.[32] I will not put on paper anything about him. But he now stands in great danger. But he has been so *unswervingly* honest, all through the years, that his Nazi friends *lie* for him, to save him! He said to me, One thing, the greatest thing I am most anxious about is that I shall not let one *bit* of hatred or poison get into my system from these experiences." And he said another thing, "I can't condemn one group and praise another. I have found that the line between *Good* and *Bad*, doesnt run *between* men, but *through* every man." I could write *much* of him. When he spoke at Yearly Meeting about *honesty* and *veracity*, it was a tremendous thing, for everybody knows his life. — One woman who is married to a Nazi is trying to avoid the *Heil Hitler*. Being a Nazi, all is going well, financially, and they live in a *very* nice apartment in a big apartment house. But she waits till she hears no one on any stairs, so she wont have the problem of the greeting. She slips furtively in and out of her own home. — I have before me the *Lebenslauf*[33] of a ~~Jewish~~[34] young woman, and I'll translate some of it. "What now compels me to seek a place in some foreign country is the following: My parents were, for many years before the war, very good close friends of a Jewish couple. My father expressed the wish, during the war, that if he should be killed in the war, I should be cared for by this Jewish couple. This occurred. And since in the same year, their own daughter died, they took me in as their own, and I have been treated as such ever since. My "crime" which has brought me continuous denunciation, the most evil calumnies, and at last the loss of my post is only this, I cannot bring myself to cut myself off from these people for whom I have so much to thank, and who stand so near to my heart. I cannot disown them simply because they are Jews." She is *not* a Jew, but mingling with Jews in Rassenschande, A race-shame. — To be born a Jew is no shame, and it breaks ones heart to see such treatment. And it breaks ones heart to see such treatment. And it breaks ones heart to see the Germans injuring *themselves* by their treatment of the Jews. In Vienna, I am told, in Aryan stores, a kind of commissar from the Party, (Nazi), stands at the entrance and watches that no Jew faces appear. To be insulted on the street as a Jew-sow is no happy experience for any woman. Placards have sometimes been put up reading, "Whoever trades with a sow-of-a-Jew is no German woman." This is a scandal to Germany. A Jew said to a friend of mine, "I'm glad I'm on the other side, I have nothing to regret." — Do you realize how aggressive Hitlerism is *outside* Germany? ------------------wife of ------------ told me that the Hitler Jungend organization in Jerusalem, among the German colony, was just unbearable, (I used a name and identification without intending to and so crossed it out. Do you think I'm foolish? Live here a while and you wait!), — You may have all kinds of questions in your mind about food, etc, No, that is no problem. All things are to be had, in the normal fashion. Oranges alone are scarce, but otherwise one never encounters any difficulty. Many of the prices are similar to ours. Shirts, ties, etc. Suits are higher. A man's suit cost $50–$60, and that means something *very* great for German incomes. And the quality is not good. An "all-wool" suit is by law 40% substitute and 60% wool. — Apparently steel is in such *great* demand for munitions that steel for building purposes is well-nigh unattainable. One doesn't go out on the open market and *look* for steel. The *government* decrees whether steel shall be granted for private purposes. One has to unlearn *so* much of such simple things.

I see no real hope, in my *few weeks* experience, except that the Party purify itself. One learns that, although the Nazis present a united front to the nation and to the world, they are much torn within themselves by various currents. Some Nazis would want to pursue a moderate policy. Others are just brutal. So far, when a matter comes to a close decision inside the party, it is said, the *left wingers* always win out. Some want to excuse Hitler and say *he* is not responsible for the extremes, he has to go along with the drive of the rest. Others say he is the worst of the unbalanced left-wingers. If may be, if no war breaks out—and Germany knows she can't risk a war inside a year or more,—that in ten or twenty years some more reasonable form of totalitarian state may develop out of this, as personalities change thru the years. —One must realize that *this* Germany, or this *government*,—I *love* the German people, they are wonderful—is *not something wholly new*. It is the old Military clique of pre-world-war days, defeated in war, smarting under defeat and the insults of the Versailles Treaty, now slipped back into power as the *sole* power in Germany. This present government is the spiritual continuation of that earlier militarism. As Albert Martin says, the German Gov. has never acknowledged that they were on any false track, at they have no sense of past sins. They see their present hard lot as the outcome of mistreatment of *by others*. They lack full honesty in facing the responsibility for the world war, and *no one* is a snowwhite lamb among black sheep. But the German gov. has not acknowledged any danger in militarism as such. That's the *hopeless part*. And in the course of centuries this wonderful people will have drained out their own blood, and sink to an inferior place. I could weep for the almost certain future. —You recall *Gusstag*, Lael, the day of Atonement, of Confession of sins, about Thanksgiving time. That national celebration is now a thorn in the side of Naziism. For the human ideal or pattern which Naziism tries to cultivate is one of pride, agressive hardness. It knows no confession of sins. There *is* no higher power, no objective standard to which we must adjust. All is human, here, in the *blood*, in the body. Religion? An exploded superstition, in the old sense. The German blood will guide to glory! Its all crazy, isn't it. But its real, and 70,000,000 people are in the grip of such a system, and too docile to rebel.

This gloomy picture *needs to be corrected* by more association with ardent supporters of the Third Reich. The Quakers are *so largely* thrown with the poor and oppressed and downtrodden. That is a glory —that they are such as are turned to by men in trouble. But it has its dangers, the danger of seeing only the dark side of the present regime in Germany. There *is* a bright side. I wish I could be here long enough to balance this *dark* with that *light*. And, so far as possible, I have tried to get out of the groove. But the overwhelming impression is dark. Yet I feel, I, too, need correcting, by longer, broader experience. For if Quakerism is *universal*, it should have a message to all, not just to the oppressed and the despairing. The German Quakers themselves need to expand their vision, and appreciate the *breadth* of this universal aspect. Many of them are extremely intolerant of any thought of good coming out of such a regime. I am not sure but what, in the years' perspective, something will grow, of real value. We're all too near it to see it clearly. There are many honest, devoted earnest, thoughtful Germans who have hope that the good will *ultimately* outweigh the evil. I pray it does.

This summer I've seen more of the meaning of suffering. Suffering of the body is only the *vestibule* of suffering. Suffering of soul, suffering of spirit is terrible. That is our mission here, I feel, as foreign visitors, — to minister, in our blind way, to this spiritual suffering.[35] Dear people, how I love them, Dear people how they suffer. — The other day, in Kassel, I met a man who had refused to teach some of the stuff he, as a teacher, was expected to teach and had, of course lost his job. I said to him Fine, that's swell, (or its German equivalent). He looked surprised and asked me why I said that! I answered, because you are a free man. You have not built a prison for yourself, within which your soul must sit for years. Yes, he said, you're right, I'm a free man now, and glad of it. — But souls are sitting in such prisons now, *bitterly* suffering because of what they find themselves compelled to do, to keep their stomachs filled, or, *more commonly*, to keep their *children's* stomachs filled. Many and many a person says to me, I could be brave and resist the regime, *if I didn't have children.* — And many young people are having spiritual suffering arizing out of this perplexity: At home their parents teach them sound ideals. They are well brought up and grounded, until about the age of 10-11-12. Then their lives get *so* much more strongly influenced from the outside world. In school and in the Hitlerjungend they hear one thing, at home another. Which shall they believe? They get confused, and troubled, and lose their way, Families are split apart. Another thing that is *so* hard, is the *hatred*, the depths of *hate* that is encouraged, and that *poisons* them. I chanced to fall into conversation with a young German on the train from Pyrmont to Kassel. He was a lovable young fellow, a chemist. But he had a Hollywood mind and when, as we talked about travelling outside Germany, I mentioned *Czechoslovakia*, he fairly hissed in his hatred. I *didn't* ask him whether the Germans were not oppressing some of their own people more bitterly and infamously than the Czecks were oppressing the Sudetendeutschen. That would have blown the lid off. But some of them recognize it. But *hatred*, unrestrained hatred, with *no* qualms of conscience to check it! Christians fall into the error of hatred. But, inwardly there is an accusing voice which, in the long run, is a restraint upon "Christian" hatred. But hatred which is *encouraged* by the *voice of the blood*, *that* kind shows no restraint and no accusing voice of the conscience. — We spent the evening at Karlsruhe talking about the *life* which, in itself, is a translation of *love* into *deed*. And afterward they said, How amazing to hear such talk![36] To us in the USA. such talk is easily a platitude. Here such talk in any *platitudinous* form, from the churches, is *rejected*, But I am convinced that it *still speaks*. When it is *genuine*. And that is one thing this *world* does to you. It strips off all but the *genuine*. It *has* to be genuine to stand up in this world of flame. And Quakers have no business here or anywhere unless they are *genuine*. But if the *reality* of the Divine life *is* in any person, *there* is a living message, and everybody, German, Japanese, or South Sea Islander can read it. If I've come to believe that the life *lived*, *in act*, is something deeper than an Anglo-Saxon trait. I used to think it this was an emphasis in Quakerism arising from its historic roots in England and America. Now I see it is an aspect of Incarnation. The life of God must be actualized *in men*, in *life*, in *lives*. —And in such lives, there is born the life of *Redemption*.

I said I wanted also to talk about the upheaval in oneself which such a summer brings. Dearest one, here I must open myself in such a personal way that it can go to no one but you. The preceding pages are more public in character, and can be read by others—by any others who will not publish them or put them into print. But now I want to talk just to you. The summer has *opened up* what was already opening up before, a new sense of unreserved dedication of oneself to a life of child-like dedication to God.[37] This comes not out of the feeling that one has, of having looked into *awful depths* of human woe, overwhelming as that is. What I want to say does not grow out of any specific external in-fluence—it seems to grow out of an *internal influence*, which is so over mastering that I can only recognize it as God working within me. Last winter you know I was much shaken by the experience of Presence—something that I did not seek, but that *sought me*. It was that which underlies the lecture on the Eternal Now.[38] When we read it first, that evening together, when Jack Cadbury and Jack Carter[39] were with us, you said you understand the second lecture on Symbolism,[40] but not the first on the Eternal Now. But this is the *real root*. And the work here this summer, or, *in the midst of* the work here this summer, has come an increased sense of *being laid hold on* by a Power, a gentle loving but awful Power. And it makes one *know* the reality of God at work in the world. And it takes away the old self-seeking, self-centered self, from which selfishness I have laid *heavy* burdens on you, dear one.[41] Help me, sweetheart, to become more like a little child—not proud of learning, not ambitious for self, but *emptied* of these things, and guided by that amaz-ing Power, which is so gentle. Yet, in the last analysis you cannot help me; except by *understanding*, and furthermore, by *coming with me*, so far as you find it to be *your way*. We have been *so* hardened, so *crusted*, so worldly-wise. I have been *so self-seeking*, and *on the surface* you have let experiences of Father Macy, and Clarence Pickets teaching, and my weakness, sharpen you.[42] I see my way now, to a richer life of serenity and child-like faith and joy. Come with me, if you see this way. You need not talk much about it. I blather on too easily. But Mother Macy must have found it, for the fruits were to be seen in her life.[43] I have been *far from this way*. Now I feel I must come home. In many ways you have always been nearer home than have I.[44] But I *long* for companionship now, in this area. And help me, dear one, to grow into that kind of self-forgetful devoted life that Mother Macy had. Don't think that I am talking now in some sudden spell of emotion. It is a maturing of spirit, which comes, sometimes slowly, sometimes in *overwhelming spurts*. I shall no doubt, fall far below what I should. So do we all. But let us keep close to the central intention, and the central life. The phrase "a child of God" has been growing on me this summer, and amazing depths seem to lie in it. Help me, dearest, to be one. It doesn't involve complicated thinking, it just involves consecrated living, and the sensitiveness of a child to the Leading Hand. Dear one, I hope I have made myself plain. Let us both, together, find the little child within us. It doesn't mean any great overturn of *outer* life, so far as I can see. But it involves a subtler change, of inner sweetening and power, and joy and peace. I seem at last to have *been given* peace. It is amazing. —Now I have said enough, darling. Reread this page and a half several times, not only with the head but with the heart.

Your own devoted Husband.

It would be easy to say that what I say here is growing out of the summer's deep experience with tragedy. One often says to oneself, what right have I to live in such comfortable circumstances as Haverford, when the world is aflame. And we *can't* live, as the average American is now living, accepting these things as naturally our right. If we use them, and live in such park-like surroundings, with priviliges I never appreciated before, it is a holy trust, out of which we must make something that is an offering to the wounds of this terrible world. But, what I have said is deeper that this reaction to human suffering. It is grounded not in time and suffering, but in the Eternal, as He breaks into us and teaches us His final nature, as *love*. But the suffering of the world os a part, too, of the life of God. and so maybe, after all, it is a revelation.

Now, Dear Wife, I've written you a long letter. *underlaid with love.* The first 9 sheets can be circulated, *but quickly.* Keep them in Maine no more than 2 days. If a group wants to gather to read any of it out loud, O.K.[45] *Don't let any get published.* Then send the 9 pages on to Wilmington, with these same directions, — that they keep them only *two* days, and do not publish anything. Then have Mary send these 9 pages to *Barbara Cary*,[46] 20 South 12th Street, Philadelphia, for her to read and use according to the discretion of the Service Committee. Then after they have had them for a time, I shall ask if I can have them returned to you or to me. I'm well, and inwardly happy and at peace, and eternally grateful for this summer's service, — not for me, but for those who have had a chance for a breath of fresh air to blow in on their stuffy prison.[47] For Germany is a prison, as well as a fortress. I said this once to a German, dass er in Gefangnis sass. Nein, antwortete er Deutschland ist ein Zuchthaus. (that he was in prison, or jail. No, he answered, Germany is a penitentiary, where one does *hard labor*). What funny German one hears here in this bi-lingual world! It's good German, but it sounds like *Dutch*, with a curious Dutch inflection and lift to the voice. Evidently the *French* training makes a difference in the throat. I haven't spoken a word of English now for several days, — since leaving Pyrmont.[48] I've been over to the Cathedral, — about 5 minutes' walk from the hotel. An amazing *spire.* Too bad the other was never finished. It is an inexpressible message in stone. I must go back this afternoon and sit a long time, and hear what it has to say. Dear ones, how I wish you too could be here with me. — But the bulk of these two days and a half are going into *writing.* All kinds of writing has to be done, postponed letters, letters paving the way for my next visits, 6–8 days ahead, — I'll bet my letters sound *funny* to the Germans! And this long letter to you, and now I must write a *long long* report of outward movements, since leaving Berlin for Hannover and Bückeburg and Pyrmont. And Hans Albrecht has asked me to write an account of the Yearly Meeting, for publication in American Quaker[49] papers. That must be done today. It's now 11:30 A.M. for tomorrow morn I leave Strassburg, ~~gove~~ go over the border to Germany to S Freiburg

Again I'm impressed by the slovenly, slapdash French mode of life, in contrast to German order and cleanness. And what a diff. in the *temper* of the people!

Boy, when you cross the border *you've crossed something.* Barbed wire, concrete gates, 4 feet thick, etc.

NOTES

1. Thomas Kelly to "My own dear wife and precious precious children," Strasbourg, France, 16 August 1938, Haverford College Library (hereafter HCL), Quaker Collection, 1135, Box IV.

2. Peter Phillips, *The Tragedy of Nazi Germany*, (New York, 1969), p. 77.

3. Thomas Kelly to Lael Kelly and children, London, 24 June 1938, HCL.

4. Thomas Kelly to Dr. Abraham Heschel, Frankfurt, 6 September 1938, HCL.

5. Thomas Kelly (henceforth abbrev. TK) to Lael Kelly and children, Zurich, 24 August 1938, HCL.

6. Richard Kelly, *Thomas Kelly, A Biography*, (New York, 1966), pp. 97–104.

7. Le and 15, rue de 22-Novembre are the last lines of the letterhead. Le, in French, always introduces the date, which TK wrote in English. Translation of the second line: 15 November 22 Street.

8. Lael Kelly, his wife, and Lois, age 10 and Richard, age 2.

9. On 1 July TK left England for Germany.

10. TK had just crossed the border that morning. He had written a letter that morning on the way, at Appenweier, a junction along the train route from Karlsruhe to Freiburg, heading on to Strasbourg in France. It was marked 10:35 AM. TK to Lael Kelly and children, Appenweier, 16 August 1938, HCL.

11. TK's previous letters to his family from Germany had described little other than sight-seeing, his health, the bare outlines of his itinerary, and his progress on the lecture.

12. Many people he describes meeting in earlier letters were never named then, either.

13. Albert Martin, wife Alice, son Richard, age 11. TK to Lael Kelly and children, London, 28 June 1938, HCL. Albert Martin held a post for the A.F.S.C. in Germany. He had been in England for the London Yearly Meeting when Thomas Kelly arrived there in June, and went over to Germany at the same time as TK. Even in London Martin had been careful of eavesdroppers, having a group speak softly in the basement of Friends House because two strangers were in the room. (As above, 29 June 1938.) As to Martin himself, TK wrote from Berlin, "And their time of service is coming now to an end, the Elkintons are already somewhere in France to take their place, and the Martins have no job to return to in the U.S.A. A possible job in Swarthmore just washed out. He used to teach at Brown University." (As above, Berlin, 9 July 1938.)

14. Translation: The individual is nothing, the people are everything.

15. Translation: Hitler Youth.

16. Translation: outings.

17. Translation: Hitler Youth outing.

18. Thomas and Lael Kelly had been in Germany with the A.F.S.C. in 1924–25.

19. The Communist Party was indeed strong in 1932 and the beginning of 1933. In November 1932, six million Germans voted 100 Communist representatives into the Reichstag. Peter Phillips argues that Communist revolution was, however, quite unlikely, and that fears were exaggerated by the depression. Phillips, *The Tragedy of Nazi Germany*, p. 70–71.

20. Translation: Labor Front.

21. A fund ostensibly for relieving hardship during cold weather.

22. Translation: blood and soil.

23. Actually, TK did mention "the woman who is to translate it, a Frl. Israel, a Jewess or half-Aryan." TK to Lael Kelly and children, Berlin, 5 July 1938, HCL. She is referred to in several of the letters afterwards, always as "Frl. I._____." The mention of her name in the 5 July letter is the first time she is referred to, and it is to be presumed that he had not yet learned to be as careful as he later learned it wise to be.

24. Elise Behrend was an old friend of the Kellys from 1924–25. TK wrote from Berlin early in July that he had had tea with her a couple of times and had noticed that she had definitely become an old woman. TK to Lael Kelly and children, Berlin, 9 July 1938, HCL.

25. "pro" crossed out. TK probably started to write "property" and then corrected himself.

26. Alfons Paquet had presided over the session of the German Yearly Meeting at which TK gave his lecture. In the 17 August letter to the Farquars, TK wrote that Paquet sent his greeting. How Paquet knew the Farquars remains unknown. He is mentioned here and in the 6 August letter to Lael Kelly in such a way as may indicate that Lael Kelly also knew him. TK to Frank and Mary Farquar, Strasbourg, 17 August 1938, and TK to Lael Kelly and children, Pyrmont, 6 August 1938, HCL.

27. Rudolph Schlesser is not mentioned in any of the other correspondence from the summer of 1938. Being mentioned here without further identification, he, also, may have been known to Lael Kelly.

28. TK had written a letter in late July in which he mentioned talking to a married couple about emigrating. Whether or not they were Jewish, he did not say. TK to Lael Kelly and children, on the train from Berlin to Hanover, 28 July 1938, HCL.

29. Translation: the Wise Stag.

30. This Haverford student remains unidentified.

31. The family, the son, and the near-Quaker all remain unidentified. This family could possibly be the one with a "tragic story" mentioned in the 28 July letter on the way to Hanover. TK to Lael Kelly and children, 28 July 1938, HCL.

32. Thomas Kelly spent the night of 28 July with Pastor Mensching and his family in Bückeburg. Mensching had four children. The oldest, a boy, 21, was studying medicine; the second, a boy, was blind and somewhat retarded; an eighteen-year-old girl suffered from epilepsy; and the third boy, 16, seemed all right. Kelly had become concerned with all suffering, not always distinguishing

political oppression from personal misfortune. This corresponds to Mensching's own non-political attitude towards evil, which Kelly quoted in the next few lines. 28 July letter cited above, note 31.

33. Translation: personal record.

34. "Jewish" written and then crossed out. Specifically, she was not Jewish.

35. Ministering to "spiritual suffering" is largely what he was doing in Germany. His lecture at the German Yearly Meeting had been about the mystical ground of religion, and he wrote on 25 July, in continuation of a letter originally begun 20 July in Berlin, that the center of his activities had become making visits to people. TK to Lael Kelly and children, Berlin, 20 August 1938. HCL.

36. In the letter written on the morning of 16 August from Appenweier, TK mentions he had "had a rather remarkably deep meeting last night in Karlsruhe" with eight or nine people.

37. This "opening" had begun the winter before with some ecstatic experiences in which he said he felt the Hand and the Power and the Love of God breaking into his life. He spoke of this in the traditional Quaker language of the Inner Light. This was a great clarifying point in his life and he soon began to write and speak of this inner experience in a way that his audiences found moving. As a result of this, he was asked to give the Cary lecture on 6 August in the German translation prepared by Hertha Israel, and, according to his own report, succeeded in touching his audience deeply.

38. TK had written the lecture on The Eternal Now and the Social Concern in the previous winter. It is published in *A Testament of Devotion*. The Cary Lecture had been a reworking of this theme. Thomas Kelly, *A Testament of Devotion*, (New York, 1941).

39. Jack Cadbury and Jack Carter were students at Haverford College. A group of students met regularly at TK's house to discuss the religious life.

40. "Quakers and Symbolism" in Thomas Kelly, *The Eternal Promise*, (New York, 1966), pp. 61–71.

41. TK had driven his family into debt in his pursuit of a Harvard Ph.D. (which he never got). In 1935, after the publication of his dissertation, he blanked on his oral examinations so badly that Harvard refused to allow him to sit again for the degree. He became severely depressed. He had spent many years in pursuit of exacting scholarship, and had moved his family repeatedly. By "the old self-seeking, self-centered self," he was probably referring to, among other things, his concentration on scholarship and the "burdens" he had laid on his wife would have been the debt, the moving, and other results of his neglect of everything else in pursuit of scholarship. In letters from earlier in the summer, he repeatedly talks of how sorry he is for the tasks which she must take up alone while he is abroad.

42. "Father Macy" was Lael Kelly's father, Herbert Macy, a strict, puritanical, Congregationalist minister from Hartford, Connecticut. Clarence Pickett was the Executive Secretary of the A.F.S.C.

43. "Mother Macy" was Lael Kelly's mother.

44. TK may have been referring to his own absence from home life during his

period of intense scholarship. More likely, in light of his references to Lael's parents, he was talking about his own relationship to his parents. His father died when TK was a young boy, and his mother remarried. According to his son Richard Kelly, he had felt that he lacked a close home life as a child.

45. Lael Kelly and her children were staying in Maine with her sister's family, the Robert Whiteheads. The group that might have gathered could have included any of the following, all of whom had homes in the small summer community of Brightwater or lived nearby: Albert and Helen Bailey, who ran a Quaker work camp in Phipsburg township and had organized a Quaker meeting there; Robert Whitehead, Congregational clergyman, close friend, and husband to Lael's sister, Miriam; Miriam Whitehead; John Filbrick, clergyman; Elizabeth Cotton, Y.W.C.A. Secretary; Roy Chamberlain, clergyman; Jerome Davis, clergyman and professor at Yale; Katherine Perry, writer; Robert Ewing, Y.M.C.A. Secretary; Leora Field, social worker. From Richard M. Kelly, 18 October 1981, HCL.

46. Barbara Cary was handling correspondence with the A.F.S.C. Her name is now Barbara Curtis.

47. July 25, on the train from Leipzig to Halle, TK wrote of his visits to suffering Germans in much the same words. They were "like a breath of cool air in a hot oven." TK to Lael Kelly and children, Berlin, 10 July 1938, HCL.

48. The German Yearly Meeting had been held at Pyrmont.

49. Hans Albrecht was TK's host in Germany. It was he who had invited TK to give the Cary Lecture. From London, 16 July 1938, he wrote home that he thought it best to tell Albrecht that he would finish the lecture in England before leaving for Hamburg. TK to Lael Kelly and children, London, 16 July 1938, HCL.

INDEX